Maureen Fallen
2nd Year
Politics UCD

The politics of legitimacy

International Library of Sociology

Founded by Karl Mannheim

Editor: John Rex, University of Warwick

Arbor Scientiae
Arbor Vitae

A catalogue of the books available in the **International Library of
Sociology** and other series of Social Science books published by Routledge &
Kegan Paul will be found at the end of this volume.

The politics of legitimacy

Struggles in a Belfast community

Frank Burton

The City University, London

Routledge and Kegan Paul

London, Henley and Boston

First published in 1978
by Routledge & Kegan Paul Ltd
39 Store Street,
London WC1E 7DD,
Broadway House,
Newtown Road,
Henley-on-Thames,
Oxon RG9 1EN and
9 Park Street,
Boston, Mass. 02108, USA
Set in 10 on 11 pt Times by
Kelly and Wright, Bradford-on-Avon, Wiltshire
and printed in Great Britain by
Redwood Burn Ltd
Trowbridge and Esher

British Library Cataloguing in Publication Data

Burton, Frank

The Politics of Legitimacy – (International Library of Sociology)
1. Minorities – Northern Ireland – Belfast
2. Roman Catholics in Belfast
I. Title   II. Series
301.45'28'204167   DA995.B5   78 – 40427

ISBN 0 7100 8966 X

For Ita and Bob

Contents

Preface

This book is an ethnography of a Belfast working-class Catholic community. It describes how the political, ideological and military struggles of the contemporary Northern Irish war are expressed within a district which is very much involved in that war. Like all ethnography the text is theoretically ordered. There can be no such thing as innocent description. This particular ethnography represents an attempt to contribute towards an explanation of the war in the Six Counties and is a product of a theoretical interest in ideological and political formations and struggles. The work concentrates almost exclusively on the patterns of ideological thought and practice evidenced within the Catholic community. This emphasis is justified because the specific problem confronted in the text is this: what is the relationship between the content of the Catholic social consciousness and the political and military activities of the Provisional Irish Republican Army?

The *partial* explanation of the present war put forward in this book rests on the connections that are specified as existing between the political practice of the Provisionals and the wider ideological structures evident within the Catholic social consciousness. The ethnography is thus ordered through these connections which have been arrived at by what I have called a theory of mediation. A theory of mediation seeks to specify, within a theory of ideology, exactly how ideological and political practice intersect. It seeks to appraise the precise connections between the content of ideological categories and ideological and political change. This has entailed the text concentrating on detailed accounts of the nature of the conflicts within this community, conflicts which represent examples of the processes of ideological and political change.

This book could not have been written without the tolerance and support of the community it describes. Many people there discussed

ix

the ideas contained in this text and everyone I met in some way contributed to its completion. Some of these contributors could be named but others must remain anonymous. I would like to thank them all collectively. My thanks above all go to Jacqueline Coote and Martin Withington who made the visit both possible and enjoyable, and to Sian Morgan, who recently has undergone many of the experiences I have documented, and in the same community. Her comments have proved extremely valuable. I would like to thank also the following people who have commented on part or all of the work: Pat Carlen, Maureen Cain, Mark Cousins, Jon Clare and Tony Fox. I am also indebted, for their academic encouragement, criticism and support, to Kit Carson and Paul Rock. Finally my warmest thanks to Ruth Nixon who has been a constant source of help and humour.

I am grateful to the *Guardian*, *Irish News* and *Newsletter* newspapers for permission to reprint extracts from several of their editions from the period 1972-3.

Glossary

An Phoblacht	lit. *The Republic* – Provisional IRA newspaper
CESA	Catholic Ex-Servicemen's Association
CRA	Civil Rights Association
cumann	branch of a political party, usually Sinn Féin
Cumann na gCailini	junior wing of the IRA; for girls
Cumann na mBan	women's wing of the IRA
Dáil	the Parliament of the Irish Republic
Fianna Fáil	lit. 'Soldiers of Destiny' – one of the principal political parties of the Irish Republic
Eire Nua	lit. 'New Ireland' – outline of Provisional Sinn Féin policy for the government of a 32-county Ireland
Fian	a member of Na Fianna Éireann
GOC, NI	General Officer Commanding, Northern Ireland (British Army)
IRA	Irish Republican Army; divided into Official and Provisional wings
Mise Eire	lit. 'I am Ireland' – personified, idealized figure of a united 32-county Ireland; often portrayed as an old woman
Na Fianna Éireann	junior wing of the IRA; for boys
NICRC	Northern Ireland Community Relations Commission
NLF	National Liberation Front
Óglaigh na hÉireann	Gaelic for IRA
Orangee (*slang*)	a Protestant (i.e. a member of an Orange Lodge)
PIGS	armoured personnel carriers (British Army)
Prod (*slang*)	a Protestant
Provo (*slang*)	a member of the Provisional IRA
Red Hand	Protestant paramilitary organization
RUC	Royal Ulster Constabulary – the Northern Ireland police force
Saracen	armoured car (British Army)
SDLP	Social Democratic and Labour Party

Sinn Féin	lit. 'We Ourselves' – the IRA's political wing; divided into Official and Provisional wings
'Sticky' (*slang*)	a member of the Official IRA
UDA	Ulster Defence Association – Protestant paramilitary organization
UFF	Ulster Freedom Fighters – Protestant paramilitary organization
UUUC	United Ulster Unionist Council
UVF	Ulster Volunteer Force – Protestant paramilitary organization
Whippet	light armoured car (British Army)

Introduction

This book is concerned with the ideological basis of politicized violence. It attempts to contribute to an explanation of the war in Northern Ireland. In particular the object of the study is to specify the social basis of IRA violence. Consequently the following analysis concentrates on only one, though a major, party to the Irish war: the Catholic population and the Irish Republican Army which springs from it. The material presented draws from a period of participant observation, September 1972–April 1973, which was spent in a working-class Belfast Catholic community which I have called Anro.

Sociologically I have approached the issue of the IRA's political violence as an empirical study in the sociology of knowledge. This has necessitated a concrete analysis of ideology. By 'ideology' I mean those representations of the objective structures of a society that dominate the consciousness of a class or social division. By ideological social relations I refer to the fact that these representations are inscribed in specific practices. To distinguish between the dominant categories of consciousness of one-half of a social division, the Catholic population, and the actual programme of a political movement, the IRA, I use the concept of total and particular ideology (Mannheim, 1968a). The text takes the form of analysing the relationship of the particular to the total ideology and the effect of this relationship on ideological social relations.

Presenting the problem in this manner has resulted in an examination of the social basis of IRA ideology through an explication of the social consciousness of Northern Irish Catholicism. This consciousness is presented as a world-view or total ideology. I shall argue that the representations constituting this world-view manifest the dominant categories of the Northern Irish, Catholic consciousness. Within the Catholic *Weltanschauung* I locate the particular ideology of the Irish Republican Army. It is the particular ideology of militant

Republicanism which allows the commitment to kill and be killed for a cause. By establishing IRA violence directly within its social context, the particular ideology within the total, the analysis gains explanatory power. The central argument is that the potential political consciousness implicit within the wider representations of Catholicism is explicitly expressed within the politics of the IRA. By firmly rooting IRA ideology within the total ideology of Catholicism, the intention is to demonstrate how the genesis of current IRA politics emanates from the structure of the Northern Irish society.

Posing the analysis in these terms represents a broad theoretical contention. IRA violence is only one manifestation of the increasing phenomenon of world-wide guerrilla and terrorist activity. The threat that national and international political violence poses, both to governments and to potential victims, has generated a widespread concern with the nature of political violence. Most of this concern – over bombings, kidnappings, sieges, hijackings and assassinations – has taken the form of an interest in counter-insurgency techniques.[1] The practical interest in combating 'terrorism' has relegated the explanation of its origin and forms to a secondary position. Indeed, the very attempt to explain the incidence of any particular form of political violence is liable to be branded by, for example, counter-insurgents as the propaganda of sympathizers. Politicized violence is, however, too important a social phenomenon to be left to the theorists of social control (Kitson, 1971; Clutterbuck, 1973; 1975; Moss, 1972).

An alternative position, adopted here, is to examine the socio-historical genesis of a political movement which resorts to the policies and tactics of violence. I argue that political violence can best be explained and understood in terms of the social and political practice it arises in.

Any knowledge resulting from this or similar enterprises might well contain policy implications for both insurgents and counter-insurgents. Policy implications will obviously vary according to the problem being studied. In the case presented here there is much to challenge the ethics and efficacy of the policies of both counter-insurgents and insurgents. The issue, however, is that the approach allows a serious theoretical appraisal of the origins of politicized violence, the activist's political cause, as well as an appraisal of the effects of such violence. The object of inquiry is an explanation of political violence, not the construction of a counter-insurgent's handbook.

Elements of a total ideology

The radical Gemeinschaft

I have ordered the presentation of the social consciousness of Catholicism in terms of three inter-connected constituent parts. The most immediate element of the Northern Irish Catholics' world is the community character of its social organization.

Chapter 1 analyses the social organization of Anro, which is taken as typical of the community structure of the Northern Irish Catholic. The structure of this community sustains a strong sense of social solidarity. This solidarity is an important factor in determining the character of the Irish conflict. Though the district of Anro is by no means homogeneous, its inhabitants do share common social traits. Kin, class, religion and territory are closely entwined within the social matrix of Anro to produce a common sense of identity. Anro displays, in Durkheim's term, a 'collective consciousness' (Durkheim, 1915, 1933).

The *Gemeinschaft* structure apparent within Anro is clearly linked to the dichotomy that exists between Protestants and Catholics in the wider society. The history of Anro illustrates how the tightness of its own multiplex social ties is inextricably connected with the general history of Belfast's sectarian conflict. Belfast, though an industrial city, remains a cluster of Protestant and Catholic urban villages precisely because pockets of Protestants and pockets of Catholics stand in opposition to one another. The emphasis of difference between the two communities serves to minimize difference within the communities.[2]

The political significance of Anro as an urban village lies in its ability to withstand and absorb external assaults. The length of the war in Ireland is partially due to the structure of the Catholic communities. This social structure is capable of 'soaking up' the attempts that are made by both the Protestant and British military forces to break Anro's own military activists. The community reaction to a number of serious confrontations has not produced a chaotic or anomic breakdown. Rather, Anro has resisted enough of the external pressure (riots, gun-battles, assassinations, internment) to make the continuation of the war a possibility. Strong community bonds not only increase the likelihood of active resistance to external threat, they also simultaneously make it possible to absorb the consequences such confrontation results in.

The sectarian consciousness

The solidarity within areas like Anro can be viewed as partially both an effect and a continuing cause of the divisions that exist between the Protestant and Catholic communities. These divisions are institutionalized at many levels of the Northern Irish society. Areas of residence, occupational and unemployment distributions, voting alignments, school attendance, friendship networks and inter-marriage rates all indicate a bifurcation in terms of religious ascription.[3] In chapter 2 I analyse how this near Orange and Green apartheid is entrenched in consciousness.

I introduce the concept of 'telling' to indicate the depth to which the Six-County society is polarized. Telling constitutes the syndrome of signs by which Catholics and Protestants arrive at religious ascription in their everyday interactions. The sectarian social division of the Northern Irish society is partially realized and re-affirmed in the processes whereby Catholics and Protestants selectively determine the religion of their co-interactionists. The sectarian consciousness is deeply rooted in the history of the economic and social policies of Northern Ireland. Telling illustrates how this history is used in the contemporary society to construct a form of ideological social relations that amounts to an ethnic difference between Catholic and Protestant. The view of the 'other side' as ethnically different I take as the second major element within the social consciousness of Catholicism.[4]

The significance of telling lies in the manner in which it elucidates the profundity of the sectarian milieu that constitutes Northern Ireland. The concept is developed because it appropriates a reality that shows the potential appeal of the politics of the Civil Rights movement for the Catholic population. Given the centrality of sectarianism in the Northern Irish consciousness, a politics which sought to expose the material basis of sectarianism was, in this context, revolutionary. The Civil Rights movement in performing such a role activated the sectarian consciousness. The result was the major outburst of rioting in 1969 which precipitated the resurgence of the IRA.

Republicanism

The final major element of the Northern Irish Catholic consciousness I refer to as Republicanism. The appeal of a united, 32-county Ireland is a well-documented feature of the Northern Catholics' political ambition.[5] But Republicanism, like most nationalisms, is more than a narrowly political goal. It carries the trappings of a cultural heritage. Irish nationalism in the Six Counties features as a living tradition in the cultural activities of the minority population. Irish dancing, traditional and rebel music, Irish sports and the teaching of Irish history represent the major ways in which the sentiments of Republicanism are culturally reproduced.

4

Republicanism has also been kept alive by the military assaults that have been made on the Northern Ireland government from the Revolution to the Civil War years through to the present day. From 1916 onwards IRA activity has provided every generation in the North with the experience of violent politics. For the Loyalist population this history was evidence that the Nationalists only ever partially legitimized the state, and that was enough to justify treating Catholics as 'second class' citizens. The resulting sectarian policies sustained the political appeal of Republicanism.

In chapter 3 I emphasize the significance of the nationalist aspirations of the Catholic community. By 1970 the Civil Rights movement and the Ultra-Loyalist reaction to it had created a vacuum of politico-juridical legitimacy. From the Catholic perspective the movement most historically likely to seize this political initiative was traditional Republicanism. At the forefront of the Republican heritage stood the IRA. Consequently as the Catholic communities began to build defence corps throughout 1970, it was the IRA, now split into two wings, which gradually came to dominate this development. The importance of this shift towards the IRA was profound. The politics of civil rights came to be expressed in terms of the politics of national liberation.

I shall examine the contradictions the subsequent IRA campaign resulted in, in terms of the arguments voiced for and against the IRA from within Anro. Such arguments are considered in terms of the IRA's own struggle for legitimacy. A brief excursion into the IRA's history illustrates that some of the contradictions of their contemporary campaign are similar to the problems created by previous campaigns. These contradictions hinge on the incompatible ideological ingredients of traditional Republicanism. The present campaign, however, differs radically in that it has managed to juggle these contradictions while simultaneously engaging the support of the Northern Catholic population.

By explicating the principal components of the Catholic consciousness and placing IRA ideology within this *Weltanschauung*, the virulence of the contemporary IRA campaign can be better understood. The politics of civil rights through national liberation produces *politically* an isomorphism with the *social* basis of the Catholic consciousness. Sectarianism, as illustrated through the concept of telling, creates and sustains the basis for the appeal of the Civil Rights movement. The political vacuum created by the impact of the Civil Rights campaign became absorbed and channelled into a modified Republicanism. Though modified, this nationalist politics was already deeply embedded in the Catholic world-view. Through the expression of national liberation, in terms of the rhetoric of civil rights, the IRA fuses politically two of the major elements

5

evident within the total ideology of Northern Irish Catholicism. The initial, definitive characteristic of communities like Anro, their *Gemeinschaft* nature, became significant for the military activation of IRA ideology. IRA volunteers not only appeared as members of the community but the community itself became a source of resistance and resilience which a more fragmented social structure could not have provided.

Total and particular ideologies as mediations

Establishing the politics of IRA violence within the wider consciousness of the Northern Irish Catholics' world-view constitutes the beginning of an explanation of IRA ideology. Specifying a particular ideology as a manifestation of a world-view has the benefit of posing explanation in terms of a more general level of analysis. This book concentrates on explicating the content of the Catholic *Weltanschauung* and on demonstrating how IRA ideology emerges from, fits into and capitalizes on this world-view. This task has necessarily involved excursions into the socio-historical genesis of that world-view in recognition of the social and historical foundations of all states of consciousness. However, the book has not provided any systematic analysis of precisely how the social meanings of Catholicism are representations of the wider material reality of the Northern Irish society. Specification of a particular ideology in terms of a total ideology is a legitimate and important theoretical task, but it can only ever provide a partial analysis.

Posing the problem in the above terms would involve the next stage of analysis in investigating Catholic consciousness as mediations of the complex political economy of the Six Counties. Treating the Catholic world-view as the mediated reality of the wider society would require a theory of mediation which could both specify the links between the world-view and the material reality, and, simultaneously, establish the degree of theoretical autonomy that existed between them: 'The major problem for the sociology of knowledge is to find a way of mediating between the evidential reality of the social individual and the societal structural aspects of his consciousness' (Wolff, 1975: 51).

Such a massive undertaking into the theory of ideology would constitute a general explanation of the Irish war and is beyond the aim of this text. However, in chapter 4 I argue for the theoretical importance of that level of analysis which documents the mediated reality which makes up a world-view. Any general explanation of the Irish troubles which fails to take account of existing states of consciousness, the level of mediated reality, is liable to produce explanations that are either programmatic or seriously distorted. I shall argue that certain press and 'left-wing' accounts of aspects of the troubles largely ignore how the significance of the war is interpreted and filtered by, in this case, the mediated reality of the Catholic consciousness. The argument in the chapter centres around the process of how the construction of the meaning of an event in communities like Anro is determined by a context which external accounts, like press reportage and 'left-wing' analyses, rarely penetrate. Knowledge of the Catholic world-view becomes vital if the contextual determination of meaning within Anro is to be appreciated.

The significance of analysing existing levels of consciousness lies precisely in the information that such an analysis provides of how a group constructs its reality and how it might interpret a series of events, such as a change in policy or tactics. In comparing an account of the contextual determination of meaning as presented in this book with the decontextualized approach of certain other accounts I am arguing for the greater explanatory relevance of mediated over unmediated analyses. The press, for example, is engaged in the creation of the meaning of daily events in Northern Ireland. In the first part of chapter 4 I compare news accounts of events that occurred within Anro with varieties of internal accounts that the people of Anro offered. The press is seen to impose a meaning onto events which frequently violates the significance attached to them by individuals and groups within the context in which the event took place.

The second set of explanatory accounts, taken from a variety of left-wing groups, seeks to specify the socio-structural determinants of meaning and consciousness but largely neglects how material reality is mediated in context. The ideological representations of any material reality can never be given im-mediately. States of consciousness in any society will differ for a variety of reasons, not least because of a class or group's structural position in that society. Moreover, there will always be lags before shifts in material relationships become registered in the social consciousness. Consequently to restrict analysis to one level, that of the socio-structural determinants of meaning, is to neglect the whole theoretical arena of the relative autonomy of mediation.

By arguing for the significance of that level of analysis which is concerned with mediated reality I necessarily raise the problems of what would constitute a general explanation. A general and inclusive explanation of the war in Northern Ireland would need to incorporate three levels of analysis. It would first need to document the mediated reality, the actual consciousness and world-views of the important parties to the war. Second, it would need to specify the social determination of these world-views through a political economy of the Northern Irish society. And finally it would need to establish a theory of mediation which was capable of linking the first and second levels of social reality. A general explanation needs to delineate both objective and subjective social reality and to analyse the dynamics of their relationships. This book restricts itself to one part of one of these areas, the mediated reality of the Northern Irish Catholic consciousness and the IRA's place within it. It in no way underestimates the serious theoretical and epistemological problems facing a general explanation of the war in Ireland. It recognizes, rather, that these problems are the identical problems facing any adequate social theory.

1 Ethnographic snapshots: the radical Gemeinschaft

This chapter has a dual purpose. Its primary task is ethnographic in that it will illustrate the social and physical structure of Anro. This will provide essential background information which will render comprehensible the content of the subsequent chapters. The initially descriptive account of Anro seeks to present a sense of the whole of the community thereby allowing the later chapters to draw on the ethnographic details portrayed below. The later analysis of Anro clearly relies on the context from which it has been drawn and it is this context that shall be made explicit in the following ethnography.

But this chapter simultaneously carries an important theoretical load. The emergent theme lies in the inter-relationship between a pre-existing culture and violent social change. The characteristics of this phenomenon are investigated in terms of their relevance for the war in Northern Ireland. What is sociologically important about Anro as a community is the manner in which it has reacted to the potential chaos of major riots and gun-battles with its Protestant neighbours and with the British Army. Under radically altered circumstances the pre-existing social structure of Anro plays a vital role in the fragile containment of disaster. Anro's solidarity as a community has been systematically threatened. Dozens of people, residents and non-residents, have been violently killed within its streets. Many more have been seriously wounded. The area has been saturated by troops and is under constant surveillance. Hundreds of the district's inhabitants have been interned or detained or sentenced to prison. Such a violent affront upon the conventional activities of the community might well have resulted in anomic breakdown. What was apparent, however, during the period 1972–3 when the assault from and on to the community was at its highest, was the manner in which the pre-existing *Gemeinschaft* qualities of Anro's social structure had stretched to incorporate and contain the troubles.

9

Though the concept of *Gemeinschaft* is frequently associated with the conservative reaction to the Enlightenment (Tönnies, 1957; Nisbet, 1970), in this context it is the very traditional qualities of Anro's community that allow it to conduct and sustain radical activities. Precisely because the community manages to contain and disperse the troubles into its institutional framework, its normative structures and its symbolic universes, it manages to prevent the dominance of external social control. In turn, the community retains enough of its solidarity to allow the militant activists to continue the politics of violence. Thus the existence of the radical *Gemeinschaft* emerges as an important constituent in the Northern Ireland war. The possibility of an IRA campaign is dependent in this respect on the social structure of its community being able to withstand the deleterious consequences that urban guerrilla activity creates.

The illustration of this theme will take the form of three parts. After describing the social and physical structure of Anro I shall illustrate the sources of potential anomie that the war has brought to Anro. Finally I shall document the inter-relationship of the community's culture with the troubles.

The task of conveying the social world of some 11,000 people in a community with over 110 years of history obviously presents methodological problems. As soon as an author writes, indeed, as soon as he leaves the community he has studied the social reality he was participating in becomes frozen into his written and mental recollections. Consequently there are only ever snapshots available. My knowledge of Anro, like its inhabitants', is partial, but more so. There are worlds, no doubt, I never knew existed, others I caught only fleeting glimpses of. Even those I penetrated often defy easy description. Some of the last may be blind alleys. Nevertheless I lived a little over eight months in Anro and became acquainted with the particular manifestations of class, religion and nationalism that existed within this community. Such knowledge enabled me to communicate and share the residents' experience. It is a knowledge that allowed me to make sense of the previously elliptical conversations of insiders; a type of knowledge which also mitigated the initially acute feelings of culture shock that living in Anro created for an outsider. More significantly it is a knowledge that suggests the beginnings of an explanation of how this community, at war and under extreme stress, has managed to cope with a massive dislocation of its routine.

I shall order the explication of this descriptive knowledge in terms of the rules and processes by which I became cognizant of the plurality of groups in the community. Where possible this will be illustrated by the connotative language that points to certain structures which the process of becoming a resident necessitated mastering.

Locating the reader: Anro's social and physical structure

Anro is a solidly working-class Catholic community in Belfast. It is surrounded on three sides by working-class Protestant communities. The 'mixed' (Protestant and Catholic) areas on the boundaries of this ring of districts have been squeezed out. The results are religiously homogeneous communities, the nearly universal position of contemporary Belfast (*Flight*, 1971; *Intimidation in Housing*, 1974). Anro's 32 streets are tightly packed into one-quarter of a square mile with approximately 2,220 houses inhabited by a little over 11,000 people, a high density. The community considers itself two areas, Old and New Anro.

Old Anro is in fact the second mill village to bear its name, the original Anro was settled a little further up the main road in 1819 with the opening of a damask factory. Today Old Anro is the remains of a village built by the linen mill owners. The first street, constructed in 1863, is still lived in. The rest of Old Anro was built between then and 1902. The 850 or so extremely tightly packed dwellings are mainly kitchen houses (two down, two up), a sprinkling of parlour houses (one extra room) and an occasional double-tenancy house. They house most of Anro's elderly and most of its very poor families. The streets are terraced without gardens. Outside in a small yard the lavatories back on to narrow entries. The rents are very low – about fifty pence per week. Some of the houses are remarkably well kept while others are dilapidated. Some are suitable for their two occupants; others are grossly overcrowded with more than ten inhabitants. Inside the houses the stamp of a family's biography can make the homes attractive. Viewed, however, from the streets the houses appear as impoverished as anywhere in the UK or Ireland, matching the stereotypical conception of the slum. The wrecked and derelict houses in Old Anro, together with its insanitary entries, both made worse by the troubles, accentuate the deprived look of the district.

Modern Anro was born in riots. Initially New Anro was built for Protestant inhabitants. Residents recalled to me the signposted slogan on the building site in the early 1930s: 'A Protestant Estate for a Protestant People.' These original intentions were frustrated in 1935, when refugee Catholics, victims of that summer's serious riots, squatted in the unfinished houses. Even today such 'immigrants', from the central Belfast areas, were referred to as 'townies' by Anro's older residents. The Catholic church bought one-half of one of New Anro's longest streets during the 1930s and is, up to this day, one of the major landlords in the district.

The terraced houses have large front gardens which bring a good deal of relief to the drab monotony of the streets of the old district.

Despite appearances, however, the living space is not substantially greater than that in the parlour houses of Old Anro, two rooms down and three up; the smallest upstairs rooms have mostly been converted into bathrooms. Rents are low, about £1 per week, and there is some owner-occupation. By the 1950s the district was 89 per cent Catholic (Jones, 1960).

A move into the new district from Old Anro was generally accepted as a move to better things. But it had not escaped many that, the gardens aside, the houses and streets, both terraced with narrow entries and outside lavatories, were not substantially different in either part of the area. One woman saw a positive disadvantage in living in New Anro. She recalled how reluctant she had been to leave her kitchen house in the early 1960s for a home in New Anro; the large windows, she lamented, were 'no good for when the riots come'.

The other main physical features of the district are the local industries which are mainly situated in the old mills, now a small industrial estate still centred on cloth making. These factories employ both Protestant and Catholic workers and constitute the only area in which the co-religionists interact. Unemployment is, however, very high in Anro. Most of the North's steep unemployment rate is carried by the Catholic population. Community workers estimate that about 25 per cent of the adult male population is jobless in Anro, which, though a low figure compared to some Catholic areas, is clearly a devastating rate for recent times.[1]

The compounding of not infrequently large families, tiny houses and one or more breadwinners out of work produces a hard core of conspicuous poverty in Anro. The apparently homogeneous class structure of the parish masks very consequential differences hinging around employed/unemployed, size and age structures of the family and housing conditions. These status differences put a family on one or other side of the poverty line. In turn such differences become signified in the geography of the district. Oldfield Street, for example, used to be classified socially at its various intersections as Heaven, Purgatory and Hell. Today, though partially perhaps in jest, the top halves of the New Anro streets are referred to as the 'better' half.

The social amenities within Anro are remarkable for their absence. There are no pubs, cinemas, swimming or public baths, parks, cafés, restaurants or libraries. The few meagre amenities in the neighbouring Protestant areas are considered to be beyond the pale of safety and are not patronized by Anro's Catholics. There are numerous shops on 'the front of the road' and several within the area, some being the front rooms of the tiny houses. Almost anything, from coal to single cigarettes can be bought in the neighbourhood shops.

Entertainment focuses on the seven drinking and social clubs. Most of these have been created out of the troubles while the rest, though pre-dating them, share for the most part their Republican associations. The new ones were built almost overnight to recompense the loss of Anro's pubs which were burnt down in the 1969 riots. The others, while not looking any less temporary, have been the traditional working men's clubs in Anro. One is connected with the Gaelic Athletic Association. Another, the 'United Irishman', specializes in more indoor sports, such as billiards and card-playing. These clubs are run by committee members mostly on profit-making lines from which the members benefit. They do a great deal of business and their members are keen to point out the 'spin-off' they give to the aged and the young in the community through their financial donations. The less capitalistically inclined saw this as conscience money. Certainly by comparison the impoverished youth club and the dingy old age pensioners' club were poor relations, and the clubs themselves were not that lavish.

Even more neglected are the thousands of young children. They may have a rich street life of their own but there is little other than their imagination to play with. Their recreational facilities consist of one or two small playgrounds, a few open spaces and one playgroup able to cater for twelve pre-school children. The adults, then, do not do that badly. The hubbub of activity in the clubs, characterized as it is by a fine mixture of song, dance and drink together with a high level of active participation can assure one of some rare times.

Standing out in marked contrast to the rows of terraced houses in various states of repair, the somewhat makeshift clubs, the handful of frequently overcrowded shops and the dour-looking mills is the impressive stone Catholic church. Built on a hill the chapel looks down on Anro from its own grounds. Its physical presence symbolizes its spiritual dominance. The order of priests in this parish[2] arrived in 1868. By 1902 they had built the large church and adjacent monastery from the donations of the parishioners, notwithstanding some setbacks such as the mass unemployment of 200 Anro men in 1878 when one of the mills closed. Today there might be up to twelve priests in the monastery. Several of them are allocated a few streets for their personal attention and are regularly seen visiting their parishioners. I found these priests to be a considerably more earthy type than those whom I have encountered in England. They know their parishioners well. Some of the priests were born in Anro. Not only do they fulfil the more conventional pastoral and spiritual roles of their profession like performing marriages, absolving sins and counselling, but they will also have a drink, share a joke and dance with the women at the parish functions. In addition a lot of people see the priests as having made Anro, as having built the parish from nothing and even dying in doing so. For example, in 1874 the Rector died from scarlatina caught while administering to the sick. His funeral, the parish history records,[3] was accompanied by the loud wailing of 20,000 people. Apart from its recent notoriety the parish has a noted history. The church choir in previous years had performed on several occasions on BBC radio. The priests' annual series of lectures always attracted, due to their controversial nature, the interested attention of outsiders. Similarly Anro was famous for its spectacular open-air ceremonies that were held on certain feast days, such as at the Eucharistic Celebration and Lady Day. During these occasions the whole community, together with many visitors, would throng the streets in processions. The church had long ago become the central institution and symbolic bank which bound Anro as a community. For several of the older women, particularly, the pride of the parish was a thing of the past: 'Anro used to be a holy place', but today nearly everyone, I was assured, went 'against the word of the priest'. Claims like this of secularization were tempered by the rush of activity on Sundays, by far the busiest day of the week, which saw the traditional surge of well-dressed individuals going to masses, of which there are nine held on Sundays.

Superimposed on the communality of residence and religion is the intricate and tightly knit kinship network within Anro. It is epitomized in the phrase 'You can't spit in Anro without hitting a relative'. On several occasions conversation in the house I lived in, particularly among adolescents, would result in individuals' discovering they were related, albeit somewhat distantly. In chats specifically about relations Paddy[4] counted thirteen uncles and aunts he knew of in the area, Cathal nine, five in one street, and James nine, all of whom until recently lived in the same street, mostly next door to each other. To illustrate this fine mesh of kinship (not managing to convince the priests I had 'honourable' intentions in my desire to see the parish records)[5] I looked at a social custom which involved the bereaved inserting a memorial of their dead in the daily paper, the *Irish News*. This somewhat morbid methodological activity is clearly very problematic, and I use the figures gleaned from a ten-month period in a way that is merely suggestive.[6] Sixty-six deaths brought condolences from stated relatives in 152 separate households within Anro (29 married daughters, 18 married sons, 16 married sisters, 20 married brothers and 69 others – nieces, nephews, uncles, aunts and so on.)[7] Each death accordingly indicated, on average, relatives in approximately three households, mostly families (with five per household) and most of these were immediate kin. This intricacy of kin in the neighbourhood seemed to be implicitly incorporated into the semantics of: 'Is she anything to you?' or more rarely 'Is he your friend?' Both questions, meaning 'Are you related to him/her?', are used by the residents.

Kin, class, religion and residence produce in Anro the classic urban village (Gans, 1962; Suttles, 1968; Hannerz, 1970; Roberts 1973; Coates and Silburn, 1972); that is, a community whose housing density makes life public and where street life together with affinity create a plethora of shared knowledge. Such knowledge underlies a great deal of social control – 'I could tell you a few things about that wee girl'. This access to biographical knowledge is the basis of much community talk; in the streets, the shops, the clubs or over the fences people continually swap and store information. It became no surprise, after a while, for example, that people I met for the first time frequently knew something about me. One old lady greeted me, 'Come on in, son, we know all about you.' Equally indicative was that often people could not tell you the number of someone's house; it was not an important piece of information as homes were located in terms of, 'It's four down from Mrs Geehan's'.

Augmenting this organization of local knowledge as a source of authority are the salient community norms. Men control the family economy and exercise their autonomy by drinking, frequently in all-male groups, often in the 'Men Only' club. There is not much evidence to suggest that it is not a woman's place to drink, but if someone has to look after the children it will not generally be the man. It would also be a matter of light ridicule for a man to be seen pushing a pram, in the launderette or with the shopping list. I recall the uncontrollable mirth of 4-year-old John chuckling with amusement at me doing the washing up: 'Ha, ha, ha, ha, ha – look at 'im, 'ee's a woman!'

Alternatively the women are by no means passive. The mother's role in particular is accorded substantial authority. Her role shares not only the connotations of the Catholic church's stress on the significance of Mary and the family but also that of *Mise Eire*. *Mise Eire*, Mother Ireland, is frequently portrayed in the form of a silver-haired, black-shawled old woman as the symbol of Irish Nationalism. The mother's authority can be appreciated in terms of the elaborate ways adolescent sons avoided mass. Rather than invoke the wrath of their mothers, which a direct refusal to attend church would create, adolescent boys (who would not hesitate to confront the British Army) would simply pretend they had been to mass. These religious truants would leave and return to the house after a suitable interim period giving the impression they had attended mass while in reality they had probably been playing billiards. Just to make sure they could pass their mother's interrogation they would also find out which priest had said mass and what the theme of the gospel was.

15

Normative behaviour, centering around sexual roles, religious obligation and the kinship duty find their expression and re-affirmation in the community ceremonies and rituals. Funerals move from the church, led by the men, some carrying the coffin, and are walked around the streets as a symbolic farewell before the burial takes place outside the district. Selected religious feast days entail the parish following behind the clergy in outdoor processions, thereby translating the streets into the church for the day. Again the parish dinners in particular were characterized by an amalgam of the elements of the community's culture. After the commensalism there were toasts of thanks to the various groups in the community who had contributed to the upkeep of the parish. Then there followed a lively series of singing and dancing to carols, Republican 'oldies', popular music and Anro's own song.[8] The other major community gatherings are the Republican marches and memorials. These now infamous occasions are suitably accompanied with bands and buntings which are more than matched by the Orange Order parades with which they are inextricably linked. Even in peace-time, Anro's culture is, of course, lent cohesion by the supposed ethnic differences (but often mirror images) between it and the circle of its Protestant neighbouring communities.[9] External conflict is critical in crystallizing boundaries and creating a semblance, at any rate, of internal coalescence. Such internal coalescence was vividly portrayed within Anro during its ceremonies and celebrations which clearly indicated the community character of its social organization.

Anro and the impact of the troubles

Anro's identity and culture, stemming from the historical and geographical roots of the district and compounded with the wider traits of social class and poverty, Catholicism, Republicanism and neighbourhood kinship, produces an interesting though not novel ethnographic blend. What is remarkable is that parts of this community are engaged in an armed struggle with one of the best equipped armies in the world as well as simultaneously being involved in an incipient war with its neighbouring Protestant residents.

Since the summer of 1969 Anro's routine organization has been systematically breached. In helping to initiate and respond to the wider military and political activity in Belfast this small community has taken and inflicted a heavy toll of death and destruction.

The summer of 1969 saw a rise in the tension between Protestant and Catholic areas. In Belfast the result had been a series of minor skirmishes and an increase in the level of intimidation of families in the 'wrong' districts. In August 1969, first in Derry and then in Belfast, these skirmishes resulted in the first major riots for over thirty years (*Sunday Times*, 'Insight', 1971). In Anro, Protestant rioters penetrated the streets. Old Anro was evacuated. Women and children were ferried from both parts of the district to safer areas. The old streets directly facing the Protestants districts took the brunt of the riot: 200 houses were wrecked, the pubs burnt and shops gutted. The sortie appeared to be led by the 'B' Specials[10] followed by Protestant rioters. Two people died, one in his house, another on his way back from work, still with his lunch box in his possession. Both were killed by 'B' Special issued guns. At least another 13 were injured by gunshot wounds. Whatever the deliberations of the Scarman Tribunal (Scarman, 1972) on the precipitating causes of the riot or the supposed judicial wisdom of its allocation of blame, the message in Anro was quite clear – the Protestants led by armed part-time police had gone on the rampage. Stunned and absolutely confirmed in their rejection of the Specials, the most frequent rejoinder to those who laid the initiative with the people in Anro was to point to the damage: 'Just look whose houses were wrecked and look whose furniture was saved and whose wasn't.' In addition, those shot were nearly all Catholics. Several residents within Anro recalled to me how the guns of the police reserve and the 'UVF'[11] (more accurately Protestant rioters) far outweighed the effectiveness of the petrol bombs and lone shotgun which, they claimed, constituted the arsenal of the Catholics. The local account was that the shotgun was rushed from corner to corner by a priest to create an impression of fire power. The guns of the IRA, I was assured, were most likely in Wales, apparently sold by the IRA to the Free Wales Army. As everyone in Anro said, there were no IRA men about, certainly none armed.

On the third day of the biggest riot since the 1930s the British Army, standing on alert, was mobilized and sealed off Anro and other areas. As several commentators have remarked (*Sunday Times*, 'Insight', 1971; Callaghan, 1973) and several residents reiterated, the British soldiers were generally welcomed as saviours. Many people recounted to me the gross fears they had had about being overwhelmed by Protestant rioters had the confrontation continued. Though much more violence was to come, and it was often more systematic, many people considered August 1969 as the most terrifying chapter of the troubles. The folk devils had been let loose in the form of the 'B' Specials and UVF. The sheer novelty of people's worlds gone awry with fear and conflict makes 1969 a key historical reference point. Three women recounted to me the impossibility of giving first aid to the men who were dying, it was hopeless; they just said an Act of Contrition as a form of last rites and turned away from them. Others recalled how the Bishop arrived and gave the whole community a general absolution.

Throughout 1970 Anro witnessed the building up of armed citizen-defence groups and this included the rise of the Provisional IRA and the re-arming of the Official IRA. This period also saw several clashes with the Protestant community. One very serious exchange of gun-fire resulted in the deaths of three Protestants. Similarly the confrontation with the British Army began in the summer of 1970 and steadily became more intensive in 1971. The early months of 1971 confirmed the British Army's new role as it initiated its first blanket (house-to-house) searches.

The second major assault on the community was on the morning of internment when in the early hours a fierce battle took place between the IRA and the British Army. In addition to several deaths, 194 houses were destroyed by fire as the few remaining Protestants from the top northwest streets of New Anro left the area. The people I heard recall the events of that first internment raid emphasized how the British Army (who had lost one soldier that evening from IRA activity) allowed the houses to be fired and prevented all attempts to stop the conflagration. Others recounted the hundreds of men, women and children held by the 'Brits' in the boys' primary school while fifty or so of their sons and fathers were lifted by the blacken-faced soldiers. Spontaneous barricading and street fighting followed. The gun-fire, the popping of the tiles on the burning houses and the screams of the army vehicles were printing on people's memories the second unforgettable offensive onslaught on their homes within two years.

Since 9 August 1971 British Army raids have been frequent occurrences and a state of warfare has been maintained in the streets of Anro. The numbers dead and seriously wounded approach 100 – IRA men and boys, British soldiers, innocent bystanders shot accidentally by both the IRA and the British Army, innocent and less innocent people assassinated by the British Army, the Protestant military forces and the IRA. The toll is numbing, as the statistics in Anro are not mere figures on the television screen or headlines in the papers, but corpses in the road, empty chairs, unworn clothes hanging in wardrobes and all the living reality of violent death.

From within and without the district is battle-torn. Of the sixteen possible ways to drive into Anro only three are now open and these are frequently manned by British Army soldiers in small breeze-block bunkers with ramps across the road. The other entrances are either barricaded with sheet metal or have 'dragon's teeth' (large conical concrete lumps) or barbed wire across them. The district is ringed with British Army observation posts – from on top of the mills, from a temporary fort, from houses in the Protestant side of the peace-lines and generally from any strategic position – about nine conspicuous ones. Though equipped with night sights and glasses British Army intelligence activities are occasionally assisted in the evenings by low-circling helicopters which beam a high-powered light on to the streets. Thus total surveillance is accomplished.

The regiments sent to Anro are stationed in a commandeered mill and bus depot from which they make periodic incursions around the streets in personnel carriers (PIGS) or Saracen tanks, or by foot-patrols. Enveloped by the 'British Forces of Occupation' and their technological paraphernalia of metal, concrete, wire and ramps and adorned with pock-marked gable-ends, Republican wall slogans and devastated houses, the visibility of the struggle in Anro is spectacular. This becomes even more evident if one sees the carpet of glass and brick, the crashed cars and the hedges and gates run over by army vehicles that follow in the wake of a riot. It is frighteningly real if you witness one of the many gun-battles and large riots. Here the streets are a mass of sound, people are shouting and screaming. Saracen tanks are whining at a high pitch, warning whistles and bin-lids are resounding, rubber bullet guns are exploding and the variety of guns in use crack, thud, whistle or boom according to their type.

Death, injury, physical and verbal abuse, internment, interrogation and torture, early-morning raids, gun-battles, riots, assassinations, and constant screening[12] are some of the more extreme developments to impinge on the everyday activity of the people of Anro over the last five years. Ironically these same extreme conditions have become part of the everyday reality of individuals in that environment. People have become accustomed to seeing armed British soldiers peering in at them as they have their tea, accustomed to walking over spread-eagled marksmen as they shop for their cornflakes, or casually watching from their front door the latest riot, only seeking safety as the lead bullets take over from the rubber. Ways of adjusting to, and making sense out of (and capitalizing on), the gross fear and continuous unpredictability have emerged. The anomie has partially been absorbed. Anomie can be considered as a condition in which our existing knowledge and beliefs are no longer able to cope with a radically new situation. A resulting struggle takes place to reconstruct both mental and moral worlds. It is to this process whereby the existing culture of Anro stretches to accommodate the unknowable and unthinkable, reinterpreting events to sustain a sense of reality and striving to maintain coherence in the face of massive disturbance, that I now turn.

Culture and conflict: absorption and change

Living in a community with ongoing internal and external threats produces a crisis in predictability and trust. In Belfast one generally walks round parked uninhabited cars with suspicion, casts unnerving glances at unattended parcels, scrambles to get home before it gets too dark, maps out safe and dangerous routes for journeys, all in an effort to evaluate risks which previously could be ignored. In the ghettos the accommodation has to go even further. An individual must get to know the dangerous streets where most of the shooting takes place, learning to avoid the outer perimeters which border on the 'peace-lines'. He must watch whom he talks to and what he says (he never knows who is listening or how it might come back on him). He must ask people, even if strangers, if it is clear of trouble where he is going; he must watch passing cars, especially at night, to see if they have passengers (if so care is required as they might be assassins). Numerous additional rules need to be learnt: do not walk past foot-patrols unless it cannot be helped; do not talk to men who are limping: they may be shifting gear (that is, moving weapons); or to girls pushing prams who are known not to be mothers, and so on. A person's stance becomes one of systematic doubt even within the familiar environment he grew up in. A tentative substitution takes place as one feeds in the new knowledge with which one endeavours to reorder the streets, the people and the activities of the changed situation. This effort to make the world safe is persistently frustrated by seeing and hearing trouble; like walking into a riot, being on the streets when the shooting starts, or losing track of your children just as the British Army raids. This order of comparatively minor impediments can cumulatively result in stress.

In addition to stress the anger of a whole community is evident when the British Army engages in a raid on one of the drinking clubs or conducts a house-to-house search picking up men and boys like a latter-day press gang. Within minutes people know the names of those lifted, and even if they are not known personally, they are located socially and spatially as 'Mrs McAllister's brother's boy from Thomas Street'. Information about how badly beaten an individual is, where he is being kept, whether he has been interned ('detained') likewise filters quickly into the district. With over fifty internees and sentenced Republicans from Anro incarcerated during my stay,[13] everyone accordingly knew someone 'doing time for the movement'. The campaign becomes translated for many in these circumstances into an intensely felt personal affront that 'foreign security forces' should intern, frequently abuse and not unoccasionally brutalize their loved ones, friends and acquaintances. Internment becomes in the cultural context of Anro a community punishment triggering off mass resentment and a strong collective commitment to free the 'boys behind the wire'. The central place of the interned and sentenced among the continued conscientiousness of the active IRA and the passive allegiance of the Catholic population, located as it is in the *Gemeinschaft* character of the ghettos, cannot be underestimated. Internment, for example, does not just produce anger and continued violence but also seriously aggravates the pool of poverty in the districts which it affects. Despite the efforts of An Cumann Cabhrach (the Prisoners' Dependents Fund) the temporary one-parent families of the prisoners do little better than their permanent partners in this well-documented poverty trap. This is particularly so after the cost of visiting prisoners and paying for the food parcels which families bring is accounted for.

The socially inclusive effects of internment and sentenced imprisonment is much evidenced by the prestige attached to the various 'Long Kesh' crafts. Republican homes boast harps, framed proclamations of the 1916 rising, worked handkerchiefs and leather goods made by the imprisoned. Initially the market for such goods was a restricted exchange between the inmate and a selected recipient who would be much honoured by the gift. More recently these artifacts have become part of a wider public market. Long Kesh iconography remains, however, an unambiguous symbol of the war in Anro.

Equally symbolic are the methods adopted to commemorate those who have died in the troubles: they also have their source in the public nature of the district. Bereavement is collective misery, there is open visiting of the dead and a steady stream of individuals will call to pay their last respects. The all-night wake will usually follow. The remembrance thereafter takes the form of the traditional cards carried with the deceased's photograph on it, and if the dead person was a Republican, often the clubs will bear witness to him by a wall plaque or something similar.

These characteristics, of varying seriousness, moving from doubt and fear to deprivation and bereavement, experienced as they are by all in the community, exact a damaging toll. Morale can reach very low depths mitigated for many only by the wide use of antidepressant pills[14] and, more conventionally, through drink. Crises by the committed as well as the uncommitted give rise to frequently heralded British Army claims and press banner headlines that a deep yearning for peace and a sickening of violence is felt by the people. This is most optimistically interpreted as a rejection of the IRA. Certainly such sentiments are often voiced: 'Anro's dying of depression', 'There's no life here at all', 'When will it all end?', 'There's a lot round this place used to love it now hate it.'

Such an unsettled existence, measured on a continuum of turmoil where the worst can happen and frequently does, is illustrated in the extensive paradoxes produced by the situation. The abnormal, for instance, becomes relativized into normality as more extreme events supersede the abnormal. Rumours become more frequent and even more fateful while scepticism towards the scaremonger similarly increases. The troubles make one preoccupied with the here and now, yet at the same time experiences are being stored which will order the past and mould the future. Amongst much else, the swiftly changing situation makes a mockery of one's attempts to hold consistent opinions, yet the circumstances demand a mental coherence. Over time I came to appreciate such characteristics of an environment where no one knows most of what is going on. The rumours, for example, were particularly alarming. There is no better way to stop a conversation than to make a claim to knowledge that 'the Orangees are coming in', 'the Brits are surrounding the place' or 'I'd stay off the streets tonight, there's going to be trouble'.

This collective anomie and the frequently radical reorientation of individuals' biographies caused by the troubles show through the culture and expose the obvious: the inability of Anro's culture totally to contain the massive violence, hence the misery, the fear and depression. The trouble is further manifested in the crystallization of different opinions and allegiances in Anro. These produce fundamental cleavages which often take on a violent expression.[15]

Yet alternatively some of the radical changes confronting Anro have been absorbed by its social structure. They have been assimilated and channelled to produce some crucial consequences. It is this process of mediation which helps account for the sheer tenacity of the campaign and why, in spite of systematic confrontation, the community has not quietly yielded to the pressures upon it. For example, I have argued that the kin network makes loss through imprisonment, injury or death a public loss which can stiffen as well as weaken the community's resistance. The same public nature of the streets can put the nature of guerrilla activity into a different moral perspective. Those heavily involved in military activity are considered in the context of the community's history and the particular individual's place in it. Passive support, like billeting men on the run, storing 'gear' (guns, explosives) and allowing the passage of transient IRA men through a house, become easier to understand in this light. A refusal to take a minor risk when others you know, friends, relatives or schoolmates are taking major risks can produce feelings of guilt. This appears to be so even when the individuals giving passive support do not fully share the convictions of the activists. The latter in a sense are cashing their social credit. The social obligations of a generalized reciprocity (Sahlins, 1965) do not lend themselves to speedy ostracism. IRA men as members of the community's networks have multiple social roles. Consequently volunteers can receive favours and credits from the communal stock of reciprocal exchanges which can be used in their IRA role – even if the donor objects to the IRA activity. Kieran, for example, carrying a gun and in a hurry, might be helped to escape, not because the neighbours who let him through their house agree with his actions but, perhaps, because they could not face his parents if he were caught because they knew him when he was 'a different lad', because he was their son's friend and so on.

Even the physical layout of the streets can be used to great military advantage. Familiarity with the rabbit warren of entries can be utilized to turn previously uninteresting corners into safe sniper positions. Knowing which way to run if pursued or which yard door will be open for you is the kind of information that is only slowly stock-piled by the British Army regiments but is intimate knowledge to the involved insider.

At a less expedient level but equally crucial is the manner in which the relevance of the religious rituals and symbols have been carried over to define and redefine the troubles.[16] This does not imply that those engaged in fighting legitimize their actions in terms of a 'holy war'. Nothing is further from my interpretation, as I shall argue when I examine the very ambivalent relationship that Republicanism has with the Roman Catholic church. But clearly the symbolic associations of Catholic thought linger on and continue to impinge upon the thinking of even atheistic IRA men. Long after the church has been rejected men respond (particularly in crises) to the God the priests and teachers and parents introduced to them. Most of the community have not, however, even rebuffed the authority of the clergy and it is to the church that many turn to order the confusion. Even young Fians[17] (one of whom had his father 'shopped' to the British Army by the Rector), who frequently cursed the non-Republican priests, crowded the chapel on the birthday of a recently dead comrade. A group of the Fians on this occasion were conversing about the 16-year-old, shot dead by the British Army, and one wondered whether he had time to say his Act of Contrition. Hard men as well as the more fearful are known to carry an indulgence prayer to St Joseph, the 'Patron of Departing Souls', which, complete with polythene case and soft metal medallion of St Joseph and the child Jesus, acts as an insurance against a violent death:

> Whoever shall read this prayer or hear it or keep it about
> themselves shall never die a sudden death or be drowned nor
> shall poison take effect on them. Neither shall they fall into the
> hands of the enemy . . . or shall be overpowered in battle.

This suit of metaphysical armour 'has never been known to fail'. As ritualistic was the old lady who sprinkled holy water around the entry after the soldiers had lifted a young man; as she sprinkled she called to the unfortunate prisoner that she would say the Rosary for him.

The solace of the church is clearest at Sunday mass. One element of religious rituals is that they can literally make one feel good, or as Frances, a Legion of Mary girl, graphically put it, 'I feel so holy it's coming out of my ears.' The several times I observed in the church I was impressed by the calmness and tranquillity of those in prayer. In contrast to the upheaval outside this stillness is soothing. The church becomes a place to unburden worries, temporarily at any rate. In some ways it was the poor man's psychoanalysis. In addition the solid familiarity of the ritual was at least one anchored institution at a time when everything else seemed to float about at its own will. No doubt many found direction in the sermons where the priests, sometimes delicately, other times crudely, intertwined the traditional gospel themes with present concerns on the immorality of violence, the arrogance of the young or the merits of authority. Certainly the bidding prayers neatly connected the expressive nature of the ceremony with the overt instrumentality of the church in times of crisis. Here God was asked to intercede on behalf of those unemployed or wrongfully dismissed that they find work, that families separated through internment be reunited and that peace with justice replace the present strife. This blending of the conventionally Catholic with the present troubles is admirably caught in the Rector's letter in the Anro parish magazine to the parishioners at Christmas 1971:

My dear people of Anro,

In this black period of trouble, one is apt to despond. One wonders will this trouble ever be over and one loses heart, but let me at once try to cheer you up.

You are true disciples of Christ, who told you to take up your cross and follow Him. This you have done and although you felt you slipped many times, you still kept your eyes on Him. Night after night you have experienced the same trials as He did. Many of your family have felt the blows and the kicks and like Christ, you have asked: Why did they do that to me?

God alone knows your destiny, but be certain that you are being made like His Son and the same reward will be given to you as was given to Him. All these troubles must come to an end. The sun will shine again, as the dark clouds go past, and you will realize that you are the beloved children of God the Father, and truly brothers and sisters of Christ. In this you are following in the footsteps of your ancestors. Countless thousands have died for their faith and their love for their country. They died and their names are now glorious. Would you want it different for yourselves? Not likely, but you would want a bit of peace. That is something

to be longed for and indeed to be fought for. Christ on the
cross prayed for His enemies, who murdered Him. Our
ancestors forgave those who injured and stole their land, so
we too must be ready to hold out the hand of friendship
to those who have wronged us so much. That is the fight we
have to make now. As we kneel at the Crib and adore the
Divine Infant, let us take His side to forgive. It is not easy.
Anro has taken an awful bashing. What a difference I can see,
I have been away from here for so long. We are going to
rebuild that. In spite of all the damage, one thing seems to
stand out as a symbol to you. Anro Church stands out. Isn't
it a beauty? And you have risked your lives for it. You
remember in the last big war, bombs were seen floating down
to destroy the Church, but when it seemed certain, they floated
away and fell in other places. God protected it and He still
protects it. Let us put our trust in Him. Let us depend
completely on Him and He will bring us safely through. Then
we can smile and dance again and, please God, enjoy the
freedom of the children of God.

May all the blessings of the Infant Jesus be shared among
you all.

It was more often this perspective the clergy espoused than a more
clearly expiatory view of the troubles. The injustice of a cruel
world should be placed into the hands of a benign God who would
bring the people through their travesties. I did, however, come
across the more piacular view that 'Someone must suffer for the
sins of this world and we seem to have been selected by God for
this task and should offer our sufferings, no matter from what
quarter they come, for their sins' (letter to the parish magazine).

Sprinkled among these various Catholic world-views of the chaos,
sporadically references would appear to less Christian superstitions
and beliefs. The banshees had caught the children's imagination.
Anyone would know there were sure to be more banshees about
with all the deaths in the district. All Soul's night might be fun to
prepare for with all the dressing up and collecting of money that it
traditionally entails, but the children assured me I would not see
them in the streets that night as the spirits would be walking. As for
the banshees the younger Fians were adamant they had seen one
and called the 'fellas' (IRA) out to 'see it off'. I do not want to make
much of this as it was superstitious nonsense for most. Yet the
community did have certain stories about quasi-religious events
such as exorcism and ghostly figures. The latter I gathered were
mostly folk devils to keep errant children in check. There was
Galloper Thompson who rode around on horseback with his head

under his arm, denied his eternal rest for spurning God and workers when, as an owner of one of the local mills he bragged he would sooner have his kingdom here than in heaven. 'The Big Man of Arden Street' was said to roam the streets tapping the upstairs windows of those soon to lose a close one. It seems this might refer to a tall tinker who used to roam around at odd hours in search of his sub-normal daughter. Then there was Screaming Anne who perished in the mill pond, or the bucket that rolled as if it were possessed and out of which a dead IRA man appeared.[18] These types of tales cluster around any tightly knit community with a history, perhaps more so if united by religion. An ex-novitiate suggested it was axiomatic that where you found faith you found spirits and talk of spirits. But I am simply arguing that the troubles increase the probability of such tales becoming conversational currency. The vivid example I witnessed was the surge of concern in the district with black magic. Rumours spread that some person ('the Black Man', i.e. dressed in black) was carrying out sacrificial black masses with the aid of butchered dogs and was generally frightening the life out of people. For a couple of weeks the adolescent boys and girls we knew were absorbed with the whole affair and enjoyed the semi-serious but adventurous task of searching the entries at night for the miscreant. It was also a good ruse for the lads to leave the 'wee girls' home. The saga was quickly associated with the Catholic church, the British Army and the Protestants. The following extracts from the 12- and 13-year-old boys' essays on the matter capture it all (spelling mistakes are left in except where the meaning is obscured):[19]

I   In the district of Anro there is supposed to be
            men dressed in black trying to do. black magic;
            whoever these madman are they are putting the
            fear god into the people, the boys said that if
            they get them they will shoot them dead. They
            would be better dead than alive because whoever
            is doing this (black magic) caper is bringing a
            curse on the district. Some people think it is
            the paratrooper who have just moved into the
            district. The paratroopers said they would get
            there own back on the people of Anro. Round the
            back of MacDongh St school two dogs were
            found with there hearts cut out. These men are
            supposed to be possessed by the (devil) the IRA
            had put out a warning that no one is to be on
            the streets after twelve. And that you are not to
            walk by yourself after it gets dark. This is

good advice if these madmen are hanging about the district you never know when they would jump on you.

II   The black man is a rumour. People say that he runs about at night and that he scrafices dogs and other things. Some say they chased him up the entry with hurly bats and sticks. Others say they chased him across the road and up the pad.[20] Some of the fellas say if they catch him he will be shot and they are to shoot on sight. If I was to go upon entry I would rather meet a paratrooper because they say the black man would kill you or he is a prod. [Protestant]. I think you would have a better chance with a paratrooper.

III   There is an Evil in Anro there is a rumour about a black how runs around with a cross turn up side down on his cloak we were all running up the entre and when we got to the middle of the entre he was away and then we started to go and look for him and a woman said that he practities the black magic she said that he used black candles and that he has a house in the Glen[21] and my sister lives in the Glen and she found black candles so she threw in the bin and threw holy water round the house and she is going to get the preast to bless the house and a wee lad seen him and him with a bottel and the bottel light up.

IV   The blackman is a load of rubbish – imaganiton excuse spelling rumours spread wildly I wonder how it started. It gives them something to talk about – ghostly stories I was sent up to get holy water I think it was a lamb she was thinking about.

V   This week there was a rumour which turned out to be true. This rumour was of a black man going round. It was supposed to bring those who were shot back to life. It had a cross upside down on his cloak. Some of the boys ran after him the other night with sticks and hurls but he was supposed to disappear. I don't know whether it's true or not. He was dressed in a black cloak and a black hood on him. He was supposed to break into Pease McAleans house [a dead IRA man] and left a black candle on the mantel piece. Is it true or is it not?

VI   If I was going along the street and I met the black man I would either run the hell or drop dead. In the district there is a rumer that there is sutch a thing as the black man but I don't believe it till I see it. I think the black man is an old man who is drunk and is trying to scare people but putting on a sute of blak. It was very funney but since the paratroopers have come into Anro the blak man has been seen. If the paratroopers were to move out then maybe the black man would move out as well.

VII   I think the blackman is an old twit who is trying to scare away the people so he will be able to do Black Mass without anyone to disturb him. Whoever is doing it is very very mad. Because when he dies he will go to hell and be with the devil for ever more.

VIII   The priest in Anro said that the devil is in Anro and he was coming round to Bless the houses for the last two nights the fog has come down awful sudden. The Man or Devil is called Black Magic. The soldiers shot at him. But the Bullets went right threw it. On Saturday night he or it was caught in the entry a lot of fellas caught it and Beat it up. Sometimes I wonder why they didn't kill it. There's two of them they sacrifice old Dogs and Do Black Masses.

The 'Black Man' disappeared as quietly as he had arrived. These essays are used in full knowledge that it was predominantly the young of the district who were fired by the affair. Though, as seen, they had their share of sceptics and several adults had in fact, one of the priests informed me, requested holy water as the stories claim. Nevertheless these extracts are very pertinent illustrations of the range of features in the community's culture and their expression in the troubles. There is the invocation of the 'fellas' as authorities; the weighing of dangers in terms of the British Army/Protestants and the occult; the extensive allusion to religious symbolism: holy water, black candles, upturned crosses, a lamb; and a concern with the efficacy of rumours and the deceased victims of the troubles. Their use, consequently, does not signify that Anro is as steeped in superstition as some of the more gullible young boys make it appear in these imaginative essays. But rather these accounts do capture the theme of this section in that they graphically illustrate, with their references to the priests, the IRA and the people of Anro, how the troubles have been assimilated into the community's culture. Indeed the troubles have become enough of a part of that culture to play a role in the interpretation and definition of a community phenomenon like that of the 'Black Man'.

Continuing the theme of the filtering and accommodation of the troubles into the pre-existing cultural forms in the community, Anro's organizations can be seen to have taken on a new importance. In addition several important new organizations have been formed. Barton (1969) suggests a stamp of disasters is that an 'emergency social system' appears which seeks to fill the vacuum created by rapid social change. This 'counter-disaster syndrome' is predominantly evident in the Anro Redevelopment Association, The Catholic Ex-Servicemen's Association and in the two Sinn Féin and IRA structures. Of these the first and last are the more important.

Both the re-emergence of the Official IRA and the creation of the Provisional IRA out of the 1969 riots received considerable support in Anro, the Provisional Sinn Féin IRA becoming dominant by 1972 in this particular area. At present I will refrain from looking at the significance of militant Republicanism in the district. The other organizations are not directly aligned to Republican parties and are more of self-help forces in the community. The Relief Committee was formed in 1968 when the first housing intimidations were becoming apparent.[22] It aims to assist victimized families, most of whom wish to move into Anro (the majority of whom have relatives in the area, which has the effect of pulling the kinship network even tighter). Its help takes the form of storing furniture, arranging transport, supplying emergency food, accommodation and bedding and in giving general assistance and information about other sources of help. As the trouble deepened its role has widened into documenting complaints against the British Army, finding out where lifted men and women are being held, running bus services to internment camps and prisons and raising money for interned and political prisoners. Its few active members are unpaid volunteers and figure amongst their ranks some of the most highly respected individuals in the community. These individuals now possess a mass of political experience and knowledge garnered from their dealings in the troubles.

To some extent the Relief Committee's role was eclipsed with the formation in November 1971 of the Anro Community Council with which it now liaises. The Council is a type of community soviet and is a fascinating example of an attempt at self-government at the local level. At its inception it distributed a non-violent Republican manifesto declaring the 'messianic role' of England in Ireland a 'presumption', claiming an understanding of the motivation of the men of violence without condoning them, and requesting the Orange Institution to 'wipe out the shame of its bigotry' so that all could seek a 'community life based on justice and reconciliation'. The Council's members are elected from the streets, with each street ostensibly voting for four women, men and children to form their street committee, representatives of which sit on the Council's committees. The children were largely overlooked in these elections and rarely did a street have its full complement of adult representatives. Apart from the street committees, the Council is composed of justice, development and welfare committees with two co-ordinating committees. While the Council does not function as it would like to because of waning enthusiasm, it does manage to publish its fortnightly news sheet and to perform a whole range of other work. This is mainly due to a caucus of dedicated individuals. The welfare committee, which I observed a few times, was run mainly by women and was particularly energetic. It organized holidays for the young and aged; it assessed, through small surveys, different needs in the area and it used its resources to battle with the outside state bureaucracy for a wide array of benefits to which the community was entitled.

The development committee in conjunction with the Anro Redevelopment Association,[23] concerns itself with the long-term plans for slum clearance in Anro. Old Anro's redevelopment is now taking place (1977) and these two groups have successfully negotiated for low-storey houses to be built in the area by arguing that the high-rise flats in other parts of Belfast have altered the social character of their communities beyond recognition. The Redevelopment Association has finished the rebuilding of the two hundred or so houses burnt in New Anro. This remarkable feat was achieved with a great amount of drive by the key men involved. However, the task of reletting the homes proved problematic. The project was done in conjunction with certain Protestant representatives of those who left the houses. The initial intention was to rehouse the original tenants. The complexity this has involved, necessitating as it does the return of Protestants to Anro, can be easily imagined. The delay in finding a solution led to the empty rebuilt houses being squatted in, the removal of the squatters by various forces in the district and the resquatting of some of the houses. The position at present in this somewhat optimistic experiment is unresolved. The development committee also concerns itself with fostering local industry and obtaining government grants for this purpose.

The justice committee closely monitors British Army activity. It issues statements on controversial incidents where reckless and illegal methods result in the ill-treatment or worse of any person within and sometimes outside the community. On one occasion, following gross assault by Paratroopers on several people in Anro, the committee sent telegrams to the Prime Minister, consulted a professor of law for advice, wrote to the press and helped organize a demonstration of protest. The justice committee was working towards a tribunal for the arbitration of internal disputes in the absence of any policing in the area. Anro had been completely free from the state policing of the Royal Ulster Constabulary since the 1969 riots. The presence of any police in the area would cause an immediate riot. Tacitly the RUC had abdicated its policing role to the British Army's security role. Members of the justice committee were not particularly concerned with ordinary criminality in Anro as they shared the widely held community view that conventional crime in Anro was minimal. Accordingly their interest in setting up a tribunal was largely concerned with hearing complaints against the British Army and the IRA. However, the IRA as the *de facto* policing organization could ignore the influence of the Community Council if for no other reason than its military strength. Nevertheless the IRA (Provisional) recognized the Council as a legitimate authority in Anro, the only one to receive such public acknowledgment. To some extent, although I could not gauge how much, the IRA was represented on the Council through the street committees. What was clear was that the Community Council was not a front organiza- tion for the IRA. The British Army's general harassment of some of the Community Council leaders seemed to imply that they were 'plain-clothes' IRA men. As it was, the Community Council boasted several bitter opponents of the IRA including members of the clergy who figured quite prominently in the committee work.

As might be expected the politics of the Council, due to the nature of the community in Anro, tended to become personalized. Issues within the Council were frequently appraised in terms of the indi- viduals who were espousing the policies. The few middle-class members, who were originally Anro inhabitants but now lived outside, hard-working as they were, came in for all the criticism ('slagging') that the aspiring and the 'foreigner' get in the district. Other active members had accusations of favouritism hurled at them: they were held to be privileged in the allocation of the better houses as they became vacant; they neglected Old Anro; they were 'cliquey'; they impinged upon others working for the community and so on. Chagrin and rivalry aside, though some complaints might be justified, the organization had effectively responded to meet several of the necessities and demands of the community. In a situation where some of the population were physically contesting the legitimacy of the State, the Council works on behalf of those who remain not so committed and those who still desire or need to negotiate with the State. Consequently it has met government ministers and civil servants, led delegations to the British Army, talked with the Housing Executive over intimidation and redevelopment policies and has negotiated with other departments of the welfare state.

I was impressed at the highly politicized nature of Anro, which is slightly untypical, even for Belfast. In particular I considered the Community Council very impressive due to the efficiency and capability of its organization and the level of participation it managed to achieve. Notwithstanding the way in which policies became personal attributes or how the limits of reformist tactics showed themselves in the face of armed soldiers, the Community Council achieved some valuable and effective community work. My enthusiasm was not particularly shared by several critical residents who thought I was in danger of overstating the degree of activity. I ought, they thought, to be impressed with the fact that the vast majority were still apathetic. If it took the crises of Anro to throw up a few committees, what had to happen before a participatory democracy emerged was even more uncertain.

Apart from the church groups (Legion of Mary, Knights of Malta and the parish committee) who concerned themselves with minor social work, first aid and fund raising for various groups in the parish, the remaining structured group in Anro was the Ex-Servicemen's Association. It was not unheard of during blanket searches for British Army soldiers to come across medals awarded to men in Anro for their contribution to the Second World War. That is, quarry and searcher had fought for the same army. Clearly fifty and more years of living as part of the United Kingdom had its effects even on staunch Republican areas and one manifestation of this was the large number of middle-aged men who had been in the British Forces, including several IRA men. The CESA was made up of such individuals who had British Army records and who though largely Republican in the sense of having some emotional commitment to a united Ireland were mainly hostile to radical Republican associations. The Association had its own club which, apart from entertainment, would be used to drill its cadets and to discuss 'security' matters concerning Anro. Many members considered CESA's primary role as that of Anro's last line of defence, a trained corps of men ready to defend the community should a concerted attack upon the district materialize. Apart from this doomsday role the organization occasionally acted as a group of vigilantes patrolling the perimeters of Anro. This would involve stopping strange cars, questioning people and generally monitoring movement in the area. CESA's relationship with both the armies in

Anro, the IRA and the British, was decidedly ambiguous. The IRA regarded it as a 'bunch of cronies', some of whom were collaborators, but it would sometimes co-operate with the Association over vigilante duty and the organization of demonstrations. There was no love lost between the two. The British Army was frequently admonished by CESA for its disgraceful troop behaviour. I was assured by one member that such behaviour never took place in other colonial campaigns. Yet at the same time CESA aided the British domination. For example, it attempted to control and stop riots and it offered an overall condemnation of IRA activity. Though not much in evidence, CESA, apart from functioning as a source of involvement for those men who are not militant Republicans, contributed to making Anro a little safer in its concern for citizen defence.

This emergence of new organizations and the rejuvenation of old ones is part of the wider process by which the troubles become expressed in terms of the cultural and institutional patterns of the community. The result of this process is the sustaining of a partial sense of social order in Anro. Though the emergency state over time becomes routinized it is not wholly successful in making the extreme commonplace. Trouble frequently leaks out beyond the tolerance of the culture to produce serious in-fighting, generally low morale and personal misery. Accordingly in the attempt to reconstruct order from the chaos there is a delicate interplay between anomie and solidarity, between the collective disturbance of the ordinary and periodic waves of the collective consciousness. Intertwined with the internecine disputes which tear the community apart common experiences of fear and danger bring the district together. Vilified by the mass media,[24] treated as a dangerous, polluted community, residents take note that their personal knowledge assures them it is not as outsiders say it is. Explicit demonstrations of insider experience, what Durkheim recognized in religious and other representations, are frequent phenomena in troubled Anro.

One clear example started with the apparently innocent observation, as I travelled from town to Anro on the bus, that none of the British Army vehicles usually stationed in the neighbouring Protestant district were in their garages. Soon I realized this was because the military had saturated Anro. Walking into the district some Fians told me the 'Brits' had shot four people and that one had died. The shootings had been an ambush. The Paratroopers had hidden in a derelict house remaining strangely unnoticed for at least twelve hours. They had opened fired on a group of men, some of whom were IRA members, at the intersection at the end of the road I was living in. The men had scattered with the first burst of fire but had been caught with bullets as they ran away. The dead man and the two badly wounded, both near death, had been thrown into the back of a Saracen tank which had moved in to support the British troops. One slightly wounded man had escaped into one of the houses and the Paratroopers had sealed off a few streets searching for him and waiting to see if the doctor appeared. The Paratroopers stayed for hours, looking somewhat pleased by their work, and effectively bottled people up in their homes. Consequently no one knew what exactly was going on and no one dared to venture out to satisfy their concern.

When finally the tanks pulled out people thronged into the streets to talk, to commiserate and to relieve the tension. The anger was fantastic, the newsmen had already gathered and several were shouted at – it was believed that they would print the official version, about IRA men being shot as the army returned fire. The non-official version of the ambush was emerging as neighbours and friends conversed with each other, with the ones who got away, with the nun who was kicked away as she tried to say an Act of Contrition for the wounded. The slightly injured man was already on his way 'down south'. The doctor had gone in the back entry to attend to him. This incident was remarkable for the solidarity it created amongst different factions of the community. Differences were temporarily suspended as thousands quickly gathered to condemn the terrorist tactics of the Paratroopers in an open air demonstration which thronged the streets.

Less spontaneous but equally unifying was the solidarity created by the Loyalist assassination campaign. Increasingly from July 1972 Anro inhabitants became victims of so-called sectarian assassinations. The effect within Anro was to limit even further the amount of time residents spent outside the district. This, in turn, heightened the awareness of being an endangered minority and consequently dependent on internal strength for survival. Evidence of the tightening of community bonds can be shown in the increased importance of celebrating things 'Irish'. Republicans organized Gaelic classes and remarked how easy it was now to sell Irish history books and literature. The interest in traditional music has also increased and contributes to what amounts to a minor Gaelic cultural revival. At another level the numerous contemporary folk/propaganda songs have immortalized some of the local heroes in Anro, which, as stated previously even has its own song born out of the 1969 riots, remembering 'those long-haired ones who stood steady and true'.

Similarly the exploits of some of the near legendary figures become apocryphal anecdotes stressing how Anro 'has been put on the world map'. Indeed the conversational capital generated by the troubles grew at such a rate that it produced an enormous increase in sociation.

As in most war situations a foreshortening and intensifying of temporal experience appears. So too in Anro, where it takes the form of the search for 'crack'. Crack is having a good time, getting a 'bit full', 'having a laugh', looking for a little extra sex and generally 'sticking two fingers up at tomorrow'. In Anro as the population bulges with the increase in 'refugee' immigrants and as opportunities for entertainment outside become less safe, the overwhelming bulk of this search for 'crack' takes place in the clubs. The effect of concentrating the majority of individuals' leisure pursuits – gossiping, dancing, singing, drinking, sexual encounters, playing music – moments from their home – is to tighten the mesh of sociability among the residents.

The collective consciousness evidenced itself in these and other ways. The troubles raised the belief in the efficacy of joint action and increased the confidence of the activists. Similarly the collective consciousness manifests itself in the crystallization of its boundaries through the condemnation of community deviance. Conspicuous non-medical drug use, homosexuality (particularly male), other sexual offences and petty thieving result in the 'offender' suffering various degrees of reprobation. Such ostracism could take the form of physical abuse, expulsion, boycotting or the milder readjustment of the community's collective memory bank about what type of person the deviant its. Probably the cardinal community crime during the troubles, though the British Army would claim not an infrequent occurrence, was that of informing. Even those who have sympathy for the motives of informants and utter contempt for the informal agents of control, frequently IRA personnel, agree that the act of informing is reprehensible: 'At least the other side stick together.' The distaste for informing runs very deep in Irish history and is traceable at least to the bitterness 'touting' caused in the Civil War years. There exists in Ireland a traditional hatred for the Special Branch which formed at the end of the last century to infiltrate Irish groups and which remains today the main organization, together with Army Intelligence, to systematize informing. In Anro informing is particularly threatening. It attacks the fabric of the community in its capitalization on what cannot be controlled, the public nature of knowledge. It is ironic that one basis of order and control in the area, the phenomenon of multiplex ties, cannot itself be controlled: knowledge is public and can therefore be telephoned in to the British Army. Systematic informing would rip the district apart and smash its tentative organizations laying it open for a Protestant or British Army takeover. This can happen in other ways such as the paratroopers' terror tactics,[25] but the initiative for informing stems from members in the community, and is the very real check that it holds over militant Republicanism.

Conclusion: culture and war

In illustrating the community's two pronged response to the rapid and violent change in Anro, that of anomie and solidarity, I have been concerned to show the principal characteristics of its culture. The length of the war in Ireland, I contend, is partially explained by an appreciation of how the features of the Catholic communities have mediated the troubles to produce a number of radical *Gemeinschaften*. The existing culture of areas like Anro which are faced with massive dislocation, has incorporated substantially different conditions into its organization and symbolization. The new 'order', though highly unstable (more accurately a series of orders), dissipates enough of the chaos to sustain the war on two fronts, that of the British Army and the Protestants. I do not suggest that the culture lends itself to the formation of a war machine or that it undermines the exceedingly ambivalent commitment to the war which most have. I claim only that the commonality of experience created by ties of kin, residence, religion and class are strong enough to disperse most of the anomie in situations like Anro. In turn this enables the war to continue. This has obvious relevance for the limits of urban guerrilla activity.

Clearly this explanation is partial. What marks off Anro and similar Catholic communities in the North of Ireland from other urban and rural villages in Ireland and Britain, and which is at the root of the war, are the social and economic realities which produce the ideological social relations of sectarianism and Republicanism. It is within these latter social forces that the possibility of the strife in the Six Counties springs. In the following chapters I shall document their centrality by drawing on their expression in Anro and then generalizing them to the wider social context. Without the existence of these societal realities Anro would be quiescent. This chapter has been concerned to demonstrate, however, that also without Anro's social structure the continuation of the militant politics thrown up by this society would be impossible.

2 Sectarianism: a category of ideological thought and form of practice in Northern Ireland

The concept of 'telling'

Critical to an appreciation of both the mundane and extraordinary activities in Anro is an understanding of the social relations of sectarianism which pervade the wider society. These relations are the conceptual and material backcloth against which a wide area of behaviour may be brought into focus. They constitute a structuring which reflects the reality of a fundamental social division. The systematic interpretation of the representations of sectarianism shows clearly how mental categories are social constructions and in turn how these categories of thought serve particular interests.[1] I intend to illustrate the manifestations of sectarianism as a normal process of thinking through the notion of 'telling'. Telling is the pattern of signs and cues by which religious ascription is arrived at in the everyday interactions of Protestants and Catholics.[2] Telling at this level is a necessary social skill for triggering the cognitive store of sectarianism. It is a trigger which brings into play the typifications and stereotypes about the nature of the 'other side'. As such, it releases the highly restricted stock of knowledge which is relevant for mixed Protestant and Catholic interactions. Telling is not a comprehensive account of sectarianism, but I suggest that it furnishes an insight into the nature and depth of a riven society by illustrating the centrality of difference as a typical mode of thought.

Telling is based on the social significance attached to name, face and dress, area of residence, school attended, linguistic and possibly phonetic use, colour and symbolism. It is not based on undisputed fact but as an ideological representation is a mixture of 'myth' and 'reality'. Aspects of the process are certainly contentious among members of the community itself. The idea that a person's religion can be arrived at merely by looking is one that is laughable to some but an obvious statement of fact to others. The significance attached to most of the cues is, accordingly, open to dispute. It makes the process of telling often unclear and open to negotiation. What is less shifting is the desire and necessity to tell. While the efficacy of the various signs fluctuates, telling as a category of thinking remains constant. This, I would maintain, is the ideological importance of the process of telling; not that it is based on differences which obtain in fact, but that it is a social construction of differences which is used to think with and to act upon. The phenomenon represents an imaginary relationship to the actual historical conditions of existence of 'Catholic' and 'Protestant' subjects (Althusser, 1971; Hirst, 1976). Telling is a central process in creating and sustaining the coherence of a sectarian cosmology. This alleged significance is partially born out in a study of 58 Catholics and 69 Protestants, all male adolescents, who claimed they could tell (Ross, 1971). Ross shows how, when presented with 80 colour slides of people and asked to assign Protestant or Catholic status, the correct ascriptions by Protestants did not correspond with the correct ascriptions by Catholics. This suggests they were using differing physiognomic cues.[3] They were thinking in a similar manner but using different signs.

In a similar vein Cooper (1958) argues that the intractable debate over whether anti-Semites can tell Jews more accurately than non-prejudiced Gentiles is resolved if emphasis is placed not on the efficacy but on the process of thinking itself. If, he argues, the testing of stereotyping is 'phenomenologically orientated', then the significance lies not in whether the anti-Semites' high scoring is due to perceptual acuity or response bias, but in what people believe themselves able to do: 'In everyday language what the person thinks he can do is just as important as what he can do.' (Cooper, 1958: 17)[4]

To those who seek satisfaction in 'really knowing' what is fact and what is myth, in the case of the Jewish studies whether anti-Semites can tell above chance better than the unprejudiced, or whether fellow Jews can tell each other more proficiently,[5] this approach may look like an abdication of analysis. But ideological representations and social relations are not founded on what 'really is'. They develop within their systems of signification sets of relations that constitute their own materiality. This accordingly becomes the object of sociological enquiry.

Thus conceived, the social effects of telling in the Six Counties may also be analysed without encountering certain quandaries. Quandaries, for example, of just how much mixed marriage has taken place since the time of plantation and how much have they produced a blurring of facial characteristics? More centrally, is it possible to assert that Scotch and Irish Celts differ physically? To what extent, anyway, has immigration confused physiological types?

Such issues are very difficult to grasp. What is amenable to analysis is how stereotypes of Protestant and Catholic are constructed with reference to race, history, politics and economics and how they are employed in the ideological configurations of the contemporary society.

Before I attempt this analysis, I want to look at the bare historical outline which makes sense of the manifestations of sectarianism I have called telling. The present day expression of sectarianism has its basis in history and in the narrative interpretation of that history by the living individuals in the Six Counties. The sectarian consciousness is profoundly rooted in the past. Several commentators on Northern Ireland have rightly emphasized the startling degree to which history is put to use in routine behaviour:[6]

> Ireland is almost a land without history because the troubles of the past are relived as contemporary events. (Rose, 1971: 75)

> To understand the present it is necessary to look to the past, for these divisions have their origins in Irish history and one of the first things to notice is that Irishmen have given to the terms 'Catholic' and 'Protestant' a meaning which would be understood nowhere else in the world. (Barritt and Booth, 1972: 1)

> An awareness of Cromwell's massacre at Drogheda and Wexford and of the decisive Protestant victory at the Boyne is socialized into schoolchildren and it becomes part of the consciousness of belonging to each faith as being black is for the American Negro. (Hickie and Elliott, 1971: 33)

It is this debate with the past that orders so much of the present meaning of sectarianism. In reading, for example, the history of Belfast, one is struck by an overwhelmingly strong feeling of *déjà vu* as the same areas, names, issues and activities which now pervade the present dominate the past.[7] Clearly people select their history to fit into their present needs. But the dialectical relationship between history and present interest has its other side, namely in the strength of macro-structural factors influencing the social reality of the individual (Marx, 1926: 96):

> Men make their own history, but they do not make it just as they please, they do not make it under circumstances chosen by themselves, but under circumstances directly encountered, given and transmitted from the past. The tradition of all the dead generations weighs like a nightmare on the brain of the living. And just when they seem engaged in revolutionizing

themselves and things, in creating something that has never yet existed, precisely in such periods of revolutionary crisis they anxiously conjure up the spirits of the past to their service and borrow from them names, battle cries and customs in order to present the new scene of world history in this time-honoured disguise and borrowed language.

The bulk of this chapter will be concerned with the manifestations of sectarianism as an ideology within the contemporary community. Clearly, though, these manifestations are the internalizations and mediations of a history of particular economic and political policies.

Aspects of Irish history: situating the 'telling' syndrome

The familiar assertion that England has been meddling with Ireland for a little over 800 years gives an idea of the massive historical appreciation needed to give justice to the complexity of Irish history. I intend, necessarily, to look only briefly at some of those issues which have an overt relevance for the depth of sectarian expression in Northern Ireland today, and which provide the raw material for the legitimation of the process of telling.[8]

The historic division between English invader and native Celt was set in the twelfth century. Though profound differences did obtain between natives and imperialists, as is evidenced in the discriminatory 1366 Statute of Kilkenny, there was a considerable degree of marrying into the native Irish by the Anglo-Norman retainers. As significant was the omission of any religious difference. If an uneasy step is taken to Henry VIII's reign, it is clear that by then the Old English settlers in Ireland had developed overtly different interests to the expansionist policy of Henry. Both the old colonialists and the indigenous population shared a strong resentment towards Henry's religious and political plans for Ireland. This admittedly minimal unity of interest was strong enough to result in over a century of resistance which was most strenuously crushed by Cromwell. For the purposes at hand what needs to be noted is that the aftermath of the sixteenth-century resistance by native chiefs and old imperialists was a recolonization of Ireland.

England adopted a solution to the problem of the decadent Old English and the still strong native chiefs by following the military defeat of the war lords with a wave of induced immigration in the form of plantation. From the early seventeenth-century (1603–8) approximately 130,000 Scots and 200,000 Englishmen, overwhelmingly Protestant, provided the buffer against further uprisings affecting the strategic alliance of Ireland in the new European balance of power (Dickson, 1966). The indigenous population was dispossessed of land and was to achieve very little security of tenure in the poorer farmlands it managed to rent. The social class of the colonists was nothing like the earlier imperialist lords. Loyalty to the motherland, which in practice meant keeping the native Irish dispossessed, was ensured, as only the land rented from the undertakers, in effect, stood between the new colonists and the natives. Conflict between, in class terms, not very different strata was contained by the existence of state and semi-private armies which separated settler and native. Belfast, for example, had a resident Scottish army for six years (Budge and O'Leary, 1973: 9).[9]

With the ascent of the Catholic King James II in 1685 there was an effort to restore the old faith in Ireland. James attempted to establish a new charter for the town of Belfast, which had by then a population of 2,000. His proposals, which would slightly have altered the predominantly Protestant character of the town, were thwarted by the invasion of Prince William of Orange. William took Belfast in 1688 and went on to win the decisive battle of the Civil war by defeating King James at the Battle of the Boyne some two years later. Like the 1641 rising, the 1690 failure was followed by severe reprisals on the Catholic population. Cromwell had extended the plantation and now the Popery laws of the next thirty years would formally exclude Catholics from the Irish Parliament, corporate offices and the limited franchise.

In the eighteenth century the native population and the new settlers came into sharper conflict. This is so despite the radical interlude of the United Irishmen at the end of the century. That episode gives one of the very rare examples of the 'sectarian' division being temporarily subdued even if not overcome. The Volunteers were a predominantly Protestant army set up to replenish the withdrawal of troops from Ireland around 1778. They emerged as a very strong pressure group which was able to exert influence on the English Parliament for increased hegemony for the Irish Parliament. Some Volunteers also championed the Catholic demands for emancipation, which, if achieved would have modified the Protestant ascendancy in the Irish Parliament. Support was particularly evident amongst the Belfast Volunteers who allowed Catholics to join their ranks. The Volunteer movement as a whole was, however, split over the exact degree of the extension of the franchise to Catholics and both the English and Irish Parliaments encouraged the setting up of new, wholly Protestant, units. The result was the hiving off of the radical Belfast Volunteers to form the United Irishmen. The main-stream Volunteer movement was left to exhibit the emergent sec-tarianism and division which came to characterize Protestant and Catholic relationships: 'And in Ulster the latent prejudice against Catholics was soon exploited since the new companies in many areas sang anti-Catholic songs and provoked the emergence of rival groups' (Budge and O'Leary, 1973: 11).[10]

One such rural clash, in Armagh in 1795, saw the emergence of the Orange Order which in later years came to dominate the yeomanry in an avowedly anti-Catholic manner (Senior, 1966; Gibbon, 1972). Where the Orange Order was strong the radical United Irishmen were weak. The Order was to develop as typical of the Catholic/ Protestant relations. By contrast the struggle of the United Irishmen, defeated in 1798, despite their strength in Belfast, remained 'a liberal episode in the history of a highly conservative city' (Budge and O'Leary, 1973: 13).

Belfast began its industrial growth in the middle of the eighteenth century. Its population increased from 8,000 in 1757 to 20,000 at the turn of the century. Its cotton industry became factory-based from 1780 (Budge and O'Leary, 1973: 8). The growth of Belfast was accompanied by settler/native differences, frequently the source of rural battles being played out in an urban industrial milieu throughout the nineteenth century.

Industrialization brought Catholics into Belfast at a fast rate, particularly over the first third of the nineteenth century. Whereas the population of Belfast was a little over 10 per cent Catholic in 1790, it was 32 per cent in 1839. The nineteenth century also saw the formation of religious homogeneous districts in the city and the beginnings of Protestant and Catholic urban riots. There was at least one major riot per decade with the exception of the 1820s. These battles resulted in approximately 58 deaths in 13 critical encounters (Boyd, 1970; Budge and O'Leary, 1973: chapter 3). The riots were most frequently sparked off by elections, usually held on King William's commemorative victory day, 12 July, or by Orange or Nationalist marches, or the more specifically Catholic processions.[11]

Elections have always been characterized by sectarianism from O'Connell's Catholic Association campaign for emancipation, through to the Home Rule contention. Rarely has the voting pattern achieved much cross-religious alignment. Belfast itself was always in the tight control of the Protestant conservatives. Although they constituted one-third of the population, Catholics managed to elect only three councillors in the fifty years previous to 1896. In parliamentary elections the familiar pattern of 1 Liberal, 3 Tories established itself from 1885. Before this it had been even less likely to produce one Liberal.

The explanation of such violent and polarized sectarianism is held by Budge and O'Leary (1973: 27) to lie in the growth and influence of the religious apartheid practised by the Orange Order in Belfast. Traditionally, authors have emphasized the historical background of a plantation system being brought into an industrializing city. In

42

turn the native/settler clashes were taken to find new expression in the competition for jobs (Owen, 1921; Beckett and Glassock, 1967). Clearly the Protestant and Catholic working classes were differentially skilled particularly after the shift to heavy engineering industry (c. 1868). Amongst other impediments the Catholic workers were allowed into Belfast, and consequently into the job market, at a late date. There were already 33,000 cotton workers in Belfast in 1811 when the Catholic population was only 10 per cent (Budge and O'Leary, 1973: 9-20, 32). The Catholics were consequently offered only menial jobs and resulting 'occupational distinctions of this kind were well able to feed Protestant prejudice already exacerbated by the alien peasant background and customs of the Catholic immigrants' (Budge and O'Leary, 1973: 33).

Agreeing so far, Budge and O'Leary then seek to undermine the economic basis of the riots by pointing out that the first one (1813) occurred before the Catholic population had increased. Moreover they argue that the other major riots do not correspond to the trade recessions of nineteenth century Belfast when it might be hypothesized that the conflict over work opportunities would be at its highest. While this is interesting and tempers the tendency to argue for a simple temporal relationship between recessions and riots it does not gloss so easily over the manifestations of the ideological social relations produced by a Protestant aristocracy of labour. This social division is clearly rooted in the division of labour. While one can agree that the ethnic and moral purity preached by the Orange Order did perform a powerful role in keeping sectarian issues alive, by harping on the supposed innate inferiority of Catholics, I do not consider it necessary to attach to the institution any theoretical autonomy. Its significance derives from the fact that the Orange Order was the ideological mouthpiece of a social distinction which was materially based. As a vehicle of ideological practice, the Orange Order was most certainly well organized and effective in combating the efforts of the labour movement to expose the sectarian character of Orangeism.[12] This was due to the particular configuration which the bonded mixture of economics, politics and religion produced in the Six Counties.

For example, apart from the Orange Order and its pale Catholic counterpart (the Ancient Order of Hibernians), Belfast has a tradition of producing extremely politicized clergymen. The better known ones are usually Protestant (Episcopalian and Presbyterian) and avowedly anti-Catholic (Roman). Wright (1973), speaking of Evangelical fundamentalism,[13] emphasizes the stream of ministers who have defined Catholicism in terms of its political machinations (real or imagined) and have accordingly ordered their Protestantism in an overtly political manner. The Rev. I. K. Paisley thus becomes the present day embodiment of a Rev. Drew, Dr Cooke, Rev. Hanna, Rev. McIlwaine or Rev. Kane. All these ministers have contributed to the precipitating events which have led to serious rioting. For example, in 1857 Drew preached to assembled Orangemen; Hanna and McIlwaine joined in the open-air sermons against the evils of Romanism and 56 days of rioting followed (Budge and O'Leary, 1973: 79). These pedagogues were also frequent visitors to the numerous commissions reporting on the riots.[14]

It was the strength of the Orange Order and the actively political nature of a good deal of Protestant religious expression which enabled the liaison at the political and ideological levels between upper- and lower-class Protestants to be achieved. This markedly important political phenomenon has only become ruptured in the present troubles. Ironically, it was the slight Liberal revival of 1868 which produced this cross-class political bloc when the Orange and Protestant Working Man's Association joined with the Belfast Conservative Association in a Protestant coalition. At the height of the Home Rule struggle the Orange Lodges had become well experienced in party political activity. They had gained a 100-seat representation on the Ulster Unionist Council which had been established in 1903.[15] This welded Orange and Conservative machine was able to resist the Irish Revolution. Its resistance achieved a partitioned six-county 'Ulster' which consolidated what had been typical in its major city throughout the nineteenth century, namely a domination by one party and one religion of that city, and now of a State.

The Civil War years following the Irish Revolution brought sectarian rioting and death on a new scale to Belfast. The experiencing of some 554 deaths, 232 in 1922 alone (Budge and O'Leary, 1973: 143) is within the living memory of the oldest generation today. Part of this memory in the Catholic areas is a hatred of British troops. In particular there is an antipathy towards the infamous Black and Tans whose legend of brutality is occasionally compared by members of the Catholic areas with the contemporary British Army presence.[16] The Northern Ireland State was born in response to and under the threat of political violence. It has been established by a police force which has occupied an openly political role as is evidenced in the paramilitary duties assigned to the police under the Special Powers Act (1922). The history of plantation and division between Catholic and Protestant, and its vicious manifestations throughout the industrialization of the North became epitomized in the creation of a separate Northern Ireland. Partition was hardly conducive to easing the *laager* mentality of the Protestant people. The border came to symbolize all the real and supposed peculiarities of the two religious groups. The polarization of political allegiance along religious lines, and the Orange, and now Unionist, hegemony was reflected in the State's intransigence: in the first twelve elections of that State the Unionist party's seats varied between 40 and 42 (out of 52), a large number rarely being contested (Rose, 1971: 93).[17]

As during the dock strike of 1907, Protestant and Catholic workers came together in the depression years of the early 1930s. In 1932 the Northern Ireland government, significantly, prescribed a hunger march to Stormont under the powers available to it in the Special Powers Act. The police fired over the heads of the workers in the Falls. The Shankill riot in support resulted in two deaths (Campbell, 1967). Three years later, however, the sectarian split re-emerged with the formation of the Ulster Protestant League. During this period the Prime Minister, Brooke, stated publicly that Catholics should not be employed unless no other option were open. Serious rioting occurred again in 1935. Over three bitter weeks of fighting brought death to twelve people and homelessness to some 400, mostly Catholic (Budge and O'Leary, 1973: 151).[18] Internment and curfews were reintroduced during the war years when the IRA was adopting a traditional strategy of trying to make the most of England's adversities. Despite such IRA activity many Catholics had voluntarily enlisted into the British Army. The comparatively recent, and in IRA terms unsuccessful, Republican border campaign of 1956–62, in which nineteen people died, has kept alive the vehemence of both Loyalism and Republicanism in the Six Counties.

The passing, however, from the premiership of Brookeborough and the later accession of O'Neill has been recognized by several writers as a major turning point in Unionism away from the 'not an inch' mentality towards a potentially less discriminating regime. O'Neill was held to be interested in diluting the strong wines of Loyalism and Republicanism (Kelly, 1972).[19] The attempt to end the cold war with the Republic, the visiting of Catholic institutions by the Prime Minister, together with the acceptance of the official opposition party by the Nationalists, did give the State, in Northern Irish terms, a look of liberalism.[20] Yet, 'O'Neillism' together with the worldwide spread of ecumenicism had the effect of bringing forth the traditional fundamentalist response, this time in the form of Paisleyism. Paisleyite demonstrations ranged from barracking Nationalist candidates to damning the revisionism of both the Archbishop of Canterbury and Prime Minister O'Neill. Catholic protest, however, took a significant turn away from traditional Nationalism. Making the most of O'Neillism, a small group of educated middle-class Catholics who were not 'Castle Catholics'[21] organized an incipient Civil Rights campaign which was intended to highlight the 'peculiarities' of this part of the British Isles. The activities of the Civil Rights movement, together with the support of the radical student movement (People's Democracy), brought the discriminatory practices of the regime to the notice of the English society. The subsequent sectarian clashes that occurred in October 1968, January 1969 and most clearly in the riots of August 1969, had the further effect of exposing the structure of the Northern Irish society to a world-wide audience.[22] The distinction between the CRA (the Civil Rights Association) and the IRA was given little credence amongst the Protestant population. Quasi-religious Paisleyism became openly political Ultra-Loyalism. Paisleyism had started as a political demonstration against the weakening of religious tenets. As the Civil Rights movement gathered momentum, Paisleyism came to represent the vanguard rebuffing, what was effectively an assault on Protestant ascendancy, an assault that was believed to be Republican inspired. The Ultra-Loyalist 'backlash' started in 1969.

Since August 1969 events have travelled at a devastating pace. The main developments have obviously involved the confrontation of the British Army with the Catholic population and the declaration of war by the Provisional and Official IRA. The resulting military campaign has created a colossal toll of death and destruction. The suspension of Stormont in March 1972 also saw an increase in Protestant military activity. From the summer of 1972 Protestant bomb attacks and the Protestant share in the large number of sectarian assassinations have been added to the heavy toll of casualties inflicted by the IRA and British Army. The Ultra-Loyalist associations (UDA, UVF, UFF, Red Hand, etc.)[23] have also had occasional skirmishes with the British Army. More significantly the Protestant para-military forces have demonstrated their industrial and military strength through the organization and implementation of successful strikes. The first major strike, of February 1973, contributed greatly to the demise of the Unionist Party. The Protestant electorate was split over the degree of power sharing which the Unionist Party envisaged extending to the Catholic Social Democratic and Labour Party in the prospective Northern Ireland Assembly. This Assembly was finally made unworkable by the tactics of the anti-powersharing bloc of Stormont (the United Ulster Unionist Council) and by a 14-day paramilitary organized strike throughout the province in May 1974. The success of the UUUC and the paramilitary forces in defeating the concept of Protestant and Catholic power-sharing at Cabinet level has had the further effect of uniting the Protestant population along traditional Unionist lines. The UUUC had overwhelming victories in the 1974 Westminster elections. The failure of the power-sharing Assembly led to a further period of direct rule and then to the politics of the Constitutional Convention. Equally, the Convention, which was instigated to create a political formula for the government of the province, has failed to agree on any form of a power-sharing Parliament. The intransigence of the dominant UUUC has resulted in presenting the Minister of State for Northern Ireland with a Convention Report that is unacceptable to the Westminster Parliament. Once again since 1976 the province has reverted to direct rule from Westminster.

On the military front internment was ended in December 1974 and the IRA Provisionals have been on a limited truce since February 1975. Though this truce has resulted in a sharp decline in British Army casualties the general rate of violence has continued largely unabated.

This patchy, crude and over-simple outline belies a mass of historical complexity. I have been forced to sacrifice the interests of historical scholarship because the detail required would deflect the analysis away from my principal focus. I merely want to introduce some of the major themes in the background of the contemporary Belfast war. It is a background of colonist/native differences being at first accentuated in the interests of the 'mother country'. Then later, the differences were expressed in terms of the development and protection of settler interests, sometimes in accord with England and sometimes at variance with English policy. The divisions, expressed in a religious form, thus compounding the complexity of the social relations, became accommodated into an industrial setting with a fervour which the labour movement was able to dampen for only brief moments. Partition further institutionalized the sectarian divide both north and south of the border. In the North the persistent concentration of political power into one party of one religion was achieved by the elaborate gerrymander, economic discrimination by the State and, when necessary, political physical force in the form of internment.[24] In the South the developing character of the Irish Republic, particularly in its relationship with the Catholic hierarchy (in moral, sexual and health spheres (O'Brien, 1974)) did little but confirm the Protestant fears of what life under the 'Papists' would involve.[25] The economic and political capital to be sustained from the continued emphasis on difference has consequently resulted in a massive sedimentation of history. That sedimentation deeply entrenches and helps to order the sectarian consciousness. It takes the form of a narrative history from which telling is constituted.

Telling: the contemporary use of history in the sectarian consciousness

The selections and interpretations of this history are manifested in the stereotypes and typifications which members of one religious group have of the other. They find expression in Northern Irish clichés about Catholics only being 'loyal to the half-crown' in that they take monetary payments from a State they do not wholly approve. A tidy house is said to look 'a bit more Protestant'. Catholics are dirty, Protestants 'black bigots', Catholics lazy, Protestants fools (for being tricked by upper-class politicians into thinking they are better-off) (Jackson, 1971). Similarly the political graffiti is historically conscious: 'Remember 1916' is matched by 'Remember 1690', a fresco of King William on the gable end of Rockwell Street is comparable in its quality to one of James Connolly in the Ardoyne. FTP ('Fuck the Pope') is matched by FTQ ('Fuck the Queen'). In clichés, on walls, in political broadsheets and in marches, there is abundant recourse to history as an armoury for the construction and maintenance of the true character of 'the other side'. As I have suggested above, the mediation of historical narrative is also found in the series of cues which make up the phenomenon of telling. That phenomenon is an integral part of the discourse of sectarianism.

Telling illustrates the representations of sectarianism in contemporary Ulster. Its signs are historical sediments that are used to reproduce 'ethnic' social relations. It is a process similar to the interactional system of prejudice which is cogently portrayed by Gerald Suttles in *The Social Order of the Slum* (1968). There Suttles, in a study of ethnic groups in Chicago, argues that ethnicity is partially reproduced through the differential relevance attributed to a widespread array of mundane behaviour. For example, the meaning of the bodily gestures exuded by Italians is interpreted as an indication to portray offence: 'I can understand why those guys [older, male Italians] can't half speak English but dammit why the hell they gotta eye-ball everybody [who] walks past' (Suttles, 1968: 139). Similarly dialect and semantic differences can lead to an interpretation of rudeness when various ethnic groups meet (Suttles, 1968: 63):

> All the subtleties that are usually incorporated into speech
> are suddenly lost. Thus persons are left adrift without the
> ordinary innuendoes, graces, overtones, and insinuation that
> play such a large part in the constant reassurances they furnish
> one another. . . . A more subtle but no less important deficiency
> is that inflection and intonation cease to be dependable indices
> that persons can use to judge the appropriateness of their own
> reactions. For older residents, this last shortcoming means that
> they cannot reliably distinguish between demands, questions
> and polite requests. A common greeting by the older Italians
> and Mexicans, for example, is a bland, 'Whadda you want?'
> Since members of the various groups in the area prefer to be

requested to meet each other's expectations, such an inability
to detect nuances in speech is a serious handicap to comfortable
social relations.

It is through the clashes of such semiologies that the everyday
hostility between the four ethnic groups in the Addams' area of
Chicago is experienced and communicated. The significance attached
to language, nuance, gesture, demeanour and general display
contributes to the cultural reproduction of ethnic difference.

In Belfast, the physical salience of ethnicity is clearly less marked
than in the Addams' area of Chicago. The two Belfast communities,
particularly those sections which form the working class, are
very similar culturally and physically. They are composed of
almost mirror images of each other. The degree of ethnic physical
visibility, to use Allport's term, (Allport, 1954) is microdiacritic;
that is, recognition of religious ascription is not as immediately
obvious as ethnic description between whites and blacks.[26] On the
other hand, approximately 370 years of not living together have made
the social construction of difference in Northern Ireland very
sophisticated. While physical differences remain microdiacritic,
the social phenomenon of telling ensures that the ability to judge
religious ascription by members in social interactions is macro-
diacritic. The sediment of history in everyday use makes ethnicity
socially visible. The semiological cues that formulate the sectarian
consciousness have created an ethnic social division out of history.

The first of these cues, the name, relies tacitly on different names
being distributed between the descendants of the native Irish and the
Scottish and English settlers. As a cue it illustrates well the nature
of telling: it uses history in terms of an imaginary interplay between
myth and reality. Its significance is accordingly varied, negotiable
and problematic. There are both surnames and Christian names
whose probability in predicting religious ascription is most likely
greater than chance. For example, male Christian names which are
Irish or Gaelic such as Colm, Gerard, Kieran, Sean, Shamus, Liam,
Malachy, and some others, Michael and Patrick, are likely to be
Catholic. Similarly Roseleen, Deirdre, Maire, Dolores, Brigid,
Bernadette, Graunia are likely to be Catholic females. Protestant
Christian names, conversely, would be unlikely to exhibit any
Gaelic connotations, while Billy, Sammy and Ian are favoured male
names. Any doubt that might arise can be minimized by probing
the names of friends and relatives of one's co-interactionist.

Surnames are more complicated. A look at any list of Catholics
will show some Scottish derivation – Patterson, Burns, Baxter,
Stewart – but a rough guide is possible: McGuinness, Murphy,
Lynch, Cooney, Mooney, Kelly and so on are more likely Catholic

49

while the more Scottish and English names – Maxwell, Taylor, Thompson, Craig, Armstrong – would more probably be Protestant. The situation is riddled with doubt because of the incidence of mixed marriage, conversion and immigration.[27] But, as I have argued, the sociological importance lies in the meaning attached to name and its usage by members in the society. Like the other cues, the significance of the name emerged for me when I had to make sense of various conversations, asides, innuendoes, jokes and experiences as I lived in Anro. I heard a little boy aged five ask his father whether he was Catholic because a woman had asked him and she had said he must be because his name was Sean. A prospective grandfather related how his own grandmother had apparently shown great interest in his baptism. She had remarked curtly, as she learnt his name was to be Patrick Joseph: 'Jesus above, do you never want him to have a job?' I did hear, in fact, of a Catholic mother deliberately calling her son Sammy, which she considered a good Protestant name, as her own practical strategy towards combating sectarian discrimination. I came upon a graphic use of this name-rule when I encountered a young Tartan gang. As I came within earshot of these Protestant youths I heard one of them shout at a lone boy ahead of them, 'Hey, Cathal' and heard them suggesting that if he turned round he must be a 'fenian' and they should give him a 'good dig'. The somewhat taken-for-granted rule of the connotation of name in peace-time Belfast was clearly being made explicit here in a search for a potential Catholic victim. It is not only such extraordinary examples which suggest the importance of name. For example, I asked a man who had just started a new job, after being unemployed for a good while, how he liked it: 'Ah, it's dead on, and about fifty-fifty I'd say, judging by the names, that is.' For him names were an obvious source and a useful shorthand for determining an individual's creed. Similarly, a young man complained bitterly that a job he had been promised one day had gone to someone else the next. He related how he had written his name as P. Burns but was asked more persistently about his Christian name before starting the job. After saying, 'Patrick', he recounted it was only a few minutes before he was told that a mistake had been made and the vacancy had already been filled. Whatever the case might have been the man interpreted, probably correctly, that he did not 'dig with the right foot' and his name did not suit his Protestant would-be employer.

While a look at the list of Catholics imprisoned/detained or at the birth and death columns of the Catholic *Irish News*, or a glance at Protestant names in the Belfast Directory,[28] will assure anyone of the complexity of name distribution, time spent in the community will show how the name can be and is invested with significance as an index for telling.

The issue of telling through the appearance of the face, dress or demeanour of an individual is similarly complicated. The historical reference for physical features being distinctively different lies in the supposed 'racial' differences between English, Scottish and indigenous Irish. These features may have been preserved by a high degree of residential segregation and religious endogamy. Sidestepping the question of the basis of physiognomic difference and the issue of the empirical exactness of segregation, I again wish to dwell, briefly, on what form the imaginary relationship of these differences takes in the applied narrative history of telling. Kieran was an always reflective and astute observer of his community. During a heated debate on this matter of telling he retorted to Pat, who thought he could tell at a glance, 'Get away, you probably think a person's a Catholic if you like the way he looks . . . like the way anyone looking freaky [that is, 'hip'] I think is Catholic: it fits in with my ideas.' The suggestion here is that telling may well involve a system of facial prejudice in which individuals assign status on the basis of whether the person under scrutiny appeals to them. On the other hand, it was put forward that what one does is simply ask oneself whether someone looks English, Scottish or Irish. If it is the last he is probably Catholic. If not, he is more than likely Protestant. When urged a little to give the salient characteristics of being 'Scottish' or 'English' even the most loquacious of respondents became inarticulate. It appeared that such knowledge does not form part of an accountable or reflexive store of information but was more firmly located in a stock of unexamined knowledge. Such references that did occasionally emerge illustrate the difficulty of talking about, rather than with, these stereotypings. Presbyterians, I was assured, had high cheek bones and a stern countenance. One particularly perceptive practitioner in the art of telling said the eyes 'were something of a give away'.[29] The 'eyes' in fact were frequently mentioned but it was also usually added that it was not easy to say how. There were no more than vague references to 'hardness' or 'softness'. Contradictory opinions on complexion also arose, Catholics being taken to be variously sallow or ruddy faced.

This inability to articulate what the alleged differences are is similar in language to our ability to speak without knowing syntactical rules. It is not solely a matter of pure bigotry. If, for example, an English person were asked to write down the visual characteristics of the English upper-class, or of Italians or Turks or some other group, similar difficulties would arise. This type of knowledge is a little like Goffmanesque sociology, it produces an 'ah! ah!' response which gives the feeling of, 'It's just like that', or, in this case, 'I just knew he was' – American, Jewish, a public school boy and so on. Analytically telling is part of the universal phenomenon of social categorization (Durkheim, 1915; Lévi-Strauss, 1962 edn.; Douglas, 1970; 1973). We all tell, and in a variety of forms, because the mapping of the significance of social cues is a required skill for social interaction. It is also an ideological prerequisite for social order. That this type of knowledge is frequently at a predicative level should not lead the sociologist to dismiss such claims as merely speculative or prejudiced but rather should constitute grounds for making the phenomenon an object worthy of analytic exposition. I shall argue later how this order of inarticulate knowledge represents the ideological manifestations of a sectarian social division.

The inability to put into words the shades of the dissimilar does not prevent them forming the bases of action. For instance the 1 May 1972 Woodvale Defence Association broadsheet (a militant Protestant publication) contains a call for the genocide of the Catholic population written by one 'Brit-Annia'. It was justified largely on the grounds of racial purity. 'Annia' claimed that the original British were Nordic and 'one look at a Roman Catholic will tell anyone they are not of the Nordic race'. Once again the troubles were making explicit those aspects of ideological formations which normally remain tacit. In my own socialization into these rules,[30] I often tried to 'tell' through facial appearance. Often the prediction was neither verified nor falsified simply because very fleeting interactions (walking past someone, sitting next to them, getting off the bus before them, waiting in a queue) rarely resulted in finding out the individual's creed. While this absence of verification may not enforce one's stereotype, neither does it falsify one's mode of thought. My own scepticism about the efficacy of the cues was shaken when I found myself employing them. On reflection this did not so much temper my scepticism towards the efficacy of cues but rather increased my subjective awareness of the importance of telling as a category of thought.

For example, one day, going back to Anro from the city centre, I stopped running for a bus. The significance of this trivial act lies in the meaning I had attached to the religious ascription of the people boarding the bus. The bus stop in question served two different buses. One would be bound for a homogeneous Protestant district and consequently only Protestants would be getting on. The other went through Protestant and Catholic areas and would have a mixed set of passengers. I determined, though not deliberately, that the bus at the stop was the 'Protestant' bus and not the one I wanted and so stopped running for it. This must either have been because I considered all the passengers getting on were all 'Protestant-looking' or that I thought there was an absence of 'Catholic-looking' people boarding the bus. Realizing why I stopped, I ran to see the number of the bus and its destination. As it happened my reading of the situation was confirmed. The importance of this simple act was not that I therefore came to believe that Protestants and Catholics do in fact look different, but that I had experienced myself thinking in that fashion. I was employing those discursive regularities which I had learnt in Anro for the purpose of explaining mundane actions.[31]

Just as it is difficult to express the symbolism of the face, so it is as difficult to distinguish the significance of the presentation of body through dress and demeanour from facial cues. Face, dress and demeanour come together to portray a front which is more likely to be read as Protestant than Catholic and vice versa. Thus Roseleen told me that a group of women visiting Long Kesh were obviously Protestant. They had an air of aloofness from the predominantly Catholic visitors. Moreover they appeared somewhat 'brassy' with elaborate hairstyles and ostentatious clothes.[32] It was their general appearance that led people to think them Protestant. Similarly, the middle-aged male Catholic is traditionally accorded the likelihood of wearing ill-fitting suits, while even middle-class Catholic men could be singled out as they looked 'scruffier' than their Protestant counterparts. Dress, Colm suggested, was not an area of life middle-class Catholic men put much emphasis on. With respect to demeanour, an upper-middle-class 'Castle Catholic', though herself of working-class origins, claimed that the ordinary Catholics could be picked out because they 'have an unconfident manner and don't hold their heads high because they are an oppressed people'. This particularly noticeable characteristic, she continued, could be eradicated. Thus, in her own case, elimination of these Catholic hallmarks was achieved by mixed marriage and, in her son's case, by an English public school education! Being a good Unionist she failed to mention that demeanour could also be changed by the military and political activities of that 'unconfident' working class. It was extremely obvious to me how those in Anro who were politically involved had a sense of purpose which was reflected in an often supremely confident presentation of self. This was in marked contrast to some of the street-corner, unemployed and uninvolved.

As I have already depicted it, there is a hard core of conspicuous poverty in Anro which reflected itself in the appearance of both children and parents. It is certainly arguable that this pronounced character of poverty would be less evident in the more fully employed and marginally smaller Protestant families of working-class areas. Yet 'Sunday best' within Anro brought out a great display of well-clad and well-dressed people. Together with the similarity of the chain-store fashions and teenage vogues these special clothes somewhat restricted the potency of dress as a means of telling. Even paramilitary uniforms share similarities on both sides of the divide –

bush hats and scarves, dark glasses, parka-anoraks, denim jeans and perhaps Dr Martin boots. Nevertheless, though dress and demeanour presented themselves less forcefully upon me,[33] they can be and are used as part of the constellation of pointers which are clustered into this system of telling. Juxtaposed with the 'face', demeanour and dress permit a decision to be arrived at which assigns the possessor to one type rather than the other. A disturbed child, for example, knew it was a Protestant who was chasing him in his dreams. The pursuer was wearing garish clothes which he illustrated in the form of checked patterns: 'He wore strange clothes and looked different from us' (Fraser, 1971: 633; 1973). A *Sunday Times* reporter felt it worth recording, in a similar vein, the objections which Protestant schoolchildren had about Catholic children: ' "You could tell a Catholic from the way he dresses", the children said. "They are all poor and have dirty faces and funny eyes" ' (Herbstein, 1973).

The various interpretations attached to face, eyes, complexion, demeanour and clothing are by no means evenly distributed throughout the population and do not constitute a generally coherent corpus of meaning. But in the attempt to answer the fundamental and almost overwhelming question, 'What is he?', people do make use of physiognomic and decorative indicators of creed. As well as being part of the unreflexive knowledge of the stereotype (about what Protestants/Catholics are 'really like') this matrix of telling seems to assist people in what Suttles calls, 'getting a "quick fix" on the relative trustworthiness of fellow pedestrians, residents and trespassers' (Suttles, 1972). Such 'rules of thumb' are nothing new to Belfast. By 1864 this discourse of ethnicity had been established. Consider for example the evidence presented to the Royal Commission investigating the 1864 riots of Samuel Black, Chairman of the Police Committee (and later to be Town Clerk of Belfast). He is being cross-examined by Commissioner Dowse in an effort to explain why only 5 out of 160 policemen in the Belfast Constabulary were Catholic (Parliamentary Papers, 1865: XXVIII):[34]

Dowse:	Can you assign any reason why the Protestant element appears to pre-ponderate?
Black:	I think it arises from the district from which the police force is here generally recruited. The great majority of the small farmers in that district are Protestant, and it is principally from their sons that the appointments happen to be made, in as much as they are the strongest class of men, generally speaking.
Dowse:	Do you mean physically?

Black: Yes, they are generally stronger than the lower class of the Roman Catholic, besides I think they are better educated.

Dowse: Have you known Roman Catholics to apply within the last five years?

Black: I certainly should think so; but I do not know them as such, nor do I know them yet.

Dowse: You look at the candidates before appointing them?

Black: In some cases I could tell a man's religion by his face but not always.[35]

Mr Commissioner Berry: Will you be so kind enough to let me know the characteristics by which you know a Roman Catholic from a Protestant?

Black: As a general rule in this part of the country, I think it is not very difficult to know a man's religion by his face. . . .

Another examiner, Sergeant Armstrong, returns to the point later:

Armstrong: It appears that these men – the constables – are known to be Protestants by their very looks?

Black: I did not mean to say anything of the sort. I said that generally speaking in this part of Ireland where there is a strong admixture of the Scotch element engrafted with the native Irish a man's *appearance* [my emphasis] would lead me to infer his religion.

Armstrong: The result is when applicants present themselves to you you can tell what they are?

Black: Frequently, I never saw a Roman Catholic clergyman whose religion I could not tell by his appearance.

Armstrong: With the assistance of dress?

Black: Even without it.

Armstrong: Did you ever see a Roman Catholic clergyman undressed?

Black: No.

Dowse: Did you ever see High Church parson?

Black: I did.

Dowse: Would you know him?

Black: I certainly would. . . .

Mr Black continues later under a new volley of questions:

Armstrong: You would know them by the shape of their face and the cut of their hair. Did you ever hear this?

'The cut of their hair/Would poison the air/
Down, down, croppies, lie down!' Did you ever
hear that tune played at the Boyne Bridge?

Black: No, but if you were long enough in Ulster, you
would know the two parties –

and with a portent for the future sectarian cliché:

Armstrong: You think them equally efficient as guardians of
property?
Black: If we could get a good class of men Roman
Catholics, I am totally indifferent as to their
religion, some of the Roman Catholics of Belfast
are my best friends.

Thirty-one years later Black, now Town Clerk, gave evidence in
front of the Select Committee looking at the Belfast Corporation
Bill (Parliamentary Papers, 1896: VII). He admitted the situation
might have changed:

Mr McInerney: Did Baron Dowse in amazement ask you if
that was so [there being no religious test for
police recruitment] how it came to pass
there were 155 to 5 and you did answer that
you would know a Catholic by looking at
him?
Black: In the North of Ireland I think yes, because
the two races were so different. The
Protestants generally the descendants of the
Scotch and English settlers and the others
are the original Celts.
Mr McInerney: There is that marked a distinction in Belfast
between the two religions that you can tell
one from the other by looking at them.
Black: Yes I think then much more so than now.

The area one lives in is of paramount importance, particularly
for the Belfast working class. Over the last six years the already
largely religiously homogeneous areas have become almost totally
confessionally pure. This has come about as a result of the massive
population readjustment that has been caused by people leaving
their homes through fear, or by being systematically intimidated out
of them. This ritualistic cleansing, believed to be the largest incidence
of European post-war intimidation (Community Relations Commission, 1971, 1974), has resulted in the bulging of the Catholic
ghettos, some incursions by Catholics into Protestant territory and
a minor glut of housing in Protestant areas and estates, particularly

in East Belfast.[36] It has also vastly increased the Six-County emigration rate. One minor outcome of this mass of misery (a misery which remains largely unreported in the press and media) has been to make territory a finer diagnostic cue. The 'what' problem is settled if one knows, for example, that a person is from the Shankill, Falls, Woodvale, Andersonstown, Tiger Bay, New Lodge areas. Though the 'tribal maps' have become especially clear over the last six years Belfast has exhibited residential religious segregation from its early industrial era. Initially areas were distinguishable between those which were populated by the English (Episcopalians) and the Scottish (Presbyterians). With the arrival of Catholics into West Belfast in the first quarter of the nineteenth century, Catholic and Protestant districts became more centrally important.[37] Accordingly the riots in the nineteenth century frequently had their battlefields corresponding to 'border' areas. A new pattern emerged in the latter half of the century when, for example, Protestant ship-workers would be attacked as they passed to and from the docks on Queen Island. Conversely, Catholics were frequent victims of eviction and intimidation in fringe areas, particularly when they were found outside predominantly Catholic domains.

The meaning of territory is consequently very basic; it has become a matter of safety or danger that is reinforced with every outbreak of rioting. The world-wide familiarity with Belfast's districts today is pre-dated with a long chronicle of infamy. The Commissioners appointed to investigate the 1864 riots began by bemoaning Belfast's notoriety (Parliamentary Papers, 1864: XXVIII: 8):

> We should give some idea of the districts that constituted on this occasion, as on former occasions of this kind, the chief theatre of the disturbances, generally known, not only with locality, but by evil fame unhappily throughout most of Ireland as the Pound and Sandy Row district.

This historical and contemporary meaning of territory accordingly finds practical application as a differentiating telling sign.

In this light, buses and bus stops are not merely aids to public transport but may also tell something about the religious status of a passenger. Buses are forced arenas for mixed interaction and can generate great tension that brings the telling cues into play. One becomes adept at talking about innocent topics which help to excise what 'one is' from the topic of conversation. Yet neutralizing the topic both enforces and illustrates the significance of relying on the signs and rules I am attempting to make explicit. A Catholic going to the Ardoyne would for instance, be safer asking for a Ligoneil bus. That destination, though mainly Protestant, is mixed. Accordingly the request does not immediately betray religious status.

Asking for Ardoyne would. Routes are considered as well, and those buses which reach one's destination by going through safe or mixed territory are preferred to those, often quicker, which go through the streets of the 'other side'. Going to the Catholic Bone area on a Cliftonville bus, for example, might be preferable for a Catholic than the Old Park bus. Both Cliftonville and Old Park are Protestant areas but the former is more middle-class and less violent while the latter has a frightening history of many sectarian assassinations. Such safety rules are not totally adhered to but may figure in the mundane decision of which bus to board. Going out of Anro one evening with a group of friends, one, an Englishman, David, with whom I shared a house, remarked that we would give the bus coming down the road a miss: it was too dangerous. Pat, a native of Anro, chuckled with mild amusement: 'Look at him, he's into the thinking pretty quick.'

My own thoughts about the bus stop one uses serving as a sign for recognizing an individual's religion was confirmed not long after being in Anro. I was sharing a bus with some Protestant youths who could be identified as Protestant because they sang, when we passed a Catholic church: 'I tell you what I think/That's Celtic stink/'Cos I'm a Rangers fan.' They took great interest in those passengers who were getting off near a Catholic area I was visiting. As I got off several of these adolescents stuck their heads out of the windows and shouted. 'Let's see who the fenians are, get a good look at them', and then directly to me: 'You fenian bastard!' The appropriate adrenal response on my own part brought home the significance of the bus stop.

Going to Anro involved similar decisions and experiences. Kieran told me part of the reason he would not get on a potentially 'dangerous' bus after I had urged him, because we were getting soaking wet, was good sense while the rest was 'not having to listen to all their [Protestant] shit'. Dolores said: 'Well, if anything happens, then at least you know there's some of us on the bus.' As frequently happened during a riot in Anro, the buses would be diverted into the very Protestant areas which the chosen bus was meant to avoid. This obviously generates anxiety for the Catholic passengers, and on a few occasions I heard people remonstrate to others to keep quiet as it was obvious that their nervousness indicated they were Catholic. This feeling which territory generated stopped a voluntary social worker visiting the Shankill: 'Because I just felt aware of being Catholic.' It made a taxi driver at night tell me to hurry up and pay him. 'I don't like hanging around this place.' It also made me apprehensive in an encounter with an unfriendly porter at a library (where one had to give one's address before gaining admission). One day out of the blue he glared at me and stated: 'Anro, isn't it?'[38]

As with the other cues territory finds its way into the telling syndrome and is used for mundane activities. For example, being genuinely puzzled, I asked some lads why they were stoning the taxis that were coming up the road. It was anything but obvious who was in them. The rioters assured me they were not stoning every taxi, just the ones that came up the left hand fork in the road because that was solid 'Prod' country. There was, however, some uncertainty about those from the right.[39]

Territory has profound importance in Belfast, as the massive shift of its population through intimidation indicates: somewhere between 6.6 per cent and 11.8 per cent (from August 1969 to February 1973) have been involuntarily uprooted (Community Relations Commission, 1974). Territory looms as an issue in the routing of marches and the location of roads, schools and social amenities. Area is even a valid reason for declining a job offered by the Department of Employment. One religious group is not expected to work in an area predominantly of the 'other side'. Its significance is manifested in the position it occupies in telling. It has a high rate of accuracy in providing recipes for activities as diverse as stoning taxis and avoiding interactions on buses. It is not surprising that the meaning it·has for Belfast residents makes it enter the forefront of cues in the sectarian consciousness.[40]

The segregation of the communities is epitomized in the separation of schools at the primary, secondary and some tertiary levels of education. Even if schools were mixed, the residential segregation of the communities would still result in schools which were in religious terms largely homogeneous. The intransigence of the Catholic church, matched by that of some Protestant clergymen, has resulted in the name of an individual's school unambiguously delineating religious affiliation. A seemingly innocent request on application forms for work can have a dual purpose when 'schools attended' is required. It was, somewhat ironically, a convert to Catholicism who bitterly complained to me that after de-mobbing he went to the Belfast Council for a labouring job and was asked for his school background. He could, of course, have given his Protestant schools: 'I told them: "What do you want to know that for? You didn't care what school I went to when I signed on to go to war." ' Similarly I was told in the gratuitous circles of freshers' weekends at Queens University the question 'What school did you go to?' accomplished least painfully the separation of the goats from the sheep.

From a comparatively concrete indicator, I want to look tentatively at a more elusive and less entrenched pointer of religious status, namely the possible meanings attached to linguistic and phonetic variations. Whether any phonetic differences obtain between Catholic and Protestants I am incompetent to say. The low rates of mixed marriage and immigration together with the high rates of residential and occupational separation again make the possibility not implausible.[41] There is always the possibility of 'something not quite fitting' in a Protestant/Catholic encounter where each status is unknown. In turn that this dis-ease may be due to a variation in phonetics is not inconceivable in a society long practised in the art of telling. Whatever a systematic documentation by social linguists might establish the social significance of differential phonetic stress lies in how the variation is used in the battery of signs that formulate telling. Like the rest of the cues which appear as statements, questions and stories, both the researcher and members have to interpret these indicators to sustain a sense of order. It is in this context that on at least eight occasions it was spontaneously put to me that one way of telling was the 'h' test. The claim is simply that Protestants say 'aitch' (/eitʃ/) whereas Catholics say the letter as in hay (/heitʃ/). Some co-conversationalists had no hesitancy in dismissing this as rubbish: 'You're wired up' (that is, weird or odd); others however claimed they had tried the test in offices and on building sites with some success. Phonetically, little else was suggested to me as being particularly diagnostic. One lad did say: 'They [Orangemen] talk different to us' but could not elaborate. A former travelling salesman (a Catholic) recounted with some mirth his encounter with a 'wee Protestant woman': 'Here she is to me, you know in that *real coarse Shankill* way: "Are you a fenian son?" ' Not surprisingly Mrs Connor, the upper-middle-class lady discussed above, was of the opinion: 'Catholics lack that forcefulness of speech, you never got a Protestant speaking so low.' There is little here, admittedly, to indicate lay awareness of phonetic variation. Yet I do suggest that there appears to be significance in that peculiar phenomenon which administers the 'religious' test in the obscure form of: 'Say the alphabet.'

Whilst not primary, linguistic differences do occasionally connote the religious preference of the speaker. Certain ejaculations – 'holy Mother', 'sweet Jesus' and 'Jesus, Mary and Joseph' – are fairly common parlance among Catholics, although not necessarily prevalent among the more orthodox ones. The force of such phrases became apparent when I was on a 'dangerous' bus with a very talkative Legion of Mary woman. The bus went over one of the many road ramps (lumps of tarmacadam which slow traffic down to prevent attacks by speeding cars on British Army observations posts and certain vulnerable districts like Anro). Margaret, not anticipating the jolt bumped her head and exclaimed: 'Oh, sweet Jesus, I nearly pulled a ricket!' On a predominantly Protestant bus not a few heads buzzed around to catch a glimpse of us.[42] Similarly a man who used to enjoy drinking with his Protestant 'cross-religionist' to me of the time, somewhat apocryphally, when he and his partne were thrown out of a Protestant pub for singing: 'A Chapel on th Hill' after being warned once to sing 'A *Church* on the Hill'. This was in peace-time Belfast. Apparently, the drink had the better of their sense of social expedience. In a slightly different fashion, the recognition of two communities finds its way into language through elliptical phrases which presupposes knowledge of a divided society: 'A nice woman, of the other side, but nice'; 'I don't know what you are, but it doesn't take long to find out what's been going on in this society'; 'Which foot does he dig with?' (Is he Protestant or Catholic?) The variations of pejorative terms for Catholic and Protestant also establish their contextual relevance in history – 'mick', 'taig', fenian', 'croppy', or 'orangeman', 'prod', 'bluenose', 'black bigot'.

Sectarian iconography is overtly evident in the Six Counties – the State even has a Flag and Emblems Act legally delineating the range of permissible symbolic expression. The annual marching seasons give full flight to colour and symbols in both communities. They allow an orgy of flags, buntings, banners, sashes, badges and bands and other regalia concomitant with one's orange or green allegiance. Even outside the traditional rioting season, there are numerous badges of Tricolours and Union Jacks (the latter predominantly replaced by the Red Hand of Ulster since the abolition of Stormont). Those flags are displayed from built in flag holders on the walls of houses which give an immediate indication of creed. Some Protestant and Catholic youths ostentatiously display their religious status. Members of the Protestant tartan groups adorn themselves, like English football fans, with unambiguously Protestant symbolism such as tartan scarves and Ulster widows' badges. Similarly Catholic adolescents might wear a tricolour or a James Connolly badge in the lapels of their denim jackets. The allusion to symbols and colour was an everyday occurrence in Anro – Protestants are synonymous with Orangemen or black bigots. Frequently it was a source of humour. The young lads who freely frequented our house were criticizing Pat's scruffy appearance: 'You can tell he's a Republican anyway: his teeth are green, white and orange.' Brigid, who worked with several Protestants, thanked one of her workmates for getting her some aspirins: ' "It's no bother, Brigid, I got them in Sandy Row, and with green shield stamps." So here's me: "If you got them in Sandy Row they'd be Orange Shield stamps!" ' A conversation about Protestants led Fergal to ask me: 'Don't you find them odd? I mean, who'd sit on their heroes?' He was referring to the cushions embroidered with William of Orange that one can buy in Protestant districts. But he was also jesting at the mass of household ornaments which display some Loyalist insignia on them such as the Queen,

ɟ, Union Jack, Red Hand or King William. I did
a man, I imagine well known, on the Shankill with a
, blue walking stick.
／ Catholic homes have elaborate, often shrine-like
, of the Virgin Mary, the Saints or the Sacred Heart. In
ɴ with the Sacred Heart an atheistic Provisional IRA man
not to read any significance into the fact that he had a
, picture of it hanging in his house. It was, he claimed, just the
, case of heart-burn he had come across (the Sacred Heart has
ɪst's heart exposed and licked with flames). Joan, a passing
ɪtor to our house, interestingly remarked when she found out I
ɪd not subscribe to Catholic dogma: 'Ah, I thought this house was
wired up, with no holy pictures and that.'

In the street it is not specifically religious icons that identify the
Catholic population, though a cross and chain might be indicative.
Thus a man who worked temporarily in the shipyard had his work
bench painted 'No Popery here' due to the unthoughtfully provocative sprig of shamrock he had inadvertently left on his coat on St
Patrick's Day. A Claddagh ring (a popular gold or silver ring with a
distinctive design that originated from the Claddagh, Galway) was
also 'fenian' in the shipyard. Despite Chris's exhortation it had
nothing to do with the Virgin Mary or any Catholic mythology but
was pagan and ancient Irish, his fellow Protestant workmates
remained unconvinced.

These selections are sufficient to illustrate how telling is facilitated
through the colour and symbolism expressed in household and
bodily decoration. The clearest manifestations of this process were
drawn from remarks made by children struggling to order the rules
of colour and symbol in their world. Two 10-year-old girls in their
Sunday best related to me their fears of visiting a neighbouring
district in case they were asked what they were: 'Well, Frank, you
know the way it's Protestant up there, but some of it's mixed; we
thought we'd say if they asked us what we were: "Mind your own
business!" ' Rosanna giggled and added: 'And me with my green,
white and gold clothes on!' On another occasion an 8-year-old was
looking through a book with me and we came across a page of flags:
'Is that your flag?' she demanded, pointing to a Union Jack. I
replied, 'I suppose in a way it is.' She rejoined, 'Huh, that's a
Protestant flag.' A 10-year-old enquired of his mother whether the
soldiers with gold cap badges were Catholic and the ones with silver
cap badges were Protestant. He had obviously established the
centrality of colour in his social world but had not quite become
attuned to its distribution and range of relevance. Thinking in such
terms can be practically applied in the distinguishing of people from
your co-religionists. Micky told me he had at least one 'Prod' friend,

as he had shown a Protestant out of Anro who had strayed in during the 1969 riots: 'You could tell right away he was a Prod, he had all the badges and that.'

I have been interested, methodologically, in showing how telling was presented to me during my stay in Anro. In trying to make sense of the significance attached to the diagnostic cues certain natural experiments were helpful. On these occasions people in the community would make the issue a topic of conversation. I will deal more fully with this in the methodological appendix 1, but an illustration of the way the concept is used and talked about might be illuminating. One Sunday I walked into the house I was living in and a group of men and boys were discussing Protestant characteristics. Gerard remarked it was easy to tell some 'Prods' but harder to do so with others, particularly the young. He knew because he had been wrong a couple of times at work and had 'only just sorted it out'. Two young lads said it was their voices but were laughed out of it. By contrast it was claimed if anything it was their looks. Raymond thought the whole discussion a joke and recalled the 'buck eejit' (a prize idiot) who after the 1969 riots proclaimed he would always now be able to tell an Orangeman. Kieran, ever reflective, said that it was sensible to 'treat everyone as an Orangee until you knew different'. Paul challenged one of the lads who was adamant he could tell with the question: 'What about the wee girls, then, can you tell with them?' There followed a confused admission that that was a little harder, though from another room a young girl shouted she could. The by now quite heated discussion passed on to the relative merits of military as opposed to political involvement in the community. From such celebrations of the notion of telling some characteristics emerge that I have argued are central to its system: it is a category of thought and practice ('I've only just sorted it out'), it is unevenly adhered to ('You can obviously tell some Prods' to 'You buck eejit'). As these come up on other occasions one takes them seriously at the expense of the intuition that appears fleetingly. In this case there is the interesting suggestion that one looks for Catholic cues if one is Catholic; that is, the process involves looking for the familiar rather than for the markings of the other side: 'You treat everyone as an Orangee until you know different.'

The sociological significance of telling as part of a total ideology

In calling the process of telling part of the sectarian consciousness I do not mean to suggest that thinking in such terms is an exclusive domain of the bigot. Clearly the very many people who are politically opposed to sectarianism in the north of Ireland may well make use of the above cues in their daily interactions. This consciousness refers to the ideological representations of a sectarian social division. This distinction has its conditions of existence located in a Protestant labour aristocracy within the social division of labour and a cross-class Unionist bloc in Northern Irish political social relations. A further caveat is that by attempting to document telling as an every-day process, I have no intention of emphasizing the differences between the two communities. Neither do I wish to lend any credence to the supposedly real bases on which this difference is constructed. The 'different mentalities' are very much ideological products. The appeal to nature (that is, race) to legitimize difference masks the fact that a race is a social category. In Northern Ireland this difference is transparently a social construction of ethnicity. A construction which is historically based in the economic and political policies which have sought to emphasize difference. The mediation, moreover, of history, economics and politics through the process of telling indicates, by the very elaborateness of its cues, the man-made character of difference and, ironically, the similarity of the two communities.

Conversely, the predominant emphasis on sectarianism as a mode of thought should not be taken to indicate that I believe sectarianism to be nothing but a mental construct, a sort of collectively induced subjective idealism. Sectarian policy is the material reality, the form of ideological social relations that underpins the social consciousness implicit in telling. Telling manages the transmission and reproduction of these relations and consequently assures the continuity of further sectarian policy. The consequences of sectarianism are discrimination in jobs, voting and housing. They are also to be found in the battlefields of Belfast's streets and in the daily toll of dead and maimed and intimidated. The structural basis of telling is patently significant in any understanding of the troubles. Neverthe-less, in examining the ideology more than the ideological social relations of sectarianism, I have been interested in demonstrating how thoroughly the management of sectarianism has permeated the social consciousness.[43] This art of spotting the other side gives an intimation of the mental barricading which accompanies the physical barricades of the contemporary Six-County society.

Telling has sociological significance at different levels of analysis. At the order of face-to-face interaction it is a necessary social skill if the embarrassment endemic in a sectarian social milieu is to be avoided. Treating a stranger as a Catholic who is in fact a Protestant, and vice versa, is not conducive to comfortable social relations. Familiarity with the intuitions afforded by telling will enable people to adjust their interactional repertoire to achieve the correct manage-ment of the potential *faux pas* (Goffman, 1967). Misreading cues can form, on reflection, the basis of humorous stories, the humour lying, as usual, precisely in the gaffe. Hugh related to me how after three weeks at a new job a fellow workmate started a conversation: 'Hey, don't we have a laugh on the twelfth [of July]?'. Hugh, a Catholic, replied that it was hilarious and you should see his mother 'having a good go at them', referring to the Orange parades that strutted past Anro. 'Still,' said Hugh adding a stoical rejoinder, 'the Queen had to kneel before the Pope, didn't she!' The stony silence was followed by the Protestant workmate retreating rapidly as both discovered their mistake. Similarly, Frances was surprised at seeing a fellow stitcher on a bus going to a weekend Catholic retreat. The girl's presence ('She looked Protestant') was interpreted by Frances as an indication that the woman was a potential convert. Over the two day retreat Frances watched in amazement as the girl in question received the sacraments, something beyond the rights of the un-initiated. Unable to restrain herself Frances asked as diplomatically as possible: 'Margaret, you'd think you'd become a Catholic.' The stormy retort was: 'Hell roast ye, I *am* Catholic!' Again Billy (i.e. Liam) a Catholic engineering worker in an almost totally Protestant firm attempted to keep his job by passing as a person who was as un-Catholic as possible. This entailed remaining anonymous and in particular not getting caught saying anything which was politically or religiously controversial. His own status as a Catholic remained of no interest as long as he kept in the background. Had he been active, as was his wish, as a trade-unionist, he feared that his views might have become dubbed 'Catholic'. This in turn might have focused too much attention on him. As it was he cut out a niche between the Catholic/Protestant worlds inhabited by the anonymous, the silent, the loners and others skilled at secularizing their social presentations.

More seriously the latent meanings of being Catholic/Protestant are made explicit when the identity of an individual is being determined for intended military, political and criminal activity. In such sinister performances, the interrogator may ask one his name or address, or even to say the 'Hail Mary' or Protestant creed. The instrumental purpose of the questions makes the cues more amenable to analysis because the phenomenon shifts in purpose. Instead of being orientated towards achieving comfortable social relations it becomes the litmus paper test, which, as the vast sum of sectarian assassinations indicates, can become the last telling trial a person fails.[44]

This threat of danger which is endemic in Belfast underlines a second feature of telling: the way it can be used to create areas of trust. As Suttles poignantly illustrates, territorial segregation amongst ethnic groups has the seeming advantage of creating personal and local pools of predictability (Suttles, 1968). Within one's own physical area there is a built-in moral arena, a normative order, which helps to structure the possible types of interaction. The potential conflict in cross-ethnic interaction is limited by territory. I would suggest that telling, in a like manner, creates order in the anomic climate of a sectarian society. In one sense Protestants and Catholics do not know how to interact. Their restricted knowledge of each other prevents communication. Telling contributes to shutting out this anomie before it can start. It provides rules of action which give an individual some glimpses of solving the basic sectarian question, 'Whose side is he on?' In this way, too, the individual has protected himself a little. By using his ready-made set of diagnostic rules he manages the extreme social climate of suspicion which distinguishes both historical and contemporary Belfast. By arriving at religious membership, a cocoon of trust and predictability is spun around a potentially hazardous interaction. What territory provides in physical terms by minimizing the likelihood of mixed social interaction, telling partially achieves outside of the comparatively restrictive areas. In this sense telling constitutes mental bricks and mortar. It is the conceptual and cognitive ghetto of Northern Irish ideological social relations.

On a more expressive level, telling may be viewed as a moral veil which invests sectarianism with legitimacy. As in all systems of stratification, there is an accompanying moral ideology which attempts to flatter the system of control with normative redeemability. In this case of sectarianism (the representational expression of a social division), the moral authority of religious ranking is symbolically played out in the ideologies constructed about the nature of the other side. These ideologies find practical application in telling. Telling becomes a purification filter which orders potentially polluting contacts with the other side. In a society characterized by near endogamy, residential segregation and patterns of exclusive sociability, telling systematizes the ritual and moral danger of one's cross-religionists. Such dangers are emitted from the structure of ideas which are based on their emphasis of polarity: settler/native, Loyalist/Rebel, Protestant/Catholic, Unionist/Nationalist. Telling assists in the drawing of such boundaries of difference. It is hardly surprising that the cues carry such an evaluative burden, for example, facial cues often being facial preference. The boundaries being drawn are the moral parameters of sectarian stratification.[45]

I have emphasized that telling is an ideological construction which serves to order the experiences of a sectarian social division. Like most ideological configurations, the shifting significance and distribution of the various diagnostic cues indicate an area of greyness where the precise meaning of the cultural artifact is open to question. I have similarly stressed that, as a category of thought telling represents the consciousness of sectarianism, and, as such, is an imaginary mediation of historical processes. Telling bears a weighty sediment of history because the history of Northern Ireland is the arena within which the social construction of sectarian rules is delimited. History, as it were, provides the material for fashioning in an ongoing and narrative manner the theories and stereotypes which each side has of the other. It is aided by the process of telling which triggers off such typifications in the everyday interactions of Protestant and Catholics. It is precisely this merging of history and contemporary interest which provides sectarianism with a very hardy root and which contributes to its pervasiveness and persistence. I have, accordingly, dwelt on this phenomenon because I consider it one of the dominant ideological representations which feature in the Six Counties. It is crucial to one major aspect of the war, namely the struggle against sectarianism, the Civil Rights campaign.

Before I move on to examine the second significant ideological pattern, that of Republicanism, I want to stress the very real difficulty that Catholic and Protestant unity poses on this dimension of sectarianism. Behind the well-meaning but often empty rhetoric of conciliation programmes lies this consciousness, entrenched, practised and closed, which makes the possibility of Catholic and Protestant debate very limited. This sectarian consciousness, partially explored in the concept of telling, seems to lead to a form of social relations which have an almost congenital inability to communicate across religious boundaries as each side immures itself in dialogue, making only 'pseudo-communication', or what Habermas (1970, 1973) has called 'systematically distorted communication', possible. In such a social situation the effects of a Civil Rights campaign were potentially explosive. In this context telling became part of the ideological raw materials for the political struggle over Civil Rights.

3 Republicanism: the IRA and the community

I have argued that the ideology of ethnicity constitutes a fundamental pattern of meaning in the community which the process of telling indicates. I shall now introduce a further element of the Catholic world-view, that of Republicanism. These ideological forces are presented here separately, purely for heuristic reasons, to enable an analytic exposition of the social consciousness of Catholicism. The contention of this text, which will be argued in this chapter, will be to re-link conceptually the ideological components of Catholicism to form the basis of an explanation of the war in Northern Ireland. These component parts will be presented as the social consciousness that constitutes the Northern Irish Catholic world-view. I shall argue that the Irish Republican Army represents a political isomorphism of the ideological meanings of Catholicism. The IRA will be presented as the bearers of a partial ideology which manifests itself as a political articulation of a wider total ideology.

The structure of this chapter will take the form of four interconnected sections. I shall begin by establishing the historical significance of the IRA within the Northern Irish Catholic community. I shall argue that although militant Republicanism features as part of a heritage within the Catholic world-view, the varied ideological ingredients of Irish separatism sustain an ideology which is doctrinally loose. One consequence of this situation has been that historically the Republican movement has been particularly prone to disagreements and splits over both the tactics and policies of its political programme. The second section is a detailed analysis of the relationship between the IRA and the community within Anro. The complexity of this relationship is presented as an ongoing debate between the militant Republicans and the rest of the community. This debate illustrates the contemporary manifestations of the splits, dissensions and problems that have dominated the IRA's history. The third part of the chapter draws the argument of the book together. It will be argued that the war in Northern Ireland arises from the fusion of the basic ideological configurations of Catholicism into a political practice. The chapter will end with an appreciation of the theoretical issues that are raised in this study concerning the wider analytic appraisal of politicized violence.

The historical significance of Republicanism

Republicanism's long history in Ireland has produced a heritage which is passed on in some families with the same seriousness that characterizes the Northern Irish Protestants' Unionism. Both political doctrines select historical events as claims to the moral superiority of their cause. This history is given vitality by the continuity of the troubles which has ensured that each generation has lived through and has stored violent experiences. Living memories stretch back to 1916, to the Black and Tans, the UVF resistance, the rioting 1930s, the 1956–62 IRA campaign, and right through to the present troubles. If the concept of a political generation can be used to explain the radicalism of particular age structures in certain situations, it would be a fair comment that in the Six Counties all generations are political generations (Zeitlin, 1967; Mannheim, 1968a). The heritage is fostered by segregated schooling, particularly, in the area of different history syllabuses (Russell, 1972; 1973; Magee, 1971). As important, though, are the shared narratives which recreate the past in ordinary conversations. There are memories like those of old Mrs Johnson who told me how, as a young girl, she had seen a man abducted by the Black and Tans. He was found dead later on in the day. Mrs Johnson sees the British troops of today in the very same street as latter-day Tans.

Another example is of Francis's mother's story about how she hated the song 'The White Cliffs of Dover'. An IRA man she had been fond of was hung in Crumlin Road jail while a group of Protestants sang that song outside. Every time she heard it, it brought back her initial feelings. Even the community alarm in these troubles, the clashing of dustbin lids and the blowing of whistles, is not new. Coogan reports (1970: 209) how in the Civil War years a scream of murder would resound in Nationalist areas when the 'murder gang' (the Royal Irish Constabulary and UVF) were raiding. Bin lids would also be banged:

> Oh she got up and rattled her bin,
> For the Specials were coming in,
> Tiddy-fal-la, Tiddy-fal-la,

69

> Oh, she got up and rattled her bin,
> For the Specials were coming in,
> Tiddy-fal-la.

From 1916 onwards the IRA stands in the forefront of the militant tradition of Republicanism. The continuity achieved by the IRA has proved to be a decisive factor in channelling the Civil Rights movement into Republicanism. Its continuity is remarkable because of the contradictory philosophies that are embodied in militant Republicanism. It is these contradictions that will be seen to find expression in the IRA's present war in Anro.

What is common amongst militant Republicans is obviously their commitment to separatism from England and a belief in achieving this through violence if necessary. What has always remained unresolved are the difficulties in reconciling the economic and social radicalism of James Connolly with the bourgeois nationalism of Arthur Griffith, and both with the mysticism of Padraic Pearse. The movement has often split over these problems of idealism versus political realism, militarism versus Catholicism, and radicalism versus conservatism.[1] For example, when de Valera went into the third Dáil (27 July 1927) the IRA considered the move a betrayal of their cause which de Valera had long upheld. For de Valera it was a matter of tactics; for the IRA's extreme idealism it was treachery to give allegiance to a Parliament they considered was unconstitutional. Rather, the IRA wished to continue the military fight for a return to the second Parliament. The forces of idealism and militarism were incompatible with concepts of political compromise. Tactics, as Bowyer-Bell (1970) says, were treated as principles.

The movement's contradictory factions were exposed again in the early 1930s. The leftist tradition of Connolly and Mellows was re-emerging through the work of Peadar O'Donnell. O'Donnell had been influential in various organizations such as Saor Eire, the Workers' Defence Corps and particularly the Workers' Revolutionary Party in 1930. The Irish Republican Army Convention of 1931 adopted the Saor Eire policy which sought to overthrow British imperialism and Irish capitalism. By 1934 the idea of a Republican Congress was being aired by the left-wingers (O'Donnell, Price, Gilmore and Ryan). The idea was to form a radical political party with the IRA at the head of it. The Congress group was vetoed in 1934 by the executive and council of the movement. The left promptly withdrew and formed the Congress outside the IRA. *An Phoblact*, the IRA's paper, captured the classic difficulty: 'Shorn of all fine phrases in which the call for a congress issued from Athlone was dressed up, the congress means nothing more than an attempt to form a political party' (Bowyer-Bell, 1970:144). This example is particularly apposite as it brought out the Catholic church hierarchy's traditional condemnation of communism. Just three weeks after the first Saor Eire convention (1931) the hierarchy from Maynooth issued a pastoral letter saying that 'the two organizations (IRA and Saor Eire) . . . whether separate or in alliance, are sinful and irreligious, and that no Catholic can lawfully be a member of them' (Bowyer-Bell, 1970: 88). By 1935, even though for two years the IRA had banned volunteers from belonging to the Communist Party, the church forbade membership of the IRA because of its involvement in labour disputes. Monsignor Byrne considered the IRA 'the most anti-patriotic and anti-religious [group] that ever attempted to be foisted on this country' (Bowyer-Bell, 1970: 120). It was not only the hierarchy of the church that was suspicious of the move to the left. Apart from condemning the swing to 'mere' politics, the majority of IRA men were not sympathetic to Communism either. The defeat of the Left resulted in the militarist offensive campaign in England in 1938.

Military failures, internal schisms and severe state reaction left the IRA much weakened by the early 1940s. Its continuity was momentarily broken in 1944. The reconstruction that followed finally emerged in the offensive against the Six Counties in 1956. Similar contradictions figure in this campaign. The left wing continued to split, losing to the IRA several more politically orientated volunteers (for example, Clan na Poblachta, Christles's own Óglaigh na hÉireann, Kelly's Saor Uladh). The IRA did, however, resuscitate its relationship with Sinn Féin, which once again became its political wing. The militarists continued to dominate the direction of the movement to produce the disastrous border campaign (Bowyer-Bell, 1970: 306):

> For ten years the leadership had put together a secret army
> for a specific task, but little time had been taken to consider
> the probable impact of their activities. Narrow-minded, deeply
> spurious of politics, limited in vision the Republicans intuitively
> and inaccurately felt their prejudices were verities, their
> aspirations analysis.

As in the 1930s, the attempt to rejuvenate the Connollyite strain of socialism led to stresses in the late 1960s. These culminated in the split into two IRA wings with the formation of the Provisional IRA in 1969. But the rupture in 1969 was complicated enough to keep some left-wingers in the Provisionals. It is popular to regard the Official/Provisional schism as a divide between the political left and right. In its most vulgar manifestation the Provisionals are thought to be 'fascist' and the Officials 'Marxist'. The rift was, however, as much to do with the equally traditional problems of electoral abstention and the role of force in politics. Consequently it is an

71

over-simplification to equate traditionalism with conservatism. Some Provisionals might be traditionalists on abstention and on the use of physical force, but they might still be social radicals. Others are traditional about everything, including contraception, pornography and capitalism. As a movement, the Provisional IRA's social and economic programme, Eire Nua (New Ireland), is based on the *Comhar na Comharsan* philosophy of 1939: a form of co-operatives (Sinn Féin, 1971: 4, 56). This policy can hardly be described as conservative. Quoting freely from its text, it calls for 'a Democratic Socialist Republic' which would (in Pearse's words):

> ensure justice for all, the means of production, distribution and exchange must be controlled by the people and administered democratically' . . . all key industries will be nationalized, an upper limit on land ownership will be implemented . . . private enterprise will still have a role to play in the economy but it will be a much smaller role than it is today. . . . Nato, EEC and Comecon, Warsaw Pact will be avoided. . . . We have more in common with the developing countries of the world . . . our aim has been to outline a social and economic system which would strike a balance between Western individualistic capitalism with its poor and hungry amid plenty on the right and Eastern Soviet state capitalism (or any of its varieties) with its denial of freedom and human rights on the left. . . . The Unionist oriented people of Ulster would have a working majority within the Province (in a federal parliament, Dail Uladh) and would therefore have considerable control over their own affairs. That power could be the surest guarantee of their civil and religious liberties within a new Ireland.

This policy would, quite correctly, not satisfy many on the left as Marxist or socialist but it is extreme to dismiss it as right-wing or National Socialist in the fascist sense. McCann (1974: 254–5), for example, is more than harsh and less than accurate in his summary dismissal of Eire Nua as 'shot through with Catholic Nationalism' and 'hare-brained'. The Provisionals' critique of the southern State may lack McCann's sophistication, but it is not markedly to the right of his own position despite his protestations. For example, it has often been pointed out, particularly well by David George (1971), that the Provisionals' position on national liberation has as much claim to doctrinal purity as the Trotskyite left. It is in fundamental disagreement with the Communist Party's stages theory,[2] adopted by the Official IRA, in its insistence that national liberation must precede a socialist Ireland and not wait on the development of a liberal-democratic Six Counties.

It is, then, possible to take issue with the right-wing label attached to the Provisionals. What may be said is that on some issues they are not as far towards the political left as the Officials. Yet on others they may well be. This apparent digression has been written in order to establish the fact that the left/right debate has not been resolved in the Provisional IRA. The competing ingredients of Republicanism, centring around the concepts of militarism, nationalism, socialism and political realism, are still in a state of doctrinal flux within the Provisionals. Their national weekly (the *Republican News*) bristles with these various viewpoints. The first editorial, in June 1970, stated the problem: 'The socialism of James Connolly, the idealism of Patrick Pearse and the unrepentant Republicanism of Tom Clarke we shall try to inculcate into our people.' This uneasy electicism is the source of difficulty in attributing a political philosophy to the IRA.

A cursory glance at any *Republican News* will show how different people will be attracted to Republicanism for different and possibly antipathetic reasons. Consider the Pearse-like strain in the following 'If you know Ireland you must love her', which reads like a nationalist psalm. Before believing McCann was wholly correct, compare 'Socialism without National Liberation is a Farce' which appeared two weeks later in the same paper. The frontispiece of the *Republican News* of 24 September 1972 read:

If we know Ireland of the great joys, deep sorrows, and holy memories, we will love her with a love that cannot be killed. If we do not know her as children know their mother, we cannot be certain that when trials come to her, we will not stand loyally by her stainless cause, willing to suffer pain, privations and sacrifices for the sake of the Motherland God has given into our keeping to love, serve and prize to the best of our ability . . . a country sanctified by the memory of brave and holy lives, whose history is one long record of noble and unselfish sacrifice, whose heart, even in the hour of her greatest sorrow, thrills at the thought of the love that has been given to her by saints and scholars . . . that country may be trampled to the earth, scourged, starved, insulted and laid prostrate under the heels of cruel enemies; but she will rise again, radiant and beautiful, for the magic of the love that has been given to her will keep her heart forever young and call to her aid a few or many in every generation to suffer and die, if need be, that she may live. . . . We urge our readers to have more faith in Ireland. We can only have that by learning to love her more. It is not enough for us to love Ireland physically, to be enamoured of her hills, her lakes, green fields and the seas around her shores. We must love her spiritually or our allegiance

will wither and our enthusiasm will die 'neath the face of
storm and seeming defeat. . . . The faith of our fathers must
be our faith, their love must flow into our hearts, their courage
and hope must be in our minds. . . . May Almighty God grant
us soon the glad end of a persecuted people's long pilgrimage
to unfettered freedom and lasting peace. God speed the day
when freedom dawns.

And two weeks later (*Republican News*, 13 October 1972: 2):

Success for the true revolutionary will come about
through a pursuance on the continuous revolution
of the mind, no less than the revolution of the streets. Given
that principles cannot be metamorphosed into convenient
tactics, the revolutionary, however, cannot cease to examine
the validity, morality and justification of the means he employs
to see these principles enshrined in political reality. Depending
as it does on the commitment of the lowest members as on the
leadership itself, the revolution will succeed if all are convinced
that the ultimate end is still through the use of present tactics.
It should be clear to all that our ultimate aim is the safe
establishment and prospering of a Democratic, Socialist
Republic for all Ireland. . . . Under the present capitalist
system only a certain amount of headway can be made towards
constructing socialism and while this in no way minimizes the
importance of socialism, we should accept that the prime
consideration must be the war of National Liberation.
Socialism without national liberation is a farce; national
liberation without socialism leaves the struggle unfulfilled.

This particular philosophy, and the priorities it entails
leave the Republican movement at variance with other groups.
Most other anti-Unionist groups in the North today are
concentrating their energies on trying to achieve democracy
within the confines of the six-county statelet. While we also
want civil rights and democracy, and while we admire their
dedication, we must also stress that we believe these groups
to be misguided and working from a false premise. We hold
that with present mentalities (the legacy of fifty years), it is
impossible to create democracy within a basically undemocratic
state. . . . The point here is that we should delve to the roots
of the problem and do a complete overhaul. The idea is similar
to that in some socialist circles as regards the rich. They
should not merely be taxed, but abolished.

The great danger about working within the Six County
system is that it dulls the penchant for complete change in the
ranks of the ordinary people. Reforms which superficially

better the lot of the people make it harder for them to see
that they are still being discriminated against. . . . Britain's
interests will now be best served by implementing imperialism
under the cloak of reform. No longer does the armed soldier
stand alone. He now stands aside the suave English gentleman
and the intelligent young businessman.

If nothing else, the minds of the members of the Republican
movement have not been dull to recognize these facts. We
wanted a change of system, not a substitution; a change of
type not form. While we have achieved much, we have not
achieved this. This war, therefore, must continue in principle,
and who can deny that the tactics employed are effective.

It is a remarkable ideology that can express its revolutionary
claims one week in a thinly veiled religious and mystical form and
the next in a style and reasoning much closer to Lenin and Mao than
Aquinas. Riddled as Republicanism is with such a complexity of
traditions, it is obviously prone to splits. The corollary, however,
is that as long as the Republican movement manages to juggle the
competing and contradictory forces within it, its appeal will be
substantially greater. So wide are the doctrinal parameters of the
IRA and Sinn Féin (Provisional) on economic and social policies
that they can contain the allegiances of individuals within communities like Anro who have substantially different viewpoints. In
the following section I shall outline the debate that is going on
between the IRA and its community. My contention will be that the
boundaries of Republicanism are soft enough to embrace many of
the arguments and counter-arguments that are to be found within
Anro. The criticisms of Republicanism, evident within Anro, are
largely for home consumption. A lot of the debate is internal. The
historical continuity which creates and sustains the Republican
heritage is characterized precisely by this phenomenon of internal
dissension. The ongoing accomplishment of the debate in Anro
will be seen to fit within the very similar lines of argument that
Republicanism has thrown up before.

The contemporary significance of Republicanism

The emergence of the Provisional IRA

The significance of Republicanism is extremely varied, but I think
the distribution of both its appeal and interpretations can most
easily be portrayed by looking at Óglaigh na hÉireann (the Irish
Republican Army) and the reaction of the community to its activities.
I would like to make it very clear that what I am writing about here

is the IRA at company level, as it appeared to me during one, now historical, period of the campaign. I am aware of the deficiencies of this account which allow me to say nothing about the Dublin or Belfast leadership of the IRA, the differences between various IRA battalions and companies, the comparisons between the urban and rural combatants and so on. Even within Anro, the secret nature of the movement and my basic status as a foreigner kept me, for the most part, on the fringes of knowledge. Nevertheless, the IRA's activities so dominate the community that they demand to be looked at – notwithstanding the unease felt at documenting formless and perhaps unrepresentative experiences, which, when written, are in danger of being reified into *the* reality of the situation. This feeling of partial knowledge is shared, in varying degrees, by the vast majority of the people in Anro who are not in the IRA. As a researcher, I was, however, able to penetrate a good deal further than I had hoped into the world of the IRA at this level. Accordingly, the knowledge made available to me is perhaps of the order of the 'Resistencia Civica'.[3] This group of the civilian population cluster around a guerrilla movement but are never part of its military operations. Being close to the activists they are more informed, but are still in the varying states of ignorance which the secret nature of the militarism necessitates.

Anro has a company in one of the three Belfast battalions which constitute the Belfast brigade of the Irish Republican Army (Provisionals). The present split in the Republican movement was the most fundamental cleavage between Republicans in Anro. In September 1969 some of the Belfast leaders dissociated themselves from the Dublin leadership. This split was confirmed by the formation of the Provisional IRA at the IRA convention in December of that year. The political wings of the movement finalized the split when, in January 1970, over one-third of the Sinn Féin delegates formed a separate Provisional Sinn Féin. The 'Provos' (pronounced *provees*) were by far the strongest force in Anro during my stay. In the summer of 1972 there was a purging of the 'Stickies'[4] in Anro which had resulted in several violent clashes. A shop run by the Official IRA had been forcibly closed; a number of volunteers had fled the district, some were shot and others intimidated. The remaining Officials were left with a much reduced role and were there only under the sufferance of the Provisionals. The violence between the organizations, a general Belfast phenomenon, seems to have come to a head within Anro because of the way in which the Provos had been treated in Official IRA areas that summer. In addition, the officer commanding Anro at that time was said to have decided that potential recruits should not be confused by the choice that the Officials' presence would give to would-be volunteers. The Official

IRA said that they had left the district with minimal resistance because Anro was too small to fight over and, besides, the violence was playing into the British Army's hands.[5] The result was, however, what any child would tell you: 'The Provos rule Anro.' The term 'Sticky' became pejorative.

As seen, this split in the Republican movement was nothing new to the history of Irish Nationalism. The IRA has repeatedly split over the issues of left and right economic and social policies, recognition of the Dáil or Stormont, or the setting up of a political party (the Republican Congress Party, Cumann na Gaedheal [Fine Gael], Fianna Fáil, Clann na Poblachta, Saor Uladh, etc.). The contemporary Official/Provisional rift stems from the middle 1960s when the IRA began to make overtures to other radical groups in the north of Ireland. It sought an alliance to bring about political change in the Six Counties. This policy led to the formation of a National Liberation Front which agreed, under certain conditions, to fight elections in both the north and south of Ireland. That decision involved a recognition of the Westminster, Dublin and Belfast Parliaments which the IRA had never previously conceded. Traditionally the IRA has paid allegiance to the second Dáil and considers itself the army of that freely elected Parliament which was 'un-freely dissolved'. It was this decision which split the movement. In addition the Provisionals blamed the NLF policy of politicization as short-sighted, leading as it did to an inability to protect the Catholic communities in Belfast in 1969. A number, but not all, of the breakaway group also objected to what they considered was Communist Party infiltration of the IRA. They alleged that this influence had produced internal purges and policies of 'extreme socialism'.[6]

Of these major reasons for the split – abstention versus recognition and participation, 'democratic socialism' versus 'extreme socialism' and the reluctance and inability of the Official IRA to protect the Catholics in 1969 – only the last was evident in the debate at the community level over the Provos and 'Stickies'. Although occasionally a 'Sticky' would be called a 'bloody communist', the Provos' ascendancy owed much to the vulnerable state which Anro had been left in by the Officials' pre-1969 policies. It was argued that those policies had resulted in a near catastrophe in August 1969. More frequently, however, the differences between the two wings were expressed within the community, not in terms of their dogmatic differences, but as more of a domestic squabble and later as a feud or vendetta. Provo sympathizers considered 'Stickies' to be people who thought they were 'better' than other people; that is, talked with a 'nice voice' or 'fancied themselves as educated'. Similarly 'Stickies' considered Provos as 'riff-raff'. The Provisionals, they argued, would accept anyone into their ranks, including Official IRA rejects and 'hoods' ('criminal types'). This apparent status difference between the two memberships was compounded with family allegiances to one side or another. The differences in the movements seemed, at this level of organization, to be much more firmly rooted in the contingencies of social status, family and community allegiance than in actual revolutionary dogma. This may partly explain the high level of violence between the wings, exhibiting as it does some of the qualities of a community feud over and above the actual political sectarianism.

The Officials became further maligned by Provo supporters because of the truce which they called on 29 May 1972. This announced a cessation of offensive actions against the British Army on the grounds that IRA violence was alienating working-class Protestant opinion. To the occasional taunt of 'communist' was then added that of 'rusty-guns'. This was not entirely accurate as the Officials did continue to operate on defensive grounds. While this lost military *kudos* to the Provisionals, it did result in the rapid releasing of interned Official IRA volunteers and to less harassment by the British Army. The Provos attempted to prevent all military activity by the Officials in Anro on the grounds that it might jeopardize any of their own operations that were being mounted simultaneously. This led, on at least one occasion, to the confiscation of weaponry from the 'Stickies', and a concomitant increase in the acrimony between the groups. This acrimony was sometimes displayed in the house where we lived when representatives or sympathizers from both sides found themselves together. These occasions were full of insinuations and innuendoes about bitter memories of confrontation. Sometimes they expanded into fruitful discussions and one or two attempts at an 'understanding' between the wings. At other times the discussions would end in threatening behaviour and heated exchanges. Thus an Official might express disgust at 'always being pushed around in this district' and a Provo would scoff at the Officials' merely elocutionary skills while they were 'going out for their tea' (that is, going on military operations which might result in their death).

Because of the salience of the Provisional IRA in Anro, the following discussion will revolve around this movement. The IRA proper commands a high degree of a volunteer's time and energy and imposes a military code of conduct on him. He has to obey orders from officers and is subject to potentially severe penalties for any infringements. These range from being fined if he loses weaponry, beaten for petty breaches like leaving a gun out of an armoury or shot for 'bringing the movement into disgrace' through committing criminal offences like theft. As a volunteer he will be paid a minimal wage. In Anro that wage was not enough to support him. In addition to friends and relatives supplementing a volunteer's income or diet, some shopowners and club managers would contribute goods and services.

The company in Anro would vary in the number of officers it might have at any one time. The officer commanding the company may well have at his disposal at any one time an intelligence officer, a quartermaster, an explosives officer, an education officer and so on. Military operations outside Anro were usually carried out by active service units comprised of men from different companies who met to execute a prearranged plan. Such a policy minimized the depletion which a company might suffer if the volunteers were apprehended. Backing up the full-time volunteers are the auxiliaries. These volunteers are not on twenty-four-hour call and are not subject to the full discipline of the IRA. This back-up force seems to date from the early Second World War years when the Belfast leaders, Charles McGlade and Sean McCaughey, reacted to the losses the Stormont government had inflicted on the IRA through internment by establishing auxianliary branch 'whose members were not required to follow the more rigid army orders' (Bowyer-Bell, 1970: 177). The auxiliaries would, ideally, have several officers with similar functions to those of the IRA proper. Augmenting these two units in Anro were the women's IRA, the Cumann na mBan, and the two youth movements, Cumann na gCailini for the girls and Na Fianna Éireann for the boys. All three groups play very important roles in the campaign, from rioting to moving weapons and planting bombs.

Closely connected to the IRA but having a separate organization is Sinn Féin, the political wing of the IRA and a legal political party in the north of Ireland. To my knowledge, there was some overlapping of memberships. For example, at one time the auxiliaries' quartermaster was the press officer in the Sinn Féin cumann. But for the most part, the military, and therefore secret role of the IRA is incompatible with the political and public nature of Sinn Féin, and this ensures a limited dual membership. Most certainly the Sinn Féin cumann supported the IRA totally. The relationship was the same as that put forward by Christoir O'Neill in 1949 at Bodenstown: 'The Republican movement is divided into two main bodies – the Military and Civil arms, The Irish Republican Army and Sinn Féin. Each has an important task to do. In the final analysis the work of either is as important as that of the other' (Coogan, 1971: 328). Anro's Sinn Féin cumann had several competent members who figured prominently on the Belfast Sinn Féin executive. They sporadically ran a community newspaper as well as contributing to the weekly Provisional paper the *Republican News*. They also organized meetings and arranged demonstrations.

79

Though some of these Republican organizations existed nominally before August 1969 they were rejuvenated beyond recognition in the months following the heavy riots of that autumn. The staunch Republicans in the district immediately warned that the role of the British Army as saviours would be of a limited duration. The honeymoon period was in fact quite short. By June 1970, the souring of British Army/Catholic relations had begun and was near complete by the end of July. In these early months the Provisionals were numerically small and still in the initial stages of policy formation. Their immediate task was to build up an armoury for defence. Confrontation with the British Army was viewed as decidedly premature. What happened in these crucial months was the continuation of large-scale sectarian violence. One particularly politicized IRA man told me that 'a brave few joined the movement to have a crack at the Orangees'. It certainly appeared that the IRA's initial rejuvenation was not because of a resurgence of nationalism but was due to the more pressing needs of citizen defence lent force by a bitterness at having suffered at the hands of the 'B' Specials and the 'Orangemen'. Though not Provisional policy, there were several gun-battles during this period in Anro with Protestants as well as major sectarian riots.

Equally, there was a great amount of Protestant violence including major confrontations with the army and police.[7] In addition the early bomb attacks were frequently acknowledged to be the work of the Ulster Volunteer Force.[8] Although a high level of violence was emanating from both communities it is instructive to see how the Catholic community came to receive the much heavier saturation of the various security forces. The 'Insight' team of the *Sunday Times* newspaper ('Insight', 1972: 176) has accorded central importance to the policies of the security forces and politicians during this period in creating the Provisional IRA. The evidence seems to support their thesis. The Easter clashes in Ballymurphy between Protestants and Catholics resulted in the British Army confronting the Catholic rioters (with, apparently, the Protestants backing them up). The GOC, NI, announced that petrol bombers (mostly from Ballymurphy) would be shot. This was the first stage of the army's deteriorating relationship with the Catholic community. Following seven deaths in riots and gun-battles in June, a mandatory prison sentence for rioting was introduced. That provision further alienated the Catholics against whom it was predominantly used (Boyle, *et al.*, 1974). Perhaps the major fillip for Provisional recruiting came in July when an illegal curfew was put on the Falls Road to assist a blanket search for arms. As well as finding a substantial quantity of arms the British Army left five dead and did irreparable damage to its relations with the Catholic communities all over Belfast. Catholics were not slow to appreciate that the changed role of the army corresponded with a change to a Conservative and Unionist government at Westminster.

From this time the Catholic/army riots became more frequent and more serious. A youth was shot dead by the army at the end of the month and, by the end of the year, snipers had started shooting at the British Army from within the Catholic areas (Deutsch and Magowan, 1973). The thesis that the one-sided or short-sighted confrontation with the Catholic community did more to organize the IRA than their own activities needs greater examination than can be given here. Reconstructing those early days it is tempting to suggest a different historical path would have been followed if the Protestant community had been severely policed and searched. That was, however, politically very unlikely.

By 1971 the IRA had been firmly established as the major threat to the State and as the major instigators and planners of violence. It was assumed that all riots were IRA-inspired, that the increasing bomb explosions were the work of the IRA and that the sniping was exclusively Republican. This resulted in further searching and patrolling of Catholic areas and a spiralling of the violence.

Whether by their own designs or through the activities of the State and its policies, the Provisional IRA had worked through its initial confusions by 1971. Its distinctive contribution was to argue that the conditions in which civil rights could be assured, and in which harassment of the Nationalist population would end, was in a united Ireland. The increase in recruits enabled it to engage in the first round of this process by instigating a guerrilla campaign of bombing and shooting. The State response to this campaign, that of direct confrontation and internment, exacerbated the deteriorating situation.

Internment is nearly universally acclaimed to have been a disaster. Not only did the level of violence escalate but it seems that the policy created more IRA volunteers than it put out of action. The gross physical assault of internment on the Catholic communities did nothing but widen the IRA's legitimacy within them. In addition it created an *esprit de corps* within the IRA as the various companies got to know each other in Long Kesh and elsewhere. I suggested to Joseph, an ex-internee who was an IRA volunteer (the two statuses do not necessarily coincide), that internment had denied the movement the political and military experience which might have prevented some of the mistakes the campaign had made. He quickly disagreed: 'Not at all; you could hold good training lessons inside without worrying that the Brits were likely to break in and carry you off to Long Kesh or somewhere . . . and you knew some of us had to be let out.'

In 1972 the IRA's campaign continued unremittingly, resulting in many more deaths of soldiers, policemen, civilians and its own volunteers.[9] The abolition of Stormont was claimed by the Provisionals as their major success. This was tempered somewhat as the Protestant paramilitary forces began to re-emerge. The summer of 1972 saw the beginnings of the second Loyalist 'backlash' in the form of sectarian assassinations. I arrived in Anro at the end of this summer, not long after Operation Motorman had cleared the barricades in the no-go areas. The war was continuing at a high pitch: the IRA and British Army were in open conflict with each other and many thought also that the IRA were at war with the Protestants because of the deaths caused through Republican bombs. The Protestant paramilitary groups were at war with the IRA, somewhat loosely defined, judging from the assassinations, as any Catholic found outside a Catholic area.

The internal debate: the IRA within Anro

These preliminary remarks provide a little of the background information to the debate between the IRA and the Catholic community in Anro.[10] Anro has experienced all the stages which the more general pattern of violence has undergone in Belfast itself: the 1969 riots, the birth of the Provisionals, the increasingly violent Protestant/Catholic encounters, Catholic/army rioting, blanket searches, increased IRA recruitment, internment and the experience of the Protestant paramilitary assassination campaign. This has produced a number of constraints and contradictions which the IRA faces in Anro. I wish to outline and analyse these in greater detail.

The major source of tension arises from the translation of the IRA as defenders of the Catholics against the Protestant population into defenders of the Nationalist population against the British Army. This finally resulted in offensive action against the British Army from February 1971: 'On the military front our fight has changed from a defensive role to defence and retaliation and then eventually to an offensive campaign of resistance in all parts of the occupied area' (Provisional IRA, 1973).

That change in tactics by the IRA was largely a response to the period of confrontation August 1969–February 1971 which had seen the British Army come into sharp conflict with the Nationalist communities. It was also due to the IRA's aspiration for a united Ireland. The British Government's Minister for Northern Ireland, Maudling, threatened action against the IRA in January 1971. Similarly in February a major-general named members of the IRA who were said to be harboured in Catholic areas. Shortly after, the first British soldier died and then later the British Army claimed its first victim in Anro following a gun-battle sparked off by a search. The IRA claimed that it was in response to the raiding of Nationalist areas that it increased its bombing campaign. They argued that the bombs necessitated the deployment of troops over a wide area, particularly the city centre, and that they consequently relieved pressure on Catholic areas. The bombs, it was argued, would also weaken confidence in Stormont, damage the economy through the destruction of capital and the scaring off of investment, and consequently contribute to the fall of the government of the Six Counties.

Such offensive action by the IRA had been operating for eighteen months by the time of my arrival in Anro, and had split the community's allegiance to the Provos. Several residents commented that the Provos had a mandate from the people in Anro for defensive action only. There was little consensus about what this actually meant. For some it meant protection against another 1969, that is, against a possible Protestant onslaught. For others it clearly meant protection from the British Army who, from internment onwards, the Republicans argued, had been used as an obvious instrument of repression. For the Provisional IRA and its staunchest of sympathizers protection for the community was not of itself enough to create those conditions in which Catholics could live in need of no protection. The IRA understood some of the community's ambivalence towards them: they were desired as a home guard – which was always the traditional role of the North's IRA units, namely to protect Catholics against Protestants[11] – but the Provos were waging an urban guerrilla war. This contradiction was clearly illustrated in the anger some in the community felt when the IRA shot soldiers in Anro. Apart from those who considered it morally wrong there were others who blamed the IRA for the revenge the soldiers exacted, often indiscriminately, on the residents. The IRA here seemed not to be protecting the community but using it as a shield. Some added that the Provos could not lose as British Army retaliation, bruising as it does the innocent, could only swell their ranks with new recruits. The partial legitimation of the bombing campaign, to ease army pressure on Nationalist areas, was in clear contradiction with using the community bases as sniping areas, because it brought excessive revenge. Sniping and gun-battles were obviously not counterproductive in other ways for the IRA. They contributed to the mounting cost of dead soldiers' lives, which, the IRA argued, would weaken Britain's resolve to stay in Ireland.

Alternatively, the IRA were called upon to protect the community when Protestant gunmen fired directly into Anro – as the pockmarked gable-ends facing the Protestant communities indicate. Several times the Protestants drew the IRA's fire. Such action brought in the British Army; the IRA would then engage the British troops while the Protestants would stop. Several IRA men had died in such battles. During my stay I witnessed occasions where such defensive action clearly endangered the lives of IRA volunteers. One example involved a British Army Paratrooper patrol coming down the street I lived in, in a manner I had not seen before and which I could only describe as aggressive. There had been no trouble in this part of Anro, although a riot was taking place in the old district. The troops ran down the street sporadically opening fire. They wounded a drunk man whom I had seen giving them the victory sign as he staggered around the street. One IRA man fired an automatic weapon from a gable end and halted the patrol; he was joined by one or more IRA gunmen and the troops eventually withdrew. This action by the IRA was partly to save face by confronting the Paras who were at that time intent on taking over the area. But it was also partly designed to stop what many residents considered was a British Army rampage.

Ordinarily the guerrilla would not have engaged in such a risky confrontation, but the demands of having a community to protect conflicted with this policy.[12] Accordingly two principles of guerrilla warfare conflict in Anro, producing an ambivalent commitment to the IRA. First there is the need to secure community support. Thus Mao talked of the sea within which the guerrilla swims: 'The defeat of the military enemy, the overthrow of the government, are secondary tasks, in the sense they came later. The primary effect of the guerrilla is to militate the population without whose consent no government can stand for a day' (Taber, 1970: 18). Second, in the war of the flea, the regime is worn down by a series of bites to the bodies economic and politic while simultaneously being unable to stamp on the flea. This analogy demands that the guerrilla can strike when and where he wants. Within Anro, the community support for the IRA is complex and variable, but it is at its highest when the IRA are in a defensive role. However, placing the IRA in a defensive role robs it of its ability to strike when it wants – because it has a community to defend and support only for defence amongst a substantial part of the community. This conflict places the urban IRA in a situation somewhat like that found in the Algerian war. For not only have the IRA no support amongst a large section of the population, the Protestants, but in addition the confined areas in which they live and which they have to protect ensure a concentration of the militia.

Taber says of the Algerian situation, 'The Draconian methods used by the French in Algiers virtually stamped out the FLN underground there, but only because the Moslems of Casbah were already separated racially and physically from the French population'

(Taber, 1970: 139). What race did in Algiers, geography is achieving in Belfast; namely, contributing to the difficulty of sustaining a campaign in a city where the security forces can concentrate on the insurgents by sealing off their bases and alienating their support.

The bombing campaign, which was designed to offset this situation partially by only using the Nationalist areas to make bombs, has not succeeded in resolving the problem. The Nationalist areas like Anro still bear the brunt of the British Army's attempts to discover the bomb factories. In turn this leads to sniping in order to keep the British Army out of the area. The resulting confrontations endanger the safety of Anro's residents and threaten the support for the Provisionals. In addition, sniping has been a part of the IRA's campaign in its own right. What the IRA sees as a false distinction between offensive and defensive action sections of the community remain convinced that there is a conceptual difference. Katzenbach (1964) has conceived of guerrilla war as being linked to time, will and space. The guerrilla fights a war of attrition (that is, over a long time), with the will of a population behind him and with the benefit of striking with surprise and then receding. The IRA, in attempting to create space in the community through the bombing campaign in the city, faces the problem of alienating the will of its supporters. In this sense the war is very much one of time: time to see if the British Army and Government will capitulate to certain IRA demands before the IRA becomes inoperable through lack of support. Or, alternatively, time to bring about the conditions in which the Protestant community will reject the Union.

Community support for the IRA is a complex variable which is in danger of being portrayed as static. Outside perhaps those third or so (c. 1972–3) who are staunchly and consistently Provisional there is essentially a see-saw relationship between the IRA and the community. What tilts the balance of the see-saw are the various activities of the British Army, Protestant paramilitary groups and the Provos' own military profile. The events of one evening, two months after I had come to Anro, illustrate the nature of this shifting support.

I was discussing with an important early respondent, Jimmy, the tension that had been created in the area by the increasing toll of sectarian assassinations. Jimmy thought the Provos should concentrate on eliminating the UDA, who, he believed, were responsible for the assassinations. He knew the Provos would not do this: they never did anything the people wanted. This thought triggered off a tirade of criticism about the Provos. He mentioned the familiar condemnations: they lived well, had plenty of money and acquired the better houses. In addition he accused them of having double standards: there was one rule for 'us' and another for 'them'. The people in Anro were beginning to see these faults and were turning away from the IRA. To support his point he recalled how that very evening a pro-British Army priest had said mass. During the bidding prayers the priest called upon his congregation to 'pray for the British soldiers who are only doing their job, Lord hear us'. There was some shuffling of feet and a rumble of discontent but the correct reply, 'Lord graciously hear us', was much louder than the murmurs of indignation. Jimmy continued at length about the sadistic and criminal element within the Provisionals who were so different from the 'Sticks', the wing he sympathized with.

Outside, a riot had started and soon the whistles and bin lids had reached a high pitch. The community alarm had gone off – the 'Brits' were raiding. The boom of rubber-bullet guns, the whine of Saracen tanks, crashes of stones and bottles and the scream of rioters soon resounded in the streets. People thronged to their doors, watching hundreds of others milling and running around. The atmosphere was mixed with fear, excitement and uncertainty. Fians were rushing around telling of three simultaneous raids on separate drinking clubs: 100 men had been lifted and screened, 12 had been detained. Some people had been 'bashed', some IRA men had been released, which pleased a lot of residents. Letting the 'fellahs' go meant, of course, that the British Army's intelligence was imperfect, and that was comforting. There were some jokes shared as eyewitnesses related how some of the community 'characters' had been lifted. These were the comedians, who, though not involved, would delight in 'having a go at the Brits' verbally. The Saracen tanks screamed back into the fort which bordered Anro. They were closely pursued by rioters hurling assorted materials at the invaders.

This large raid produced a bitter response in Anro. People were seething with fury. Once again with gross effrontery a 'foreign' army, equipped with the whole gamut of technological warfare, had penetrated the drinking clubs and carried off selected individuals. These offensive incursions by the British are forms of community assault. They weld many previously cool residents into warm or red-hot supporters of anti-British Army activity. The rioters, men, women, boys and girls, assembled outside the fort and rushed in waves at the gates. Each attack was repelled by heavily clad riot squads. Others were singing anti-army songs:

> To-ra-to-ra-to-ra-loo,
> They're looking for monkeys up at the zoo,
> And if I had a face like you,
> I'd join the British Army.

Sinn Féin was broadcasting through a megaphone details of what had happened in the unlit streets. It called upon the women to collect their men from the fort. At about 11 o'clock, over 100 women lined up and marched quietly to the fort and demanded their men. The women included old grandmothers, draped with their black shawls, some of whom could barely walk, alongside fashionably dressed and attractive teenagers.

The overall spectacle of this march, the riots, the bystanders, was one of resurgence. The people demonstrated they would not take their repression lying down. Not all of those involved that evening would change the adverse views they might hold about the Provos. But the raid and the reaction to it was enough to stay criticism about the Provos, underlining as it did the basic vulnerability of Anro. The Provisionals would still have difficulty reconciling their twin approach of defensive and offensive action. But beside the British Army's contradiction of claiming to 'root out the terrorists' while also protecting the Catholic people, the Provisionals' problem seemed less acute. The British Army's policy was hopelessly incompatible. Rooting out the terrorists means offensive attacks and these attacks confirm the Catholic people's views that the British Army is anti-Nationalist and consequently anti-Catholic.[13] The absurdity reached its height when the Paratroopers were running amok one day and posting cards through residents' doors offering their assistance in any way they could help the next.

The raid that evening served to relativize the type of criticism that Jimmy was making. Even those who thought badly of the Provos would think worse of the British Army during such periods. This was very evident in the fury of a Legion of Mary girl I met that evening. I was later able to realize that she loathed the Provisionals' activities and generally followed the anti-Republican views of some of the priests in the parish. That night, however, she burst into the house alternatively cursing and asking the saints to forgive her language. Her fury had been roused: she had been prevented from walking down her own street by a soldier: ' "Only keeping the peace," he says; here's me, "Go and keep the peace in the Shankill." And to think I was praying for the likes of him at mass *and* feeling very holy about it. Who do they think they are . . . Jesus, I'm no Republican but the way I feel now I must be.' Susan had been only on the fringes of the trouble and was disturbed about being ordered around, and found herself talking about Republicanism. For those directly confronted with the raid, who had been pushed around and abused, the anger was considerably stronger, leading to more than indignation and possibly to military revenge. During such British Army incursions, the Government's call to Catholics to reject the men of violence had a bitter ironic ring to it in Anro – they were rejecting them in the form of British soldiers.

Offensive and aggressive British activity, whether or not in response to IRA activity, had the effect in the community of tilting the balance of allegiance towards the Provisionals. In between times of offensive action by the British Army the debate over the Provos would be much more apparent. It is to this medley of argument and counter-argument that I will now turn.

Argument and counter-argument: the anti-Provisional perspectives

One aspect of the following criticism levelled against the Provisionals is that they are, as it were, for 'home consumption only'. It is a different matter entirely for outsiders to criticize the IRA, even on similar grounds to those of insiders. Outsiders may fail to grasp the intricacy of the debate and, in isolating criticisms, become mere propagandists. In Anro voicing anti-Provo views does not entail a commitment to the British Army, but it is frequently taken as such by the press. Moreover, the situation is so fast-moving that views and allegiances need constant reappraisal. People in the community can view their situation militarily at one time and politically or historically at another: each will produce a different perspective. These perspectives in turn will be modified by recent events, producing yet again different conclusions and adherences. For example, the IRA is the object of a communal stock of knowledge from which various selections can be made. The contingencies effecting any individual's choice range from his political views, his idiosyncratic experiences with any Provos to the military profile currently adopted by the Protestant or British Armies. The selections designate the IRA variously as 'mad-bombers', 'hoods', 'cowboys', a necessary evil, to the vanguard of the People's Liberation Army. The debate in the community is between the holders of these divergent views and it is about the process by which a view becomes dominant. As such, the debate is illustrative not only for the anomic climate of Anro but also of the essentially political nature of guerrilla warfare. The shifting allegiances within Anro demonstrate the boundaries within which the IRA can continue to operate.

A frequently voiced criticism of the Provos concerned what people considered to be a cynical use of children and adolescents in their campaign. A young Fian had been shot dead by the British Army as he opened fire on a foot-patrol with a shotgun, a hopelessly inadequate weapon. This near-suicidal act was explained by residents as possible only because the 15-year-old was of slightly subnormal intelligence. Two other young men, both under 17, have since joined him; one at least was shot dead while 'operating'. Such incidents had given vent to a strain of anti-Provisional feeling that accused the IRA of using children in their war by ordering them to or letting them riot, and adolescents by allowing them access to guns. Even some Fians, in a fit of pique, assured me that the 'fellas are a lot of drunken pigs ordering us to riot while they stay in the houses'. Susan bitterly attacked the IRA 'for having poisoned the children's minds with Republicanism. They teach them how to die for Ireland but never how to live for it. . . . They accuse the Catholic church of indoctrinating the children but look what they've done. Meanwhile they just sit and drink in the clubs.'

The clubs were frequently the scenes of conflict with the British Army and several IRA men had been 'lifted' during raids on them. This produced further criticism: why did the IRA not keep out of the clubs and therefore avoid being picked up? Moreover, how could they afford the drink and why did they drink so much? pat, a teetotaller, found this behaviour unforgivable. Pat considered himself a Republican but disagreed almost completely with the Provos. He was a respected man in Anro, particularly because of his contribution to the rebuilding of the burnt-out houses in the district. Pat had been to America to collect money for Anro and had also persuaded the higher clergy in Ireland to make contributions to the rehousing programme. Once he started talking you could not stop him. He condemned the clubs as places where too many decisions were made under the influence of too many drinks. He deplored the fact that the IRA tolerated such behaviour from its volunteers:

'These Provos have ruined the ideal of Republicanism. They're gangsters ruling with guns and if you say so you get your knee-caps blown off. You can't rule this district with a gun, you can't protect people like that. . . . They're paying now for scraping the bottom of the barrel. The old IRA would never have allowed these hoods in the movement who spend their time in these clubs. These drinking clubs are an evil, they are capitalizing on people's needs in these times of crisis. The members are capitalists who rake off the profits and go on holidays with it. . . . They cause fights, it's like Dodge City some nights outside the Mellows [a popular club frequented by Provisionals]. . . . Provos outside Anro have been approached to take the district over from these hoods; they're gun happy and when orders come from Dublin to dump arms I don't believe they will. There are too many young men having a good time without working; they won't want to give that up. . . . It's people like these who have created informers; and what have they done? Got rid of Stormont? I don't believe they did . . . they've done nothing but create seven hundred empty chairs.'

Pat's extensive and vitriolic criticisms of the Provos were frequently voiced. I did hear that on one occasion he was cautioned by the IRA, but it never stopped him reiterating his views. Most of the critical would not talk at such length as Pat, especially to an outsider such as myself. For example, a course was held by community relations workers in Anro over several weeks to try and provide 'community leaders' with certain basic skills. These would enable them to present the authorities with information that would be helpful to Anro in bargaining for such things as government grants. One week the course was examining the concept of power, including power within Anro. Though most of the participants on this course I knew were anti-Provo, the most anyone would say was: 'I wouldn't say they speak for all'.

The reluctance to engage in diatribes against the IRA does not stop the criticisms being privately aired. Many complained in casual conversation of the overwhelming sense of misery and anxiety the war was creating in the district. Shortly after the paratroopers shot their first victim in Anro, a woman on the welfare committee was reminiscing about the dead man. She finished speaking, sighed and then added: 'Anro's dying of depression.' The toll of anxiety exerted on the people of Anro, as I have observed, was evident in the 'nerve pills' found in so many houses. A war weariness created by extensive grief and loss brought about a desire for peace at almost any price amongst part of the population in Anro. The Provos were blamed for continuing the strife. In a bout of melancholy Susan thought, 'We'd all be better off Croppies[14] lying down, better off as second class citizens, because the way it is now we're no citizens at all. I'm sick to death of being hemmed in by these streets.'

The overall effect of trouble – the crack of gun-fire which makes one jump, the occasional bomb that gives one's heartbeat a miss, the fear that the latest death is a loved one, the struggle to survive with a spouse interned – can produce a gross feeling of futility. The deprivation and unhappiness involved in the campaign can make even the Republican-minded call for not even 'peace with justice', but just for peace. It was conditions like these which Geraldine suggested were responsible for producing informers. There were those, she assured me, who informed for 'badness' and those who did it for money. A third type of informer, however, gave information about IRA leaders to speed up the ending of the war. In this way they hoped their own girl/boyfriends or wives/husbands or relatives who were involved in the campaign would be spared, simply because the war would be over.

There seem to be two different moral frames of reference involved in this debate. For the Provos and their sympathizers, who arguably suffer the most anyway, there was a tendency to consider the suffering

90

in terms of the campaign as a whole. The suffering was a tragic, though necessary, part of a historical struggle in a country's fight for self-determination. The belief in the right to wage war and the strength of Republicans to bear the consequences were part of the moral qualities of the Republican tradition. The morality which made possible the continuation of the campaign in Anro was that of the cause, the nation, Eire Nua. And one could not, as a volunteer assured me, 'make an omelet without breaking an egg'. For others, these ideals contradicted a more personal morality. This morality emphasized a duty to one's family and friends which the historical morality of the cause violated. To those who put their sphere of personal morality first, the campaign morality appeared unemotionally pragmatic. Mrs Meehan recounted with venom how the 'boys' had taken her brother's van and put a bomb in it. The van was known in certain Protestant areas and was presumably chosen because its use in these districts would not arouse suspicion. The IRA used the van to blow up a target in a Protestant area. The owner was warned not to say anything for four hours. He was then to telephone the police and say it had been hijacked:

> 'You see they just don't care. Not everyone's going to believe on the Shankill or in the shipyard that it was hijacked. So there's my mother and I always worrying when he's a few minutes late that he has been assassinated in revenge . . . when that happens they'll say there's another one who died for Ireland.'

The same view was offered by Francis, a man who had been shot and seriously injured by the RUC. He had also seen close friends and relatives die in the troubles:

> 'Perhaps in historical terms the Provos are right, perhaps we'll look back and say, 'Yes, it was their campaign which got rid of Stormont', and even, who knows, achieved a united Ireland. They might even be glorified in tomorrow's history books. But as for me, living through it now I've seen enough of the shit that's involved, I can't stomach any more; I just don't think it's worth it.'

This remark illustrates that one aspect of historical accounting can be its tendency to snuff the meaning of the struggle involved in periods of militant social change. Bowyer-Bell describes the guerrilla attacks and counter-attacks by the IRA and the Black and Tans in the 1920s as 'a series of pin-pricks' (1970: 24). Historically they are pin-pricks, but those same pin-pricks involved then, just as they do now, dead men. It is such 'pin-prick' theory that captures the differences between the campaign and personal moralities.[15]

Some argued further that the Provos' violence had brought about the retaliatory tactics of the Protestants. Those tactics had resulted in massive intimidation and a grisly toll of several hundred assassinations. The IRA had overstepped their traditional role in the North as a defence corps and had jeopardized the safety of those Catholics who lived in Protestant and mixed areas. This was a particularly frequent complaint put forward to me by those intimidated Catholics that I met who lived outside Anro. In addition, even the Catholics within the Nationalist areas were frequent victims, mown down as they went to work or shot dead when coming home. Anro had several of its people fall victims to the assassination campaign.[16] The indictment that the IRA had brought about a Protestant backlash, fairly quiescent since 1935 (if 1969 is excluded), had not escaped people in Anro. I heard some bitterly ironic comments that the IRA, far from being protectors of the Catholic people, were rather creating the conditions under which they were needed for protection. As Sean put it: 'They blow the fuck out of the city centre, madden the Orangees, bring down the Brits on our backs and then claim to be our protectors!'

It was not only the grave risks that people bemoaned. There was also a feeling of claustrophobia. Anro looked like an open prison, it was easy to get out but it probably paid in the long run to stay inside. While staying in the district minimized the risk of assassination it created a series of petty inconveniences. Not being able to visit friends or to take the dog for a walk, nor to play any sport or to go to the cinema safely, nor do anything spontaneously, led people to say there was no life in Anro anymore. The absence of these taken-for-granted freedoms gives the ghettos a feeling of meanness which at times could be blamed on the IRA.

Just as the British Army operations would swing support to the Provos, the Provos' own activities could alienate the floating climate of allegiance. The various anti-IRA views would appear in all their manifestations in the conversational streams that followed an IRA offensive operation. Michael, a very committed Fian, was disturbed by an incident in which he found out that the Provos did not always admit responsibility for their acts. He had just seen a farmer shot in the leg by the Provos. The farmer was in a Landrover similarly coloured to the British Army ones and was shot because he was mistaken for a soldier. The Provos denied shooting the man but Michael echoed the sentiments of those who believed them to have been involved: 'I think the people of Anro will turn against them.' An incident in which an elderly woman was shot dead by the British Army (who admitted the mistake) also brought out familiar criticism. The British Army claimed the IRA were about to operate. At least three people had died in Anro either through being caught in crossfire or through IRA mistakes. Events like these accidental shootings elicited a swell of condemnation against the Provos.

A similar wave of revulsion came from the beating and hair-cropping of three young girls. I knew one of these girls' brothers very well and he kept me informed on the events as they unrolled. The girls had been accused of giving information to the British Army in exchange for money. Henry's sister had been forcibly taken away from her parents and kept in a hideout for three days while she was interrogated. According to Henry, though the IRA said she would come to no harm, she was abused and frightened. She signed a confession and was told to leave Anro. Henry, 14 years old, had a wonderful imagination. I had heard the same stories told by him several times in very different ways. Given his capacity for embellishment, I have not quoted the extensive allegations he made. Certain 'facts' remained, however, There was Henry's sister, hair-cropped and soon to leave Anro. Henry's house had had its windows broken. And Henry, once a loyal IRA supporter, was now talking about joining the British Army to 'get his own back'.

The examples can be multiplied. Thus two 'UDA' men were seriously wounded in Anro. One of them, I learned from a friend who used to work with him, was probably educationally subnormal. For example, he had been sent to get a tin of tartan paint and had gone. There were numerous incidents of rough justice and casual disregard for life which found their way into the barrage of anti-Provo feeling which could be turned against them.

The most poignant illustration of the community's relationship with the IRA lies in the age-old clash between Republicanism and Roman Catholicism. These two sources of allegiance in Anro were persistently at variance. From Fenianism onwards the Catholic church hierarchy in Ireland has a fairly consistent record of condemning militant Republicanism. This is true despite the belief in a conspiracy theory between the IRA and the church held by some Protestants (Smyth, 1972). Alternatively, a tradition of militant Republican priests does exist but it has always been a minority.[17] During the early years of the Provisionals, the Catholic church made no condemnation of the movement. The doctrinal complexion of the Provisionals was unclear and the church would not quarrel with the immediate task the Provisionals embarked upon, that of citizen defence. The development of the IRA offensive soon brought out the traditional critique from the church on militant Republicanism – a stance it was very quick to appreciate was different from a Catholic defence ideology. With the church behind them a good deal of anti-IRA sentiment was to be found among the more religious residents. Anti-Republicans I met tended to be more religiously orthodox. It was not wholly surprising that the crystallization of anti-Provo feeling came from the pulpit, or more accurately from the parish bulletin. The priest who edited this weekly newsletter claimed he had been pressed for some time by his parishioners to speak out against the IRA in Anro. In the middle of 1972, in the name of 85 per cent of the parish, he condemned the

> active violence being perpetrated in the parish. . . . The IRA are now intimidating you, trying to get you to act against your conscience. What a vast difference between these misguided, deluded men and the people of such noble character as Pearse, Connolly and Plunkett. . . . Thank God the vast majority of people in this parish are splendid and holy and it is tragic that they should be held to ransom by gunmen the calibre of those now operating in our parish who seem to know not what patriotism or Christianity or even the care for others mean. . . . The means being used by these men are an abomination and their inspiration is not from the Holy Spirit, and in some cases (God forgive them) they are passing their diabolical ideas onto their children.

The Reverend Father concluded by exhorting parishioners to close their doors on the IRA and to make their views known to the Anro Community Council, the democratic body in Anro.[18]

The Provisional IRA's reply

At this juncture I want to introduce the perspective of the IRA together with other sympathetic militant Republicans in the community. So far the debate has been one-sided. The issues raised have been those espoused by the critical. The rift between the Republican movement and the church is a convenient point to begin looking at the counter-argument put forward by the militant Republicans in the community. Their perspective contributes to the total context within Anro in which all criticism has to be located.

The immediate reaction of Republicans in the district to the priest's bulletin was to demonstrate outside the church. This unique event culminated in the crowd (one estimate was of 200) delivering a letter to the clergy:[19]

> The people resent your absurd accusation and have come to protest peacefully in support of this delegation. The people of Anro have suffered far too much to be slandered by one of their own priests . . . we defy you the right to force your own policies down our throats. . . . By seeing us assembled here you are seeing the true reaction of the Anro people who are deeply hurt by your accusations.

The next bulletin thanked the petitioners for their concern but denied they represented the people of Anro as the Reverend Father did. The issue did not rest. Shades of opinion in the community used the daily *Irish News* to bolster their arguments over the following weeks. The press officer of the Community Council reprimanded the priest for 'his efforts to use the Community Council of Anro to support his own particular opinion'. He pointed to England as the cause of the violence and said 'it was at best a waste of time and at worse a source of even greater violence' to lay the blame at the feet of either the IRA or UDA. The article stressed the Council had never either wholly supported or wholly condemned the IRA, but mentioned that (*Irish News*):

> In our situation in Anro we have found that since 1969 the
> incidence of civil crime has been reduced. While some members
> of the IRA in the area have been guilty of misbehaviour,
> these failures in discipline were, for the most part, punished.

Two days later someone who signed himself 'Republican, Anro' took the Community Council to task. This 'Republican' was clearly unsympathetic with the Provos, and most likely with the Officials as well. He or she illustrates the complexity of allegiance in the district – a pro-church, anti-violence Republican. The correspondent asserted that the priest did not accuse the IRA of being the essential cause of violence but was pointing out that immoral acts done even in the pursuit of a just cause were still wrong (*Irish News*):

> Surely a time comes when we have to stand up and accept
> personal responsibility for our actions. If not we might claim
> responsibility for nothing. Don't forget that reasons have been
> given to justify the use of euthanasia, abortion, birth control,
> etc. Anro as it is today is not a nice place to live in. There
> may not be an increase of civil crime since 1969, but is it a
> democracy? Certain groups have taken positions of power and
> issue statements claiming to speak for the majority. Who
> elected them? Did the Council, the elected representatives,
> ever contradict these claims?

The Reverend Father was speaking out for those who suffer intimidation, robbery and damage to property by these people (*Irish News*):

> He wasn't attacking Republicanism. He was attacking acts that
> are a disgrace to Republicanism. How the Council view this as
> a waste of time or a source of even greater violence is a mystery
> If the United Ireland of the future is anything like the Anro of
> today, few people would want to live in it. . . [moreover]
> Father —— stated that he was *not* giving a personal view. For

months, he said many *thousands* of people had been pleading with him to give expression, somehow, to the silent majority in Anro.

Other letters accused the Community Council of having no mandate without consultation to reply to the priest who had made 'his stand against the evil that is our community today' (*Irish News*). 'One who really loves Anro' was similarly disgusted with the Council for laying the blame solely on the English: 'God knows, we cried out for the British Army to be brought in to these districts to prevent what would have been a massacre' (*Irish News*).

I arrived in Anro a little over a month after this public discussion. I experienced at a Sinn Féin meeting in Anro the first major illustration of this increasingly bitter rift. The open-air meeting had a fluid attendance; as people joined, others wandered off. A man spoke in Gaelic and few understood him. The second speaker warned of the British Army's implication in the assassination campaign. The British Army murder squads, he argued, were creating an unofficial curfew, thus avoiding the international embarrassment which a legal curfew would bring on Westminster. The new press officer of the Sinn Féin cumann made her maiden speech. She was having some difficulty in getting her views over, but the audience was tolerant: it was largely a meeting of the convinced. Finally, 'one who needs no introduction' was heartily cheered. This IRA man had just been released from Long Kesh and was soon to be interned for the second time. He invited 'the Reverend Gentleman on the Hill' (the priest's residence looks down into Anro) to come into Anro because, if he did, he would find no evil men, because there are none in Anro: 'I have heard the Reverend Gentleman say we are using children to fight our war. The Irish Republican Army has no need to hide behind children. From today there will be no more rioting on the front of the road.' From that Sunday there was no more daily rioting on the main road which separates Anro from a large Protestant district. There were occasional breaches but the previously daily event, by which one could time one's watch, was a thing of the past. In stopping the riots that occurred after the children finished school the IRA had responded to one aspect of the community's grievance towards them. Adolescents and children were not to be so frequently allowed to riot.[20]

Towards the end of my stay, the same priest felt compelled to speak out again. By this time I was in a better position to hear both sides of the debate. During the first half of my visit I heard mostly anti-IRA views and in the second half I heard both, but probably more pro-IRA. The second attack on the IRA was posted through everyone's door on a printed sheet; it bears reprinting here:

Dear Parishioners,

In July 1972 I issued a statement which began: 'It is quite evident that 85 per cent of the Catholic people of Holy Cross Parish totally reject the ACTIVE VIOLENCE being perpetrated by the Provisional IRA in our parish IN THE PRESENT CIRCUMSTANCES.' I knew this was the VOICE OF THE PEOPLE who dare not publicly express what they thought because of intimidation by the same IRA.

Because of the terrible situation in which we now find ourselves I realize it is again essential for me to give expression to the views of the overwhelming majority of the people. In 1970 and 1971 some men of character, of high ideals and of generosity joined the IRA, because it THEN seemed to be the answer of defence against injustice. I felt certain that these men (and women) never realized that this organization would degenerate as it has done. The men and women of high ideals are now away or have abandoned the organization in complete disgust. So, unfortunately, we are left with men and women, who, could not possibly be considered your 'Protectors' or 'Defenders'. Nevertheless they still claim they are acting in your name and for your good. Tragically, they seem to have lost all sense of 'RIGHT' and 'WRONG' and would appear to have accepted as their own the principle of Karl Marx (Founder of Communism) – 'WHATEVER SERVES THE CAUSE IS RIGHT: WHATEVER DOES NOT SERVE THE CAUSE IS WRONG'. Hence, to kill, to bomb, to shoot down soldiers as they guard your schoolchildren, to torture men and women and even children, to drive people from their homes and force them to emigrate, to hand guns to youngsters and teach them to hate – is 'GOOD' because it is done in the name of the people and for Ireland.

So, what you good people said, through me, in July 1972 is even more true today. BEFORE YOUR EYES, WHILE YOU SEEM TO STAND HELPLESSLY BY, THESE PEOPLE ARE DESTROYING THIS ONCE WONDERFUL PARISH. They are using some of YOUR boys and girls and distorting their immature minds for evil purposes. Many of the members, through it all, are better-off financially than they ever were. THEY NEVER HAD IT SO GOOD, AND THEIR CONSCIENCES SEEM DULLED.

For some reason, best known to themselves they call themselves 'FREEDOM FIGHTERS' and they like to say they give the 'TRUTH' about a situation. So, it is important to clarify the meaning of these two important words.

'FREEDOM' means 'the right to do what one morally ought to do'. Freedom – for the men and women of the Provisional IRA means – 'the right to do what we tell you'. When we tell you to clear the streets; when we tell your children to start a riot; when we tell you to get out of your home – you are 'free' to do these things. What price – Freedom? The reason you are 'free' in their eyes is best summed up by the Head of the Chinese Communists, when he says: 'POWER COMES FROM THE MOUTH OF A GUN'. His doctrine seems not to have been lost on these people. 'TRUTH' is defined as '*the conformity of thought and expression of thought with objective reality*'. For those people who try to rule your lives in this parish 'TRUTH' means 'what we say happened'. A real (and tragic) recent example may illustrate this. When Mrs Smyth was shot, immediately the word was spread: 'there were no gunmen present'. After a full examination of witnesses the objective fact (truth) became clear: '*The Army while dealing with gunmen accidentally* shot Mrs Smyth'. It is possible that those who first spread the lie did not know it was a lie, but if they did know, they are bound to repair the calumny. The eighth commandment reads: '*Thou shalt not bear false witness against thy neighbour*'. *Of course* we have examples of the army doing this; BUT that does not justify another lie. Jesus Christ said, '*YOU* SHALL KNOW THE TRUTH AND THE TRUTH SHALL MAKE YOU FREE.'

Parents, once again as a priest, I plead with you that you walk worthy of the vocation to which you are called. Make sure you know where your children are at any time and what they are doing. MAKE SURE THEY ARE NOT BEING USED FOR RIOTS. Point out the worthwhileness of *LIVING* for Ireland.

To the Provisional IRA and affiliated organizations and their few followers, I plead with you, as we come near the feast of our National Apostle, to turn back to God; repent and accept the Gospel of Christ and return to the Sacraments and the practice of your Faith. People hate what you do, because it is so evil, BUT they do not hate you. I, or any other priest, will give to you the mercy and the love of Christ if you repent even at this eleventh hour. Remember, the people asked for the British Army in 1969. Much has happened since. BUT THE PEOPLE STILL NEED THE BRITISH ARMY. Should an all out attack by any extreme Protestant group come, remember there are in our parish, men of character, nobility, courage who are ready to stand together with the army in defence of the people – men who will not shoot the army in the back while the army is defending the people. So, remember, the CATHOLIC PEOPLE OF ANRO *reject* what you do and have *no need* of your active violence.

Gentleness, kindness, patience and *persistent persuasion* have all been extended to you over a long period. You have been asked so often to listen to the VOICE OF THE PEOPLE. In God's name I ask you once more to cease what you are doing. Remember that many people are working very hard by peaceful means for the peace with justice which all desire. If you fail the people now they have no choice but to band together against you. I shall personally do anything I can to help you return to God.

The morning the broadsheet was posted marked the first incursion of the Paratroop Regiment into Anro. The Paras were received with the familiar riot any foot-patrol would expect. The atmosphere was very tense. The Paras' reputation had come ahead of them, many feared they would use force in the undiscriminating way which they were renowned for, from Bloody Sunday onwards. Others could not wait to fight them. Many people were watching the riot from their doorsteps, not bothering about the rubber bullets that were flying around. This was partly because the troubles were by now routine but partly because this was the opening skirmish with the infamous regiment. A blast-bomb racked the streets – a pound or two of explosives well nicknamed 'frighteners'. A few shots rang out and people quickly dispersed. An hour later the trouble had ended.

Being Sunday morning most people were up and about and the stream of callers to our house had begun. Jimmy dropped in from mass to find Joseph, a volunteer, in the house. Jimmy took a dim view of Provos being around and it was likely he would not stay for long. He thought the priest's letter was a little crude but 'nevertheless it seems to be the way most people are thinking'. John, who spent most of his spare time helping out at the church, echoed similar feelings: 'It's not as strong as before, but he's dead on; I think it'll do good.' Joseph had heard both these remarks but he had too much on his mind to argue with them. He had reckoned that now the Paras were in the district he had three weeks before he was either lifted or shot. He was thinking, as usual, about how to avoid getting stopped by the British Army and what to say if he were stopped. He had some thirty streets to lose himself in and he did not like his chances. Like the other volunteers he was not the complete guerrilla. He had no space to operate in or to lose himself in. Right now he was more concerned about surviving than anything else. He did not want a cup of tea: 'No, thanks, I'm practising for a hunger strike.'

He would be found, he assured us, under the floorboards if the Paras came in. His continual witty rejoinders hid a concern about staying alive. He knew from those interrogated by the British Army that he was wanted. Still, he had a very alert mind and reacted very quickly under pressure. Once he had convinced the Special Branch that they had the wrong man, it was his brother they wanted. He told the interrogators how he hated his Republican brothers: they had caused the death of his friend. He gave all the right dates and details which he had conscientiously learnt. He had talked himself out of a second spell of internment by passing as his brother.

Another time he was sleeping with his wife, a rare luxury as his house was under surveillance, when a heavy bang came to the door. He heard his wife explain to the police detectives that Joseph was not in. She had separated from him, she told them, and it was embarrassing as she had her boyfriend with her. The police were unconvinced and wanted to come in. Joseph shouted down the stairs: 'Tell that bastard Quinn, to pay his own debts; hang on, I'll be down in a minute; how many more debts does he owe?' He had created an impression that the irate boyfriend thought it was another debt collector in search of money which the separated husband owed. The detectives stalled and Joseph jumped out the back window over the entry walls and escaped through another house. There were many such exploits. He began talking about the priests, he was very anti-Catholic in the religious sense. The Reverend Father in question did not want to marry him so he liked him the less for that. His bride Sandra was a Protestant and she had been expecting a child as well. The Reverend Father appeared none too charitable. Joseph accepted he might have had good reasons to frown on the marriage:

> 'But the thing that makes me hate Catholicism is the way the priests instill fear into you. They bring you up to fear God but not to love him. Like the way when you're fifteen and your hand slips under the blanket and then you think, "Oh, my God, what I have done!" . . . the fear is there when you're in the back of a Saracen. You know you're in for a digging so you start to make bargains with God: "Look if you get me out of this I'll start going to mass again." That's the way it gets you; you think you're wised-up but then you find yourself doing that – bloody praying.'[21]

The fear and guilt aside, Joseph was exasperated at the myopia of the church as far as the war was concerned: 'It's always the same with folk who live on hills; they're always looking over people's heads. A blind man could see what is going on down here: the priests just don't know what it's like.'

Tom, another Provo who like Joseph was now an auxiliary (both previously having been full-time members), was maddened but not surprised by the bulletin: 'Last time it was that we were different from Connolly and Pearse; now it's the men of high ideals that are missing. The way he carries on you'd think they used humane bullets in the past.' Tom was a very complex character who was generally assumed to be a bit 'away in the head', that is, slightly crazed. He was very frightening when he wanted to be, and that was quite often. He projected a fiercely militant personality which would stun people into silence, particularly during his accounts of certain acts and his portrayal of personal views: 'You just put the hood on, shoot them, and watch them shudder. That's it. All this talk of conscience is a lot of shit the Catholic church try to put into you.' That the near-psychopathic image was a front took several months of close contact to appreciate. I came to realize that most of Tom's utterances were deliberately designed to shock.[22] He was a master at this art and his reputation was founded on the front he presented. He recounted how he had once given some reporters what he thought they liked:

'You could see they wanted something sectarian, so here's me: "My dream is to stand on the Bone [a Catholic area] and see the Falls [this would involve wiping out the Shankill]. Maybe you can't bomb a million Protestants into a united Ireland but you could have good fun trying."'

It was this type of remark which led him to be considered at best a fool, and at worse inherently evil. He was by no means either, but one could understand why some thought so.

The same day as the bulletin, a man named Kevin, an IRA officer, came to the house to ask us some questions. These vetting procedures were something we had now got used to. The questions were always very routine and conducted as if there was no real reason to ask them. He did not talk about himself much except to say he was a socialist. He mentioned the priest's letter in passing, merely saying a reply was being distributed that evening. This, too, was hand-delivered:

To the people of Anro:
We would like to take this opportunity to issue a rebuttal to the opinions expressed by Fr. ———, editor of our local parish bulletin. We hope that everyone notes that we use the word 'opinion'.
   If this attack on the Republican movement is consistent with the Rev. Father's beliefs then no one can fault him.

However, perhaps this priest before launching himself on such crusades should collect and understand the facts surrounding the situation.

He, for instance, calls into question the character of the members of our movement, stating 'that men of high ideals' and generosity 'once graced our ranks'. He of course says these things knowing full well that his position as a priest does not permit us to voice our opinion of his character, whatever it may be.

It is not our intention to enter into a slanging match with a Roman Catholic priest. But as we have mentioned we will inform him of some poignant facts which seem to have escaped him.

To condemn the Republican movement of Marxist or Communist connections is ludicrous. We point out in large letters, NO VOLUNTEER MAY BELONG TO THE COMMUNIST PARTY, OR ASSOCIATE HIMSELF WITH ITS IDEALS. This is a standing order of the Irish Republican Army.

Next, Fr. —— accuses us of financial gain and insinuates that this is a reason for carrying on our campaign against the British Occupation Forces. We hereby challenge anyone to have the utter gall to stand over that statement. Any man worthy of the name will take a very dim view of anyone who presumed to call him a thief.

One disturbing ingredient in his statement is his call for men to stand beside the British Army. It is our contention that Protestant extremists are already enjoying that vaulted position, and for our part we can not see any other outcome to such action other than further subjugation and treachery. The Rev. Father is correct. Many men of this parish are prepared to actively defend our homes. They in conjunction with ourselves must recognize that it will take much more than Fr. ——'s derisive bulletins and collaborations with foreign thugs in order to defend those homes. What we need in many respects, Father, you cannot supply.

Father —— quotes a rather strange account of the murder of Mrs Smyth. We refuse to use the tragic death of this woman to bolster our own argument. But honesty makes us repeat, 'No Volunteer was engaging that army foot-patrol and her death was accidental only by grace of the fact that the Army meant to murder someone else.' We do not hesitate to accept responsibility for our actions, but we do not accept responsibility for murders committed by our precious British Military.

Fr. —— goes on to quote, 'Power comes from the mouth of a gun' he adds that this Marxist slogan is the basis for our theology. We will answer now that if any other way in our opinion were open to us, other than the use of arms to oust this cancerous political system, we would gladly use it, and the sooner our goal is achieved and the weapons are relinquished the happier we will be. Power comes from the people – Power is the people – This is our doctrine.

Finally we are sorry that this reply was necessary. But we can not allow even a man in a position such as Fr. ——'s to slander something so dear to us as our patriotism and our comrades. As for our return to God, I need not remind the good Father that conscience and natural reason are the jury which decides whether an individual acts in a manner which is right or wrong. We are and will continue to be so very grateful for his religious advice and his administering of the sacraments. For it is in this context that we value his advice. His political opinions do not interest us.

SIGNED: 'G' COY.   5th Batt.

ÓGLAIGH NA hÉIREANN.

The reply was perhaps representative of the Provisional movement The volunteers I encountered, however, were more agnostic than the sheet implies. I did not find the dictum that Provos went to mass once a week and 'Stickies' once a year at all an accurate indicator of religious conformity. I think the Provisional movement is, as a whole, anti-clerical, while the individual beliefs of its volunteers vary. In *Freedom Struggle* (Provisional IRA, 1973: 22, 41) the tension being played out within Anro is generalized to the body of the movement: 'The duplicity of the Roman Catholic hierarchy and its lackeys can be shown in many ways . . . against British imperialism one of the most treacherous forces has been the Catholic Church hierarchy.'

Three famous Provisionals in Long Kesh took the priest to task in the *Republican News*. In the name of their comrades who had died in Anro they reminded the Reverend Father that the IRA had protected the population in Anro from both the Protestants and the British Army: 'Even the scandalous writings of a man of God can't change that. . . . You say that freedom means "the right to do what one morally ought to do"? Well, is one not morally bound to defend one's family and home?' They dismissed the allegations of personal gain and reminded their readers of the death and suffering the movement had endured. They finished by wishing they were free to join the men outside. 'We are with you in spirit, and as practising Catholics and Christians, we offer up our prayers for you and hope

103

you will keep up your good work, as we know you will' (*Republican News*).

The intricacy of the arguments used by both sides in this debate is important. It shows that even in this fundamental division over church authority there is no simple position. The plethora of opinions make it possible to take various standpoints. The Provisionals argue they can be good Catholics by appealing to the ultimate sanctity of the conscience. They strive to make a distinction between religious and political dogma and they reserve the right to use violence in a just war. Alternatively, the priests reserve their right to judge dulled consciences, to appeal to the consequences of violence and to interfere when political activity impinges on matters of faith and morals. Theologians make a great deal out of all these matters. For my purposes, I would stress that this lack of crystallization produces a fluid area where there is room for manoeuvre. The mere complexity of the views assures that there can be no easy way to determine or justify one's allegiance. It is in this conceptual battlefield that the debate takes place and where the struggle for support is waged. It is this element of ongoing accomplishment that characterizes the IRA's relationship to the community.

These claims and counter-claims represent ideological struggles within a discourse of legitimacy. They are political arguments striving for moral authority in the community. The Provos grasped this in their policing role in Anro. At one level the IRA said it was necessary for the success of their campaign that they control certain types of behaviour, like informing. Non-political crime similarly endangered their own security. The RUC they alleged, bargained with ordinary criminals along the lines of 'Tell us who the terrorists are in Anro and we will co-operate with you on this charge of theft.'

These issues are evident in the following broadsheet put out by the IRA:

Report to the People on General Social Conditions in the District
Firstly, our schoolchildren:
It is no service to the cause we claim to serve to allow our children to roam the streets when they should be in school. The schoolboard has approached Provisional Sinn Féin who have agreed to co-operate with the schoolboard in the matter of school attendance. We seek the full co-operation of the parents in this respect. No punishment will be meted out by the teaching staff to a child who returns to school after a period of absence.

It has also come to our notice that children have been seen abusing senior citizens, breaking windows and committing other misdemeanours. We would point out that control of children is the responsibility of parents. However, if the parents abdicate their responsibilities we will be obliged to take corrective measures. At all times we will hold parents responsible for the conduct of their children.

Secondly, removal of rubbish from streets and entries:
The condition of our streets and entries leaves much to be desired. To facilitate their cleansing, provision is being made for 10 skips to be placed at strategic points. All groups in the area are co-operating in this effort. The disposal of household rubbish in entries will no longer be tolerated. After the skips are in position, it will be an offence (which will incur a severe penalty) to dump rubbish other than in the skips. Advise us if you are unable to dispose of large quantities. Na Fianna Éireann will assist you in this work.

Third theft:
Thieving and its attendants, the buying and selling of stolen goods, will no longer be accepted as being part of normal life in this district.

We pledge ourselves to take whatever measures as may be necessary to eradicate this blot on the character of our community. As and from now, THEFT MUST STOP. Anyone found thieving will be severely dealt with.

Fourthly, informing and drug-pushing:
CRIMES AGAINST THE PEOPLE: we have no hesitation in labelling INFORMING AND DRUG-TAKING as 'CRIMES AGAINST THE PEOPLE'.

These crimes are the poison in our community – the rotten apple which corrupts all around it.

We also have no hesitation in linking them together, since we have evidence to show they are not unconnected.

We warn everyone, especially parents, to be on their guard lest this evil embraces our youth in its tentacles. Once hooked on the 'soft' drugs it is but a short step to the unspeakable horror of heroin addiction.

A drug addict will go to any lengths to procure supplies to satisfy his craving, even to selling the life or liberty of his neighbour at the nearest post of the British forces of occupation.

We therefore give due warning that anyone found guilty, by the Courts of Óglaigh na hÉireann, of Crimes against the People, will be shown no mercy.

SIGNED: O C
'G' Company,
5th Battalion.

Here, interwoven amongst the clearly instrumental motives for policing Anro, is an awareness of the symbolic importance of appearing as community police. As the *de facto* power in Anro, the IRA flouted any moral authority possessed by the State. It was precisely this nature of the 'no-go' areas that infuriated Protestant opinion: they constituted alternative political realities which openly mocked the regime. In addition, the IRA took this stance not only to flout but to usurp the moral authority of all other contenders within the community. The Provisionals claimed the right to bring to court not only their volunteers but any civilians in Anro as well. In the 'no-go' period, Tom said, the IRA even had a makeshift prison where 'felons' were temporarily held. Even these rudiments of a judicial system, courts and prisons, were generally inoperable because of the war. The IRA considered that the situation demanded speedy trials and punishments. Accordingly the justice was military. Taking this, together with the traditional IRA disciplinary methods, their justice appeared, and often was, barbaric: death sentences, knee-caps shot, tarring and feathering, beatings and public humiliation.[23] Many people, ranging from the conservative counter-insurgency theorists to others of a more liberal, humanitarian or even radical persuasion point to such incidents as evidence that the IRA are terrorists who will kill or terrorize their own people if and when needs be. While there are people in Anro and elsewhere who have suffered terribly through the IRA's summary punishments, it is too simple to generalize from these individuals' contention that the IRA's relationship with the community rests on naked political force. Though the rough practices offend any enlightened principles of jurisprudence and penology, they need to be located in their total social context. It was not, for example, only the IRA who had suspended the due process of the law. Internment and detention may be legal, but the process carries the same scant regard for normal legal procedure as found in the IRA's kangaroo courts.[24] Laws such as the notorious Special Powers Act (NI) 1922 and the Detention of Terrorists Act (NI) 1972, which replaced the Special Powers Act in November 1972, and the current Northern Ireland (Emergency Provisions) Act 1973 sanction a whole array of activities which communities like Anro condemn as repressive. If the legal climate can and frequently does result in death, internment and invasion, it is not surprising that there is an absence of a moral commitment to British justice in those areas where the activities of the security forces is greatest.

In Anro the whole of the law enforcement process becomes compressed into the armed soldier. After some retrospective legislation he can now legally be policeman, judge, jury and executioner in a split second interaction.[25] As Boyle *et al.* (1974:90–1) have remarked, this licence

constituted an effective abrogation of the rule of law in the sense
that under them [NI laws] the security authorities retained
the power to arrest and detain anyone they pleased without
having to give any justification and without fear of being
called to account in respect of any decisions later to have been
unjustified. To that extent Northern Ireland had always been
and remained a potential police state.

The law's legitimacy is not contingent merely on the content of
law. Equally damaging to the politico-juridical legitimacy of any
state is the illegal enforcement of laws. British justice is recognized
within Anro not only by the stamp of repressive law but by brutal
enforcement. Soldiers not only apprehend and detain suspects, they
beat them. They interrogate with illegal methods ranging from ill-
treatment to torture. They wreak vengeance for their dead comrades.[26]
This 'enforcement' can be terrifying, as when the Paratroop Regiment entered Anro. Reports came in hourly about the latest beating,
intimidation or act of destruction. A discotheque was interrupted by
a foot-patrol who attacked the teenage dancers, putting one boy
back into the hospital from which he had just been released. He had
the stitches from a routine operation on his stomach reopened by the
troops. A baker's hand was broken by the soldiers as he went about
his delivery round. A store of furniture belonging to homeless,
intimidated families was wrecked during a search. Local mill workers
were kicked in the genitals as they were searched, twice daily, as
they went to and from their workplace. I was hit in the ribs with a
rifle as two Paratroopers asked me if I was in the IRA. I said that
I was not and they replied, 'Well, fucking well join so we can shoot
you.' The friend I was living with was beaten up in the back of a
Saracen tank by a Paratroop sergeant. After being interrogated and
cleared he was taken back to Anro by the same soldier who apolo-
gized, 'I'm sorry about that lad on the way down, we do it to everyone. People soon start talking after we soften them up.' In addition
to these and hosts of other examples, four people were shot dead by
the regiment in heatedly disputed circumstances.

Aggravating the illegal activities of the militia in their enforcement of the law was the whole issue of differential enforcement
between the Protestant and Catholic communities. People in Anro
felt very strongly that it was the Nationalist areas that were being
selectively searched, Nationalists who were being interned and
detained, given longer sentences when dealt with in the courts and
generally bearing the brunt of the security forces' energies. Much of
this feeling was entirely justified. The Cobden Trust's report into
the allegations of differential enforcement (Cobden Trust, 1973: 66)
concluded:

> We found that no discrimination was involved in the treatment of non-political offences, but that there is some justification for allegations of discrimination in dealing with political offences. The evidence for this is clearest at the pre-trial stage. Different standards would appear to have been applied as between Roman Catholic and Protestant defendants in the selection of charges, especially in fire-arm cases, and in the advice given to courts on the granting of bail. At the trial stage, there would appear to be a greater readiness on the part of juries to convict Roman Catholic defendants and to acquit Protestant defendants of 'terrorists' offences. There have also been some differences in levels of sentencing. It is not clear whether these are to be attributed . . . to some element of conscious or unconscious discrimination.

The difference in approach has been well drawn by Boyle *et al.* (1975) when they emphasize that generally the Protestant community has received a police-prosecution, due-process approach while the Catholic districts have received an army security response.

Whatever the ostensible reasoning behind these tactics, officially claimed to be linked to the higher level of violence in the Catholic areas, the consequence is clear. Differential enforcement sustains differential commitment to British law in the Six Counties.[27] The political and military reality behind this may well lie in the British Army's inability to contain two paramilitary forces attacking it, one from each community. Differential enforcement at this level prevents the Protestant militants attacking the British Army, which they have demonstrated they are willing to do if necessary.[28]

Repressive law, illegal enforcement and differential surveillance were the three characteristics which contributed to the revulsion against British justice in Anro. Living in this environment on a day-to-day basis, the people in Anro were less likely to share the moral indignation that outsiders expressed at the rough justice meted out by the IRA, particularly when the same indignation was absent or constrained concerning British Army justice. Within this context, IRA justice appeared, at the worst, only of the same calibre as that of the British Army. The climate of justice was determined by the war in Anro and there were two parties to that war. Propaganda about IRA methods was accordingly viewed in a different light within Anro.

Moreover, part of the context of the IRA's summary punishment would be understood in Anro in terms of traditionalism. The continuity of the IRA is maintained by its traditional practices which include such activities as hunger strikes, jail breaks, outrageous funeral appearances by wanted leaders and non-recognition of the courts. Its military punishments are a similar hallmark: they stamp

108

out the mythologies of the movement. This traditionalism is ritualized in the tarring and feathering procedure. That act is effectively an expulsion ritual. The punished individual knows that the act requires his or her leaving the district. Pointing out the connotative association of the traditional aspects of IRA punishments is not to justify them but to establish their social significance. Part of the moral opprobrium outsiders attach to such activities lies in the apparently anachronistic features of the punishment. This is not wholly shared by insiders. Further, harsh as the punishments are, there are some in the community who are not outraged by them. This is particularly true of the lesser sentences of public humiliation when offenders are accused of violating community values, like engaging in non-medical drug use, thieving from within the district or under-age drinking. The general level of penal enlightenment in Anro is probably no higher than a lot of other communities. In this sense, for some crimes the IRA's punishments offended no one's moral sensibilities.

Finally, the IRA did show an awareness that for the guerrilla, social control is a double-edged sword. Though their authoritarianism frequently contradicted the will of the community, the IRA appreciated that there were boundaries of tolerance which it could not overstep. If the movement persistently violated community norms, doors would stop opening, billets would be harder to get, informing would rise and their isolation would increase. Volunteers understood this because they were themselves part of the community.

The debate I have been outlining here has so far persistently juxtaposed the IRA and the community. But IRA volunteers were rarely imported into Anro: they were men and boys who had grown up within the district. In 1969 they had been some of those who defended Anro during the riots. The only difference now was that they were organized into the IRA. It is an over-simplification to project the IRA as conscious propagandizers insidiously injecting their real values (Republicanism) into the community. Most volunteers in the IRA did care about Anro and took their role as protectors and policemen seriously. It is too easy for the counter-insurgency theorists to impute bad faith to guerrillas' motives and ulterior reasons for their activities. For example, Tom took the mentally-ill husband of a distraught woman to a psychiatric hospital. The woman had implored Tom to help her as her husband was hallucinating. Tom was not at all anxious to do so; he never left the district because he knew he was wanted by the British Army. Nevertheless, partly to save face and partly through genuine concern, he took the risk and drove the man to the hospital. Similarly, Provos would be called upon to stop a non-political fight in a club or to intervene in a violent domestic row. Joseph was continually tying ropes around lamp-posts for little girls so that they could play their favourite game. This insignificant act is worth recording as it brought an ironic comment from him: 'How can I be a meany, tough, hard-faced terrorist when I do that all the time? It's bad for my image. I'll have to start kicking those kids.'

These more positive acts do not find expression in anti-IRA criticism, whereas putting people out of houses, threatening shop-keepers and hijacking vehicles did. It is possible to overstate the punitive and authoritarian features of the IRA in their own community. If the tapestry woven by the press, or indeed by the anti-Provo elements in Anro, were a true picture of the 'rah', my two English friends and I would not have survived in this militant district. It is instructive that critics of the IRA within Anro did express surprise that we had not been run out of the area.

Situations in which the IRA have used harsh and bitterly cruel methods on their own people are not hard to come by, but that is not the whole picture. The policing role of the IRA rests on their total relationship to the community, only part of which takes the guise of naked force. Empathetic sociology is always in danger of being read as apologetics. Criticism which sees the above analysis as a condoning of the IRA is wide of the point being made here. The issue is not whether I am condemning or condoning but whether the IRA's relationship with its community is realistically appraised. Politicians and military men who operate with a crude notion of this relationship are living in a fool's paradise where the IRA are always nearly beaten and the Catholic community always sick and tired of the Provos. These two half truths recreate little of the social reality within the communities but help to formulate policies which result in an ever-increasing death toll.

It will be apparent that there is another side to the IRA/community debate which is not evident from the arguments put forward by IRA critics. I want to continue this theme by looking at the perspective of some active volunteers. That perspective tempers the definition of the situation offered by their antagonists. 'Being connected' with the IRA for example, was a source of prestige in Anro. Being a 'rah' man had connotations which veered towards romanticism. It not only established volunteers in the mainstream of Irish history but also gave them a sense of involvement, excitement and purpose. Volunteers would join for such varying reasons as an intellectual conviction to Republicanism, a commitment to defeating the British Army, to destroy Stormont, to revenge the dead and the interned, to 'have a crack at the Orangees', to be as good as the next man and so on. Whatever the reason for joining, volunteers demonstrated a sense of purpose. This could actually be seen in the glow of involvement IRA men radiated – a quick-walking 'busy' appearance.

In stark contrast to some of the retired and unemployed, un-involved men who stood on the street corners chatting, IRA volunteers had an aura of urgent activity about them. I mentioned this to Francis who knew exactly what I meant: 'Aye, even the dogs in this place look as though they're going somewhere. It's like a network of James Bonds, everyone running around scheming with wee plans.' He also suggested one could tell who the 'rah' men were by the way they acted. Their style and demeanour gave them away. This was a mixture of the surreptitious, murmuring and consulting in the clubs, and the *machismo*, the confident portrayal of 'manliness'. There were some who played at the role of the IRA man for any prestige they might receive. These individuals affected the deport-ment and manner of volunteers. Though they were not members of the IRA, the appeal had attracted them. On those occasions I met such individuals, they would drop hints to intimate their importance. Jimmy assured me one day, 'It was not our lot shooting last night,' which did not surprise me because as I understood it he was not in anything. Fergal talked loudly in Dublin about all the Provos he knew in an effort to get a little capital from those in earshot of his Belfast accent. Paddy used to talk so low in pubs that you could not hear him: it was his way of making sure the Special Branch did not pick him up. I had heard from many people that these three were not volunteers. The fact they sought to mimic the aura of involvement indicates that being an IRA man does carry a degree of social status.

One criticism of the detention tribunals which were instituted after the Diplock Report to replace internment with detention (1972) was that they failed to differentiate between these two cate-gories of people. So scant were the safeguards of the legal process that an individual might be detained for playing the role of the IRA man. This was possible because the traces of evidence offered at these tribunals could be that of the hearsay evidence of informers. A legal institution which rests on the hope that informers can distinguish between the presentation of self of some IRA men and the presentation of self of 'would-be' volunteers invites its own mockery.[29]

That it was prestigious to be in the IRA or to be closely connected with it made knowledge about the organization possible. As an organization the IRA has plans and tactics which are secret. Formally there existed a code of secrecy, as the posters on the gable-ends and club walls illustrated: 'Stop your blabbering' and 'Silence is golden'. Yet the IRA were a dominant topic of conversation, and those who dropped knowing snippets of information would be assured of an audience. Through the formal code of secrecy leaked a source of social status – 'being in the know' – which made information about the IRA public, as well as other numerous rumours, exaggerations

111

and scares.[30] Tom frequently, and with great pleasure, broke this rule of secrecy. Sometimes it was pure bragging, sometimes to shock people and perhaps initially to warn us we had better be what we said we were or we would have the likes of him to contend with. He was aware of this dialectic of prestige, knowledge and secrecy. On one occasion he threatened a woman who addressed him, 'Now, you're in the movement . . .', for being a security risk. At another time a Fian accused him of being a 'blabber-mouth', and he replied that it did not matter as the 'Brits' knew everything anyway because of informers.

The prestige flowing from membership of the IRA, the glamorous side of being 'one of the boys', might make a 'living legend' of some volunteers. Anro volunteers had a particular forte for being jail escapees. This had put them on the headlines of the world's newspapers and had given Anro an international reputation. There was an anthology of tales which underlined the daring and panache of some volunteers, making them into community heroes. One OC of the district took five soldiers to restrain and capture him. Another officer escaped by dressing up as a woman. Two Provos gave the impression they had a foot-patrol surrounded when they announced through a megaphone: 'This is the Irish Republican Army: lay down your arms, we have you surrounded'; the foot-patrol had beaten a very hasty retreat. These and similar tales contributed to the living folklore of the IRA.

Less romantic were the stresses and strains of being on the run, the thoroughly unglamorous situation of being hunted. Several volunteers knew that they were wanted by the British Army and lived under constant fear of apprehension. Even those IRA men unknown to the British Army faced problems of survival. They might know the blind spots on the streets where the observation towers could not penetrate, the safe houses to billet in and the convenient escape routes, but there was always the chance of being caught during a random raid or of walking into a hidden foot-patrol. Mundane activities like shifting weapons became very hazardous, unless the rifle was an Armalite, which folded. Ordinarily a rifle had to be carried down a trouser-leg and it obviously impeded walking. Apart from being accosted while moving 'gear', a volunteer might easily be shot dead if he continued to operate. He was not infrequently blown up by his own bombs if on active service outside the district.[31]

An important factor in a volunteer's chances of survival was the regularity of foot-patrolling by the British Army. One light infantry regiment in Anro had fairly intermittent patrolling which enabled the IRA to attack it frequently without too much risk to apprehension. Moreover, the community alarm (whistles, bin lids) would warn the patrol and the rioting would contain the offensive intentions of the foot-patrol while the 'fellas' made themselves safe. Under the Paratroopers matters were very different. By terrorizing the district through shooting dead an innocent man, firing live rounds at rioters, shooting to kill suspected volunteers and waging a campaign of random beatings, they managed to saturate the area with almost constant patrolling. This penned the volunteers in and put them on the defensive. With little room to manoeuvre and the community alarm silenced (whistles could not be blown all day), the Paratroopers depleted the Provos' ranks by ambushing them when they did appear. In one sense the Paras 'cleaned up' in Anro. Those volunteers not dead or maimed were interned or went underground. A few went south. Shooting incidents declined and finally almost stopped. Troops walked in and out of clubs without a riot breaking out. 'Intelligence' presumably soared. Anro was certainly a different place. Yet other regiments must have an ambiguous relationship with the Paratroopers; they leave a district flattened but revengeful: a 300-pound bomb welcomed the incoming regiment. In the short term the Paras might succeed but at the cost of alienating moderate opinion. Other districts have emerged and regrouped from the Para experience and Anro is unlikely to be an exception. The short-term victory, which, anyway, embarrasses the liberal ideology of Westminster's policies, will most likely lead to a long-term increase in the level of violence.[32]

The Paratroopers exaggerated the normal conditions of British Army policy in Anro and consequently highlighted the perils which a volunteer faces when on the run. Tom had his hair cut, ostensibly 'so they can't pull me along the ground by it', but really in a vain attempt to change his appearance. Kieran had his hair dyed several times. Others changed their clothes frequently during the same day to confuse the British Army's photographic list and radio descriptions of wanted men.

In addition, volunteers suspended taking things for granted. All possible meanings were read into an occurrence. A whistle sounding would make an IRA man apprehensive: was it a child playing or was it a raid? A knock on a window might alarm a volunteer who was hiding in a house: was it a foot-patrol? why weren't they knocking at the door? Occasionally I would find myself in a house with wanted men when a foot-patrol would go by. My own nerves were frayed; I did not expect troops to sympathize with participant observation. How the actual men felt who would be 'lifted' did not require much imagination. A feeling of helplessness, of being trapped, pervaded the atmosphere. People sat and tried to look cool, but it was impossible for some and not easy for anyone. Joseph would try to crack jokes if he was there: 'Ach, you don't get famous hiding in houses or under floor boards. Besides, I'm giving up the war, I've decided to take up the piano instead.' He then proceeded to bash the piano keys as the soldiers passed by. Another time a Fian ran to a house where there were several 'fellas' hiding to warn them of a coming foot-patrol. The men saw the Fian had attracted attention to the house; it seemed they must raid now. All talk stopped except a few mentions about the Kesh. As the foot-patrol was diverted by a riot, Brendan remarked to an obviously shaken new recruit: 'You should try a year of it.' Brendan's own first year had seen his friend shot dead looking 'like a red cushion' next to him. He had also been designated the task of telling a young girl her boyfriend had been killed.

Being on the run is mentally exhausting: it systematically denies a volunteer relaxation. Walking up the street involves sending scouts to see if it is all clear. Even that can go wrong. Joseph had a female scout twenty yards ahead of him one evening. She was to turn right if she saw a patrol instead of going ahead. She did turn right but he found himself too close to the patrol to avoid being stopped. He ran up to the girl and asked if they could not make it up and shouldn't they stop rowing so much now they were engaged? The foot-patrol laughed: it was a lover's tiff, which Joseph had manufactured from nothing. Such incidents are illustrated here as examples of the tensions that may be produced by being a volunteer. The culmination of the constant pressure to keep mentally alert in situations of anxiety has its toll. In my opinion, this stress was the single most important reason why the Provos would indulge in what others called binges. Being drunk was the most effective way of sloughing off the tension. It was all unofficial, of course. Formally volunteers were restricted to a volume of alcohol which would not get most people drunk. Tacitly, the collective strain was recognized and getting drunk was, even if forbidden, one way of snatching a few hours of release and remaining sane. However, it was material for the anti-Provo critique in the community that the IRA men drank too much. The drinking in my experience was not that excessive and was mostly restricted to weekends. But the critics of the IRA pointed to examples where drinking had led to breaches of discipline. This does not mitigate the fact that others in the community knew what the actual living conditions of volunteers were like and could offer alternative arguments.

Paradoxically, intermingled with the fear and tension there was an element of boredom in the volunteer's life. Long periods between planning and executing operations were spent inside safe houses with little to do. This boredom itself can pull the IRA into the clubs where so many have been captured. Part of a volunteer's day might also be spent in mundane activities far removed from the glamour of the IRA. Stopping cars as they come into the area can not only be dangerous but also very uncomfortable in the rain or cold.[33]

Evidence for the charges of personal gain made by the British press and the Catholic church were not conspicuously apparent at this company level. IRA men seemed to have difficulty in getting enough money to buy cigarettes and beer. Joseph's family barely made ends meet. Sandra, his wife, had taken out a separation order so she could receive Supplementary Benefits because Joseph could not take the risks claiming involved. After deductions had been made for the arrears of rent and rates strike, she just managed. Joseph cared about his appearance and was never scruffy, but he did not tell too many people he was wearing borrowed shoes. Tom refused the IRA wage for some unascertainable reason, claiming that his reluctance was based 'on principle'. He never had any money. Brendan had exchanged a well-paid engineer's job and his own house (outside Anro) for a revolutionary fugitive's life and so on. The only volunteers who appeared to gain anything were the young adolescents who were previously unemployed, their first job being an IRA soldier. It is this type of knowledge that weakens the critics' allusions to IRA girlfriends having expensive rings and volunteers being comfortably off. This is not to deny the possibility of some volunteers' being involved in corruption, but it is to argue that there is minimal evidence to suggest that such practices are widespread.

That there was a gap between the world of the active volunteer and the one portrayed by his critics was clearly recognized by two close respondents, Aileen and Francis. Aileen on my first day in Anro assured me, 'The Provos are nothing but yahoos, running around trying to be little James Connollys, but they have no mandate from the people.' Francis, who had been threatened at gunpoint by some Provos, was not enamoured of them either. He said that you could not trust the Provos to defend the area; it was the Fianna anyway who were doing the shooting now; the IRA were a bunch of cowboys.

All three of us got to know several Provisionals at the same time. While I would not claim Aileen and Francis became pro-Provos, the critical edge of their old arguments became blunted. Joseph and Francis had some good times together, they talked over the Provo 'Sticky' split. In the end Francis agreed with Joseph that his conception of the Provos was misplaced: 'You didn't really believe that Provos were running around with plenty of money ready to shoot "Stickies" on sight, did you?' Even with Tom, Francis ended up arguing in a friendly manner despite Tom's early threats: 'I'll knee-cap you, Francis, and it will leave horrible blue scars.' On his own admission Francis agreed that he had been wrong in his opinions on some issues concerning the Provos, although he continued to condemn the ideology and tactics of the movement. Similarly Aileen made a point of telling me she had changed her mind about them after seeing some of the men behind the labels.

Access to and appreciation of a volunteer's perspective aside, there is one final factor to be grasped concerning the totality of the IRA's relationship to its community. With most people they share a stubborn resistance to be typified. I am not at all sure what the typical IRA man is. Perhaps Tom most clearly matches the popular conception. He had a non-political criminal record, was extremely violent, authoritarian, uneducated and fanatical. Yet Tom, who talked and acted so violently, had attempted suicide because of the depression induced by the troubles, particularly because of the loss of close colleagues. His formal lack of education had been supplemented by private reading. His criminality had been politicized. He was capable of writing coherent political statements and articles. His violence was, of course, selective and he was capable of sensitivity and friendliness. His fanaticism did not mask the dangers he undertook and he appreciated he had little time to live. He had his memory cards printed when he saw the way the Paras were behaving. He was shot dead shortly afterwards by that regiment and buried in the Republican plot without, at his own request, any religious ceremony.

Joseph, a few years younger, in his middle twenties, was markedly different from Tom. His intelligence and ability were immediately apparent. He could argue very cogently and had a firm grasp of the political situation: 'Look, there wouldn't be any trouble or IRA if the Catholics hadn't been denied civil rights. This is a Civil Rights war; what's different is that we reckon we can only get these rights through national liberation, so it's a National Liberation war: the two go together.' His humour had made him a popular cell mate in Crumlin Road jail and in the Kesh: 'I tried to make harps and that in Long Kesh, but they always came out as titties and fannies.' His preoccupation with what he called 'style' made him a popular man with women, but he was 'married sometimes'. His own flippancy was interspersed with bouts of depression about what he was doing, by being involved, to his wife and children. His wife Sandra had reached the stage where she told me: 'I wish he would get caught. because that way I'd see him alive even if it was twenty years' time. The way it is now, I never know whether I'll see him again.' He finally went south. Had he stayed he would very likely have been interned or worse. The decision was made partly because Sandra was pregnant again and partly because he had no real chance in Anro to do anything but be caught. In a more open society Joseph would most likely have been highly 'successful'. As it was he left school early against the teachers' advice and became a skilled craftsman. In between his revolutionary activities he occasionally read Blake's poetry and seemed to be fond of Beethoven's music (his bombs went off 'boom-boom-boom-boom', he said, in the manner of the Fifth Symphony).

Gerry was different again, less outgoing than Joseph but extremely confident. He was possessed of a great amount of technical knowledge which he contributed to the IRA company. He was extraordinarily cool and little could ruffle him even though he was a very active volunteer. He was less politicized than some volunteers and seemed to want a united Ireland now as he felt if union were not achieved the troubles would only break again in the next generation.

Mick was in his mid-twenties and near the top of the command structure. He said he was a socialist. His quiet commitment brought the respect of many volunteers and he was a stabilizing influence on the more wild young recruits. He spoke a little Gaelic and appeared well-read in both Irish politics and history.

Brendan was similar to Mick though middle-aged. He had the most clearly articulated ideology. Personally, he was quite well-off with a professional job and his own house. He gave these up 'to fight for justice and equality in ghettos like Anro'. He liked to debate about politics. Like Joseph he was prone to the 'Big Ds', that is, bouts of depression.

Alternatively there were some young volunteers who were extremely naive about most things except violence. Kieran was barely seventeen and one of the most active Provos, high on the British Army's wanted list. His politics were very simple, as Joseph put it: 'He knows he wants a 32-counties State, but that's about it, really.' He listened one evening to anti-Provo criticism about their death toll, intended or unintended, and replied: 'Every one can have their own views . . . the Provos have done some terrible things but this IRA has done more than all the other IRAs in the last fifty years.' He believed he had a spiritual communication with a dead colleague, a close contemporary friend, who was acting as his guardian keeping him out of the British Army's way. His military ability was by far his most developed talent. He fitted into a strain of IRA men throughout the century: young, militant, loyal and not too questioning.[34] There were several other young volunteers who as a whole were more abrasive than the Josephs, Gerrys or Micks. They were the source, perhaps, of the 'yahoo'-type criticism. But even the 'hoods' in the movement were not of a type. Joseph said some of these were still wild men but others who were noted 'hardcases' before the troubles had been politicized by the IRA and straightened out of their non-political criminality by the Republican movement.

The IRA is judged by outsiders in terms of its actions. The judgment of its host communities assesses the organization by its actors as well as its actions. It is consequently a source of confusion to have a variety of different people in the IRA as this inhibits one single conception being formed about IRA men generally. The young, informed and highly perceptive member of the battalion staff who questioned us was as far removed from Kieran, the aggressive teenager, as Tom was from Joseph. This variation militates against the formation of having consistently opinionated feelings one way or the other towards the 'fellas'.

This account has been concerned to illustrate the nature of the IRA's relationship to its community. The anti-Provisional criticisms are numerous and serious. At the same time, these criticisms tend to mask the other side of the debate concerning support for the IRA. By illuminating some features of the IRA's perspective, I have intended to provide the reader with the larger social context which is accessible to the community. The community in Anro does not hear merely one side of this debate, rather it is one side that outsiders more frequently document. The relationship is kaleidoscopic. The absence or presence of support for the IRA is embedded in a series of arguments and counter-arguments, in a multiplicity of moral claims pitched against other moral claims. The ethical right to engage in political violence is contested by those who point to its consequences. Arguments over the representatives of the IRA, their tactics and personal qualities, are countered by Provo supporters who insist on the IRA man's idealism and disregard for his own life. Callous punishment is seen, for example, by others as a necessary enforcement of discipline carried out by an individual who is safe-guarding his colleagues' lives. Stories of personal gain, high living and criminal behaviour are matched by those of IRA men existing meanly on the run, fighting for a highly politicized cause.

At any one time these various arguments can lean towards one pole or another. What is important to establish is that this debate is constantly in progress in the legal, political and moral vacuum of Anro. Behind the overt power struggle – the physical battle that is being waged in Anro, principally between the IRA and the British Army – there is a running ideological debate about legitimate authority.

The limitations of counter-insurgency theorizing

It is this many-sided reality which exposes the counter-insurgency theorists' writings on Ireland for what they are: bad sociology and political theory, thinly veiling the right-wing sympathies of military men. The theory which authors like Moss (1972), Clutterbuck (1973, 1975) and Kitson (1971) operate with portrays the civilian population as manipulable. Communities like Anro are held to be malleable to the hands of Machiavellian guerrillas. The community is terrorized into submission. Any other view is represented as either an illustration of sympathy with the terrorists or of political naivety. There is passing reference that guerrillas are dependent upon community support, but much greater emphasis is laid on how shallow the water can be in which the fish swims. The rest is accomplished by the rule of the gun. Kitson, for example (1971: 190, 41, 29, 17) persistently portrays the guerrilla as Shakespeare's Iago. The civilian population is 'cajoled or terrorized'. Insurgents commit 'carefully calculated acts of revolting brutality designed to bring excessive government reaction'. They select their causes 'because the real reasons for the campaign may not be such as to attract the population ... if no cause exists it will have to be invented'. The invention of a cause is made possible by the mass media: 'the means of mass communication are being used which concerns the general conditioning of people throughout the world to accept subversive ideas so that they will act upon them when the time is right'.[35] There is no suggestion that the guerrilla is part of his community or that his causes can be intellectually grasped and rationally embraced by that community. The matter is simply one of propaganda and coercion.

Similarly Clutterbuck's political science is simplified beyond value. He says of the Provos (Clutterbuck, 1973: 94):

> They know that the urban guerrilla is most vulnerable to betrayal by the public amongst whom he lives and fights, and this can be discouraged by fear or terror. That is why more civilians have been killed than soldiers and police, and why more of the civilians were Catholic than Protestant (though the time bomb does not discriminate).

As a comment on both the toll of sectarian assassinations and the IRA's relationship with its community this is uninformed and speculative nonsense.[36] He continues (Clutterbuck, 1973: 94–5):

> The Provisionals also calculated that violence and terror would induce clamour for repressive counter-measures which would bear hardest on the Catholic ghettos on which they were based, so that amongst the people in these ghettos the fear of the IRA man would be mingled with respect for him as their protectors and a growing hostility towards the soldiers and the police who would act as the cutting edge of the repression.

Such ahistorical conspiracy theory omits the possibility of the community sharing the IRA's conception of the police and British Army as armed aggressors. Clutterbuck attempts to make his point by relating an incident where the IRA is purported to have rung

119

up the British Army and given them six addresses of IRA men.
(This incident is fully reported in the *Sunday Times* 'Insight' book,
Ulster, published in 1971.) The army duly lifted these men with the
roughness they are renowned for in Ireland. The men were patently
anything but IRA men and the whole community knew this. The
British Army soon realized this and released them. The damage
had been done, however. The district was outraged, unaware that
the raid had supposedly been initiated by the IRA. What Clutterbuck
is doing here, and he shares the technique with other counter-
insurgents, is employing the often-used artifice of discrediting
the insurgent by an over-concentration on their tactics and an
under-emphasis on their cause. By writing in detail, as he does, of
those who have been killed, maimed or punished – his omniscience
is confident enough to assume his examples are all IRA acts – he
draws a picture of the IRA as cold, calculating or stupid.[37] Such
concentration on tactics and a neglect of the history and context of
the cause conveniently neglects the complex debate I have sought to
outline here. One way of writing about Northern Ireland is to
describe and to list the dead, the bereaved and the horribly dis-
figured. An author can bring home the reality of bombs, bullets and
intimidation in such a way that the humanity of his readers would
react with a horrified repulsion. This method, adopted by Clutterbuck, excises analysis for a polemic based on the production of an
affective response in his audience. It is my contention that such an
approach is abortive. I have no need or desire to deny the horrors
of the war in England and Ireland, but I am committed to an
understanding of the so-called lunacy and evil behind these acts.
The counter-insurgents come nowhere near to this: the IRA remains
a pathological conundrum.

Catholic social consciousness and political violence: the political activation of elements within a world-view

In contradistinction to the counter-insurgency theorists I shall
locate the rise of the Provisional IRA in terms of the ideological
conditions from which it has emerged. The contemporary debate
about the IRA within Anro re-establishes and reproduces the
historical heritage of Republicanism. It illustrates the significance of
Republicanism as a central ideological component within the
Catholic social consciousness. Republicanism and its associated
issues permeate the Catholic culture. But the ideological centrality
of Republicanism *per se* cannot account for the rise of the Provisional
IRA. There is a danger in only looking back to stress the IRA's
continuity as an explanatory factor of the contemporary war. The
major problem to be explicated is the fact that for the first time in

fifty years the IRA has regained substantial support. More to the point, that support is overwhelmingly from the Nationalist communities in the North. And the goal sought by the northern Catholics was initially that of civil rights. Volunteers in the IRA between the 1930s to the 1960s were fighting much more of a National Liberation war, while those today are fighting much more of a Civil Rights war expressed in national liberation terms. Support in the North did not originally emanate from the desires of national aspirations but from the drive for civil equality. Without the civil rights consciousness there would be little support for the IRA's traditional goal of a united Ireland to be obtained by force. With civil equality there would be nothing like the allegiance to a united Ireland that there is in the Catholic communities. The debate in Anro would have remained tacit. The irony in the Unionist jibe that 'CRA' (Civil Rights Association) was just another way of writing 'IRA' was not that it was true, because the IRA never totally dominated that movement, but that civil rights were later to become expressed in terms of Republicanism.

The two fundamental ideological representations of Catholicism have been merged politically in the present war to produce a spectacular and devastating response. The politics of civil rights and national liberation have been able to fuse because they represent the ideological manifestations of Catholicism in Northern Ireland. The phenomenon of telling is possible only in a discriminatory society. The social significance attached to religious affiliation exists because the religious groups are stratified. Telling would be unnecessary in a society which did not differentiate in terms of 'religion' for jobs, houses and social honour. The power of the Civil Rights movement was that it exposed the social practices behind telling by making explicit discriminatory policies. The Unionist violence that accompanied this exposure helped to solidify the Civil Rights movement among the Catholic population.

What the Civil Rights movement lacked, however, was a strong enough organization to contain and channel the political enthusiasm it had activated. At this time, in 1969, there were consequently three major attacks on the legal and political order of Northern Ireland society. There was the Civil Rights campaign which struck at the base of a discriminatory society, there was the Ultra-Loyalist Protestant backlash and finally the state violence by the RUC and 'B' Specials. The IRA filled the vacuum that these attacks on the moral, legal and political order created. Unprepared as the IRA was in 1969 it represented the only political force that was deeply rooted in the Catholic community, Republicanism. The IRA so successfully stepped into the politico-juridical vacuum because its heritage was alive in the consciousness of the Catholic minority. Republicanism represented a further major ideological component of Catholicism. This fact was as important as the policies it finally put forward, that of achieving civil rights through national liberation. Consequently the particular ideology of the IRA in no small measure combined the major, total, ideological elements within the Catholic *Weltanschauung*. In addition, the doctrinal looseness of the Provisionals has enabled them to balance some of the contradictions which their campaign resurrected. The corollary of the contradictory dogmatic ingredients of the IRA's particular ideology is that while it manages to juggle these contradictions the movement will continue to attract supporters who, on particular political and economic issues, will be of different persuasions. The debate within Anro is exemplary of this balancing process.

Given the recent historical conditions which have produced this isomorphism of total and partial ideologies, the *Gemeinschaft* character of the Catholic communities has provided a material basis for the activation of the ensuing political and military campaign.

It is this significance of the IRA as a potential merging of the fundamental representations of Catholicism that stands in the way of the community's rejection of them. Far from terror and fear, as the counter-insurgents would have it, the main reason for their existence and persistence is the centrality of their movement in the Northern Irish Catholics' consciousness.

Catholic social consciousness and political crime: some theoretical issues

Irish Republicanism has a phrase – 'felon-setting'. It is used to describe the enterprise of those people who, in classifying IRA violence as ordinary criminality, attempt to deny its political essence. The phrase raises a number of issues about the nature of politicized deviance which I intend to examine. By politicized deviance I mean any illegal act which is committed for political reasons. The politicized deviant is an intentional actor whose motives are expressly political. This narrows the subject matter to exclude the political nature of ordinary deviance. Non-political deviance, as theorists from Durkheim onwards have shown, contributes to the drawing of moral boundaries. In any society that is a political process. What is defined as illegal and immoral, what comes to be designated as a social problem, is frequently imposed and can often be shown to be in the interests of the powerful. The transactionalist or labelling perspective in deviancy theory has also emphasized the political nature of ordinary crime in its illumination of the consequentiality of social control. The variety of agents of control are seen to be at their least discreet in the enforcement of law amongst the 'dangerous classes'. But it is precisely when deviant behaviour becomes purposively political, when effect becomes intent, that distinctive characteristics emerge which set off conventional from political crime. The theoretical positions developed to understand the former require reappraisal to appreciate the latter. This in no way underestimates the importance of a clear analysis of the politicality of conventional deviance. It is to suggest an interpretation of politicized deviance must start with this distinction between intent and effect.[38]

This definitional problem features as a characteristic of politicized crime in the actors' world. The antipathetic will deny, for example, that there is any politics at all involved (Rose, 1971: 350):

> By defining opponents as pathologically anti-social the regime
> can justify treating the demands made by those opponents as
> of no political consequence. To admit that those who attack
> the regime differ from anti-social criminals is to recognize
> the disaffected as political criminals, a label with important
> and disturbing implications.

A verbal war over terminology develops as the essential nature of the deviancy is negotiated. The Burntollet Civil Rights march in January 1969, which was attacked by Ultra-Loyalist Protestants contained a fair representation of the most actively political students in Northern Ireland. The then Prime Minister O'Neill did not, however, share their definition of politics: 'But in the event. . . . Some of the marchers and those who supported them in Londonderry itself have been shown to be mere hooligans ready to attack police and others' (Egan and McCormack, 1969: 64).

This verbal war over terminology is particularly evident in the tribunals, reports and inquiries that have emerged from the various stages of the troubles. Cameron (1969: 72), writing of the Derry riots of October 1968, asserts:

> The RUC in Londonderry had a most difficult task to
> perform in the maintenance of law and order and in the
> control and repression of outbreaks of violence and riotous
> conduct which came mainly from youthful and hooligan
> elements. Those elements were activated not by personal faith
> or motive but were ready at any time to take advantage of a
> situation to cause disorder.

Liam de Paor (1970: 171) illustrates what a counter-definition of the riot, in political terms, would look like: 'The brunt of the street fighting with the police had been borne, not by any traditional Nationalist element but by the Young Socialists who had shown great courage.' The Hunt Report (1969: para. 10), however, stuck to the non-political definition of rioters:

> In particular we would point to the growing cult of violence in society, the increasing tendency of a minority to flout the law, undermine authority and create anarchy . . . to some extent it is a symptom of general *malaise* amongst youth.

As the troubles deepened, the effort to ignore the political content of the confrontation had to be given up. The major 1969 riots were treated in a different fashion. Politics were involved: it was the conspiracy of Republicans. 'Republican elements were behind all that had happened, men deliberately seeking to subvert a democratically elected government': so the Prime Minister claimed in 1969 (Hastings, 1969: 170). The CRA was, according to Chichester-Clark, a Republican front which engineered the 1969 August confrontation in Belfast: 'Well disciplined and ruthless men working to an evident plan attacked the police at a number of points in the city' (Hastings, 1969: 170).

Having allowed the political motivation behind the acts in Northern Ireland the regime began to discredit the nature of the 'politicians' behind it. The trouble was recognized as political but it was variously criminals, psychopaths, mad bombers and child murderers who were behind it. Faulkner's view of the IRA is representative: 'cut-throat, anarchical villains . . . with criminal backgrounds' (Boyd, 1972: 25). The most persistently political label has been that of 'terrorist' which has been invoked with the same moral disgust reserved for the criminal.

The various attempts to 'felon-set' can be viewed as efforts to arouse the social reaction that exists in all communities against the 'terrorist'. By blurring the categories criminal/political criminal there is a possibility that militant activists will suffer from the same moral revulsion that the public already applies to deviants. It is a marked feature of politicized deviants that they take up the challenge to define their activities as essentially criminal, not political. In the most successful cases of militant politics, as in a *coup d'état* or revolution, the ability to write the official history and to define situations authoritatively passes into the hands of the insurgents. This not infrequent phenomenon turns the terrorists into freedom-fighters and the bastions of the old regime into war criminals.[39] In the majority of less successful cases (the IRA, Palestinians, Baader-Meinhof, Tupamaros, etc.) the activists have to make do with newsprint, perhaps radio and their own symbolic activity. In the IRA, both the symbolic defiance of non-recognition of the courts and hunger strikes for political prisoners' status serve to emphasize the politicality of their cause. As far back as 1867, when the

124

Manchester Martyrs (Allen, Martin and O'Brien) were executed, there was an outcry in Ireland because they were buried in the lime-pit. Such a burial did not set these Fenians off from the ordinary criminal.

There exists, accordingly, a consciousness in volunteers which provides an immunity to the imputation that their activities are criminal, mad or merely 'Irish'.[40] The Republican movement attempts to instill into its volunteers self-conceptions which are counter to the 'terrorist' stereotype. The volunteers must see themselves as soldier-politicians. Indeed the labels offered from anti-IRA sources are frequently rendered ironic by the volunteers. Tom used to conjure up amusement when taking leave of company by prefacing his exits with: 'I'm just going out to do a bit of terrorism.' Joseph remarked once on the gall of a stray cat which had soiled his shirt: 'Fancy a cat pissing on a terrorist's shirt!'

Any identity change that the military and political actions of the volunteers induced was consequently likely to be that of a revolutionary rather than a deviant nature. In this context, 'doing time for the movement' was considered an occupational hazard. Far from criminalizing a man, the experiences undergone in prison resulted in a passing of the revolutionary colours. Volunteers were respected if their commitment had been tested by imprisonment. As Colm, a 15-year-old I visited in a detention centre, remarked, his sentence was 'a way of becoming one of Anro's famous men'.

As important for the self-perspective of the volunteer was the degree of social reaction he faces from within his community. Identities are not self-constructed. It is precisely because the community does not endorse the definitions of IRA activity offered by the British and Protestant societies that this important source of identity change, social reaction, is weak. The debate between the IRA and its community can be seen in this light as a series of attempts to resist and establish the social reaction of felon-setting. To a large degree the IRA's definitions of its activities approximates to the Catholic communities' definition. The communities from which the IRA springs have experienced state violence; this has weakened the moral authority of the regime to impute criminality to others. The community has experienced punishments of CS gas, rubber bullets, water-cannons, British Army saturation, raids, internment and detention.[41] The community experience of direct repression as well as its experience of the social consequences of the suspension of due process have seriously damaged the legitimacy of the law in the Catholic districts. Law and order, which were only ever partially legitimized by Nationalists, are seen now as unabashed force.

Into this void of legitimacy the IRA have injected their own quest for moral acceptability. The political struggle in the community is precisely the attempt to gain authority for their own law and order.

While the IRA cannot claim to have more than partial allegiance their legitimacy is sufficient to frustrate both external and internal attempts to felon-set. Even those who are critical from within Anro would recognize, for the most part, the IRA as different from 'criminals'. The social reaction required to make the label 'criminal' stick is held in abeyance.

The relative lack of social reaction against IRA men together with the ideological convictions of volunteers can be seen as preventing felon-setting. These factors suggest a modification to the labelling theory of crime if it is to incorporate the politicized deviant into its explanatory framework.[42] Political deviance needs to be understood in terms of the social and political practice in which it arises. The ideology which allows the moral release to destroy and kill for a cause needs to be explicated. The social consciousness of Catholicism in the North of Ireland has been analysed here to account for the IRA's ideology in the historical context of the Catholic world-view from which it emerged.

However, facile criticisms which see the labelling perspective as unable to deal with politicized deviants, or any deviants who rejected the identity offered them, are overdrawn. The theoretical boundaries of the labelling perspective have already established the possibility of active rejection of the imputation of the label 'criminal'. J. Lofland (1969), for example, in a book, *Deviance and Identity*, which is somewhat neglected by those critical of the social reaction theorists, has stipulated the perspective's limits. Here Lofland addresses himself directly to the conditions in which social reaction will and will not be consequential, the so-called 'facilitants of escalation' to a deviant identity (Lofland, 1969: 179):

> to the degree that orientation of the cognitive field is accompanied by moralization, actors are resistant material in escalation. They will have less doubt about themselves in response to negative imputations by others. They may even seek to mobilize sympathetic others against the negative imputations and by so doing transform an initiated issue of deviance into a purely political struggle.[43]

Similarly, Rock has stressed how the process of becoming deviant depends on the structure of the moral world the individual finds himself in (Rock, 1973: 63, 122).

Moreover, it is anyway a rare individual that can totally resist a wide gamut of criticism. The volunteers I met, equipped as they were with alternative definitions and partially immune as they were to community reaction, were still occasionally subject to periods of self-doubt, the 'Big Ds'. The 'Big Ds' were induced by a number of factors such as war fatigue, prolonged anxiety and setbacks. They were sometimes, though, brought about by moral doubt and reflection on the labels that bombarded the volunteers from the media and sometimes from within their own district. Joseph remonstrated after hearing the news, ' "Terrorists"! For fuck sake, the way they go on you'd think we were putting bombs down people's backs. We don't bomb the married quarters at Aldershot, do we? Or the Shankill for that matter.' The label was getting through to him. Even more poignant was the internal criticisms, whether it was Francis's mother throwing potatoes at them or the Reverend Father firing bulletins at them. Gerry said, 'The people of this district make me sick . . . we ought to just get up and leave: they want peace at any price.'

An insistence on the actively purposeful nature of the politicized deviant should not obscure the theoretician from appreciating that even the most purist ideology has chinks in it into which can creep the imputation of moral unworthiness. The experiences a volunteer undergoes do have consequences for his self-conception. It is true that these are unlikely to be those calling him a 'hood', 'criminal', 'mad bomber' or 'terrorist'. The rejection, however, does not imply that he will not be bothered by the labels. He will wage a counter-attack but occasionally he may entertain the idea that the labels are correct and withdraw from the movement.[44]

It is important to look at the actual ideology which a volunteer does embrace. The concepts 'guerrilla', 'freedom-fighter', 'revolutionary' all suggest a fusion of the political and the military. The IRA as a movement has always had difficulties in striking a balance between these two types of activity. This has led to splits as one group saw 'politics' as the betrayal of the cause while others saw continued militarism as unthinking idealism. To the extent that volunteers embrace the role of soldier over and above their role as politician the movement is in danger of losing contact with the political consequences of their military activity. While this view can overstate a volunteer's commitment to violence, suggesting, almost, it is done for its own sake or through 'goal-displacement', it does illustrate the difficulties that a military campaign has in grasping the opportune time for political initiatives. It is a commonplace but important remark that the experiences undergone in fighting a war can contribute to the intransigence of the combatants to compromise. IRA volunteers, war-weary as they might be, will view anything less than the end of internment, now achieved, and the withdrawal of troops as an insult to their dead comrades and a mockery to the toll of suffering. It is this essentially militarist conception of the war that equates political compromise as treachery which is the familiar dilemma for the IRA.[45] In this sense the volunteer's self-conception is an important element in the tactical development of the campaign.

The identity change produced by being 'one of the fellas' may well not be that of deviant but what it actually is, soldier or politician, is not of merely academic interest.

Conclusion

As I have previously noted, for the last six years the political and legal order of Northern Ireland has been under attack from three major directions. From the Catholic community the law has been challenged by the Civil Rights movement and, more seriously, by Republican violence. The Protestant community's assault on the rule of law has, from 1969, taken the form of an Ultra-Loyalist 'backlash'. The third source to weaken the authority of the law has come from the illegal activities of the Royal Ulster Constabulary and the British Army. It is within this context of a variety of threats to the legitimacy of the State that the IRA have instigated their own attempt to construct an alternative social order.

The attempt is immediately forced to confront the vestiges of legitimacy that remain attached to the criminal law within Catholic districts like Anro. Before the IRA can begin to compete with the ideology of the law it must establish that it is challenging the legitimacy of the law and not just breaking the law. Consequently the IRA's resistance to the imputation that their activity is merely criminal is the first stage in their own struggle for legitimacy. The debate within Anro illustrates precisely this issue: the argument over felon-setting represents the beginnings of the confrontation with the ideology of legality.

How the IRA has come to be in such a position to challenge the juridico-political legitimacy of the Northern Ireland State has been the *explanandum* of this book. I have argued that it is precisely because the particular ideology of Provisional Republicanism has been able to fuse the social consciousness of Catholicism into a political practice that its challenge has been so prolonged and so profound. The IRA has managed to activate, from the favourable social structures of the Catholic communities, a politics of civil rights through national liberation. This formula derives its potency not only from the fact that those political forces have been the twentieth century's most powerful ideologies, but primarily because it mirrors politically the Catholic social consciousness. That consciousness has been engendered through the experience of living in tightly-knit communities possessed of a Republican heritage while simultaneously being located within a wider sectarian social structure.

4 Leaps into the dark: views into and from the inside

Contextualized and de-contextualized theorizing

This text has sought to ground the phenomenon of IRA violence within the ideological formations of the Northern Irish Catholics' world-view. The theoretical position adopted has been to explicate the total ideology of the Catholic social consciousness and to demonstrate how the particular ideology of the Provisional IRA reproduces politically the dominant features of the Catholic *Weltanschauung*. This world-view has been presented in terms of the three constituent elements of communalism, sectarianism and republicanism. These forces within the Catholic social consciousness have been fused and activated into a particular ideology that has produced a virulent form of political violence.[1] In an attempt to locate the genesis of the IRA's political violence within a historical and social context, IRA ideology has been specified as a political manifestation of a world-view.

I have arrived at the categories of thought, which I argue constitute the Catholic *Weltanschauung*, through an analytic study of Anro's ethnography. The analyses of the community reaction to the troubles, the entrenched nature of sectarian thought and the significance of Republicanism have been drawn from this context. The enterprise has involved documenting and theoretically appraising the manner in which Anro's residents have interpreted the material reality of their society. The ideological meanings of Catholicism have been contextually determined through an analytic exposition of the mediated reality of the Catholic consciousness.

I intend to discuss the limitations of un-mediated or decontextualized accounts in this final chapter. Such accounts of the Northern Ireland troubles, for a variety of reasons, tend to gloss over the complexity of the issues involved. I shall argue that these accounts

129

are characterized by a false conception of generality and externality. The purpose of this discussion will be to formulate the problems that face a partial explanation becoming more inclusive. Anro, important as it is, is not *the* Northern Ireland problem. To go beyond what is essentially a partial explanation (even of the Catholic perspective) is to extend analysis into areas where the theorist's knowledge becomes progressively more skeletal. To weave into the Catholic perspective offered here the equally important dynamics of the Protestant population, the British connection and the Irish dimension, necessarily entails a great deal of not only empirical, but also theoretical and epistemological work. Such a problem proceeds from a particular level of analysis and it is the obverse of that confronted by those who seek a general and inclusive explanatory approach. For researchers such as myself analysing mediated reality, the level of analysis severely inhibits a total perspective. It is not, after all, the intent of the study to furnish total explanation. This predicament does little, however, to mitigate the necessity of forming a broad understanding of the war in Ireland. Yet those approaches committed to this task tend to suffer from an opposite difficulty. Their very breadth deals cavalierly with the manner in which their theses and prognoses account for the construction of reality found at community level. Their obvious fault is that, in the effort to portray *the* problems, such analyses are prone to do violence to the complexity of the social worlds they claim to have mastered. The result is banality, partiality or selective amnesia.

This problem is a familiar one, particularly salient in the Irish debate. It is concerned with the difficulties general accounts (theories, explanations) have in incorporating, without parodying, other perspectives and other partial accounts. The problem is whether it is possible to transcend the relativity of perspectives: whether an abstracted view can successfully subsume all insiders' views of outsiders together with all outsiders' views of insiders. To the extent an analysis can incorporate other views, I would argue it grows in theoretical stature. The focus of this chapter is on precisely the difficulty that general and external accounts have encountered in their attempts to render faithfully partial and internal perspectives. My specific view will be the community reaction to the troubles in Anro. I shall be examining two examples of external and general accounts, those of the press and those of the Irish and British political left.

It will be appreciated that while this exercise emphasizes the hazards of general accounts, it does, of course, also highlight the very problems which limited analyses, such as my own, have in going beyond their particular focus. In this sense the problems raised here are precisely those which have to be faced if the Protestant,

English and Irish complexities were to be combined with the Catholic viewpoint presented in this thesis. Consequently I am arguing for the recognition of the theoretical importance of analysing mediated social reality. That is, that level of reality which constitutes the social consciousness of a class, strata or group. I shall argue that attempts to ignore the content of a consciousness within a total or particular ideology will produce accounts that remain programmatic. To treat as unproblematic the process by which objective material reality is contextually defined is to make the unwarranted assumption that the ideological representations of a society are given immediately.

Alternatively, to raise the possibility of a general explanation demands delimiting the theoretical autonomy of the contextual determination of meaning. To argue for the significance of how reality is interpreted by existing levels of social consciousness is *ipso facto* to raise the matter of the structural determination of meaning. As I have argued in the Introduction, to construct a general explanation of the war in Northern Ireland entails the resolving of such epistemological matters. A theory of mediation is required which can link the various world-views of the parties in the struggle to the material reality of the Northern Irish State. The following demonstrates the significance of only one element within this matrix of theoretical problems. It necessarily raises the others.

Limitations to knowledge (1): Aspects of press reportage on the troubles

The presentation of a full appraisal of the newspaper coverage of the Irish troubles since 1968 is a massive undertaking that is well beyond the limits of this study. As a pragmatic compromise I have decided to examine mainly the English (Manchester) newspaper, the *Guardian* frequently described as being the 'liberal conscience' of the English press.[2] The period of coverage will be the months in 1972/3 which coincided with the time I spent within Anro. This has involved a content analysis of the total *Guardian* reportage of Irish matters during this time. References will be made to the specific reporting of Anro given by the two Belfast morning dailies, the *Irish News* (Catholic) and the *Newsletter* (Protestant). Even such a restricted project requires a much fuller qualification.

What will be under focus here are the boundaries of what the press can and cannot manage to know. These limits deny access to certain types of knowledge. I shall argue that the journalist adopts strategies that are designed to minimize readers' awareness of his own real areas of ignorance. In elucidating these strategies many other important aspects of the newspaper world will remain untouched.

For example, I shall neglect those aspects of coverage which concern not what is knowable but what is likely to end up in print. Here the inter-relationships of the economy and the press are studied to ascertain in what manner the physical links of capital influence the ideological contours of the content of news.[3] Nor shall I be analysing how this ideological content is a form of cultural power which helps to reproduce the normal climate of consciousness in society.[4] At another level I shall also underplay the importance of the role of the bureaucratic organization of the news world in determining how news and the news value of events is established.[5] These crucial issues of interest, selection, bias, censorship and influence will not be the object of study. The central concern is what some of these processes build upon. The construction of news is contingent upon what is communicable to outsiders and what can be conveyed in news articles. Even if *Guardian* reporters were free agents who subscribed to the notion that there exists an objective and reportable account of an event (two great assumptions), there is an order of knowledge which is stubbornly resistant to reaching the journalists' minds or to taking shape in an article.

There is nothing peculiar in this; it merely refers to that order of constraint which is involved in translating the meanings attached to an event in one social world into the medium of another social world. In this sense the journalist faces the same problem in communicating with Protestants and Catholics as they have in communicating with each other. In chapter 2 the depth of this communication chasm was illustrated and 'telling' was offered as one indication of it. The consequences are the progressive ignorance each group has of the other despite their sharing of 'basic social characteristics'. The Protestant militant broadsheets of Anro's neighbouring community illustrate this ignorance in their grossly inaccurate portrayal of Anro. I am aware, of course, that these war-cries are fundamentally intended to serve propaganda purposes, not function as sociological descriptions of neighbours. Accordingly they may well be intentionally exaggerated. But sophisticated propaganda, like the cartoon, makes use of knowledge that appears true; it seems plausible, if exaggerated. The rhetorical extremes of these broadsheets bear no relationship to anything going on in Anro – variously referred to as 'the septic boil', 'the mau-mau jungle', 'the cannibal village' and so on.[6] Two examples will draw the point:

> The propaganda machine of the Rebel scum of Anro is again in full production. An army officer stated this propaganda does not deserve comment, he could be right but we take this opportunity to give this a little mention. The sick twisted minded creatures claim the Army in the area are on drugs

and also charges them of drunkenness, no need to comment any further. Now here are the true facts; the same rebel scum who after a night of riots in Anro stretched themselves down on the roads and pavements in MacDonagh Street and had a real booze up. They drank like animals from fruit and bean cans which they filled with scrumpy taken from buckets. Cheap wine was consumed by the ten glass bottle, some sat, some sprawled, some crawled while shouting abuse at their own people who were forced to step over outstretched drunken hooligans as they made their way to mass at the Sacred Heart. It is not so long ago that this would not have been tolerated. Ex Fr. Hurley Stick would have sorted a few of these animals out, that is of course if he had not received an invitation to the party himself.

Following a piece of information that the destroyed houses in Anro were to be rebuilt by the 'RCs', the same newsheet later commented:

So we ask all those who are to rebuild these houses, for goodness sake have them like Protestant homes and please do not be putting the coal in the bath or using the stair rails to kindle the fire. Just two more requests: don't be using these houses as stick breaking and bundling factories or rag stores and keep all handcarts out of the garden.

A lot of typifications are revealed in such statements. I want to suggest merely that the stereotypes invoked here are the product of separation. The distancing of the communities and the accruing ignorance make this absurdity possible. The attempt at humour is lost; the images are incredible. Just as the two communities do not know each other and have difficulty in producing credible propaganda, the journalist frequently comes over as knowing neither Protestant or Catholic communities, and he shows difficulty in producing faithful accounts.

It is on to this ignorance that the reporter attaches his conscious and unconscious views of the world. In turn those views are shaped by the processes of selection, relevance and interest to result in a news product. This product, apart from constituting a major source of information for outsiders, is received back into the community from where it supposedly originated. Insiders are avid readers of external accounts of their affairs. Within Anro the daily newspapers and the television and radio news reports acted as constant sources of conversation, particularly when the reported incidents were local.

Faced with a problem of access to knowledge (reporters live outside the communities) the *Guardian* journalists can be seen to have adopted certain ground rules to temper their situation. The *Guardian* offers a most suitable example for analysis. It has largely avoided the sensational excesses found in other press coverage of the violence emanating from the troubles. Its reporters are considered to be influenced by high journalistic standards, its readers to be somewhat critical and its editorials 'responsible'.[7] In such a newspaper, unconstrained by a flagrantly commercial approach and with a commitment to serious reporting, it is easier to see the ground rules which are followed in its organization of the Ulster chaos. What follows is a presentation of some of these rules, after which selected events that occurred in Anro will be scrutinized in conjunction with the *Guardian*, *Irish News* and *Newsletter* accounts of these events. This juxtaposition is designed to argue how such rules are contingent on the predominantly external nature of press accounts.

Northern Ireland is full of news in terms of happenings but equally it is full of confusion as to the meaning and consequences of these events. Nobody knows exactly what *is* going on in Northern Ireland. That is a defining characteristic of the war. However, the reporter's dilemma is precisely to portray coherence. The order which he produces in his frequently hurried texts leans necessarily towards sources of information that are available to him. The most consistent and clearly articulated views, stemming from constant sources, come from the British Army and party politicians, including fringe parties. This results in the reporter taking the line of least resistance by constantly using these wells of information. This leads, however, to an over-concentration on official views of the kind that may be found in party statements, army claims, political speeches and broadsheets.

This process of talking to the amenable and listening to the talkative creates an assumption that such people represent the principal actors; that the people who matter are the people who are amenable and available. This is not to deny the existence of 'twilight contact' with the unofficial paramilitary men. Reporters do have them, even though their sources are frequently press officers. However, I shall discuss this below. I do suggest, though, that one consequence of taking the line of least resistance, particularly with British Army press releases, is to enter, perhaps unwittingly, into the propaganda campaign.[8] The *Guardian* always echoes the army line. This goes beyond the standard form of: 'The army claimed. . . . Residents, however, say', to a stream of claims that residents regard as contentious. These vary from British Army assertions that the war is going well, officers in the IRA are being arrested, British Army victims are gunmen (except if they are elderly or women), to claims that contrary allegations are mere propaganda. I am not asserting that the *Guardian* uncritically follows the army line, yet I would claim that one of the consequences of the over-dependence on articulate sources is that there is always a place reserved for the British Army view. Sometimes these views are contested by the paper and sometimes they are not, but they are always there. The following extracts from the *Guardian* support this contention:

A consolation for the security forces has been the knowledge of an important IRA capture. It is understood that one of the five alleged IRA gunmen . . . is commanding officer 1st Battalion Belfast Brigade. Two more of the Battalion staff were also arrested on Tuesday and two company commanders. . . . One of them is believed to be an explosive expert (10 November 1972) Another leading Provisional IRA man has been arrested . . . and is believed to be the adjutant of the Provisionals. (23 November (1972)
The latest important arrest was . . . one of the most wanted men in Ulster [from] one of the most successful IRA units (13 January 1973)
The total of men now believed to be active around 150 is strikingly fewer than the 500 known to be working directly for the IRA in spring and summer last year . . . the number of arrests has risen remarkably. Nearly 300 officers have been put in custody since Operation Motorman. . . . In spite of all this though there is no evidence that the IRA is on the brink of defeat. (10 April 1973)

At least twelve such reports of arrest successes occurred between September 1972 and April 1973. At that time the death rate was in fact nearly at its highest. There were no references to the scepticism shown in the Catholic communities about all these successful arrests of 'officers' and 'most wanted men in Ulster'. There was also little reference to the social consequences of the raids that preface such arrests.

It is instructive to see how the newspaper reverts to external indicators of the pattern of violence. With no real possibility of penetrating the secret organizations, much is read into the statistical vagaries of the death rates, explosions and shooting occurrences. Playing the numbers game is, however, unpredictable: the rates hide whole sets of unknown processes. The *Guardian* of 25 January 1973 reported:

The total of deaths and explosions is significantly down and although destruction is continuing at a rate clearly unacceptable to most people in Ulster, there is increasing optimism that the forces of terrorism are being successfully contained, if not defeated . . . the level of destruction has fallen off considerably since July last year . . . the death rate has also dropped. . . .

The RUC has also been heartened by the recent spate of arrests. Eleven days later (5 February 1973) the rates change and the analysis follows suit:

> The situation in Northern Ireland is now dreadfully bad and there is virtually nothing the Government can do about it. This has been expected for some time, the only surprise is that the deterioration has been so sudden and so rapid . . . eighteen people have been killed in a seven day period.

The vacuum of knowledge coupled with the pressure to produce an air of knowingness results in a further technique – the rule of Thomas's dictum. Here the reporter reverts to the face-saving formula: if people define something as true, then it might as well be, because people act upon their definitions of situations. I happen to think this can on occasions be good sociology. Its application in the *Guardian*, however, is used to suggest the irrationality of a claim and to cast aspersions upon the veracity of the complainant. Faced with a situation which the reporter has no possibility of appraising, where he has no access to the debate surrounding an event, claims and allegations are important only in so far as these people believe them to be true. For example, following the October clashes (1972) with the British Army, the Belfast Protestants made several allegations about the troops' behaviour (*Guardian*, 19 October 1972):

> How many of the claims and stories are true it is not possible to say. Some may be invented, most of them are probably exaggerated. But what is important is that the people in Protestant areas believe them and a climate is rapidly building up in which they will elaborate them and where they will attach credence to wild rumours which may be deliberately circulated.

When the irrationality is not stressed Thomas's dictum is used as a distancing device which invites the reader to treat this respondent with scepticism. A particularly unhappy example is provided in the following (*Guardian*, 2 November 1972):

> In the living room of a cramped flat a woman who looks much older than she really is lies quivering with fear or nervousness on a couch, cuddling a neighbour's small child for comfort. Her husband is also nervous and stammering and together shakily but politely they explain that the army has just been in for the sixth time since Friday (six days) to look for their 16-year-old son. He was picked up on Saturday and held for six hours and they say he was tortured. He was thrown down some steps, had wire put round his neck, and skin grazed off his

hands, they say. He was too scared to come home, they say, but they hoped he would be back for supper. It is impossible to say if any of this is true but the important thing is that this elderly frightened couple believe it. So does their grown-up daughter who comes in later and bursts into a fit of hysterical tears.

The distancing achieved by Thomas's dictum (and the continual qualification 'they say') is also behind a further strategy whereby the reporter builds a hierarchy of credible respondents. As outsiders who rarely witness events but endeavour to capture reconstructions of events, reporters are vulnerable to being used for what might loosely be called 'propaganda purposes'. Individuals and groups within the North of Ireland certainly attempted to manage the media. To counter this twin disability of having to rely on witnesses but wanting to avoid partisan views, the reporter looks for respectable eye-witnesses. In Ireland this category of the credible contains, preferably, the non-Irish and/or the professional classes. The consequence is the increasing scepticism of the everyday Protestant or Catholic whom 'everyone' knows to be partial. Accordingly, there is an increase in the distance between reporters and residents. If the role of the credible respondent is fulfilled then not only is Thomas's dictum superseded, but a licence to criticize is established. The widespread complaints of Paratrooper activity in Ballymurphy have to be taken seriously when deep in this heart of Catholic Nationalism an English Protestant, also an ex-Marine, endorses the complaints of brutality (*Guardian*, 30 October 1972):

> Allegations of brutality, misbehaviour and harassment by the Parachute Regiment have long been commonplace on the Ballymurphy estate in Belfast. Most people there, Republican and Nationalist to a man, hate the army in general and the paratroopers in particular, and it is easy to be sceptical of their lurid and often illogical complaints. But it is not so easy to dismiss the claims made yesterday by Mr Smith. . . . Mr Smith is an English Protestant with twelve years service in the Royal Marines. He is also articulate and moderate.

Similarly sixty-five priests constituted a plausible group. Half of Belfast's clergy accused the army of brutality, including the shooting of unarmed civilians by non-uniformed soldiers (*Guardian*, 21 November 1972):

> Charges like these have been made many times during the past three years. But previous claims have been made by hysterical women, committed Republicans, or politically motivated groups, and it will not be so easy for the military

or the Government to dismiss the claims. . . . The priests
spend almost all their time in areas where the army operates
and while they may fairly be said to have emotional and
political sympathies with their parishioners it is hardly likely
that they would or could fabricate such an overwhelming
range and number of serious allegations.

The issue here, amongst others, is that the reporter is unable to
assess standard allegations. His knowledge of army behaviour in a
ghetto is nearly always second-hand. Though the journalist's own
eye-witness is always acceptable, it is in the structure of his profession
that these occasions will be rare. Condemned to dependence, he
applies his various criteria to respondents.

The quest for the aura of knowingness reaches its height when the
reporter plays the role of the impartial expert. Here the journalist
writes authoritatively on a subject which turns what is essentially
opinion into hard, inside fact. This is particularly plausible in the
Irish troubles because the person with a coherent, confident analysis
looks as if he can penetrate a situation loaded with so many un-
knowns. The authoritative account of what is happening ('really'
happening) inside the ghettos, within the secret organizations, or the
British Army headquarters makes compelling reading. It also
frequently creates a dissonance amongst those upon whom they
comment (*Guardian*, 5 February 1973):

In effect the IRA and the Protestant extremists have launched
a game of poker in which the ever-increasing stakes are the
lives of innocent people. Both believe they can bluff the other
into defeat and both are quite evidently wrong. In the ghettos
the mood is the most dangerous of all – fear combined with
anger. People are resentful of authority and convinced that the
army and police will do little or nothing to protect them. They are
turning again to the gunmen to give them a false sense of security
and to provide them with the revenge they apparently crave.

Such near fantasizing is not infrequent (see the *Guardian*, 10 March,
10 April 1973) but by far the greatest invocation of expertise rests
in the editorial statements. Here the mixture of reportage and
comment found in the main body of the paper is exchanged for
pure comment. Editorials are as complex as any part of the newspaper world. They do not have to accord with the views of their
own reporters, as was shown when Simon Winchester's report on
the Widgery Tribunal was clearly different from the editorial in the
same edition. Frequently their comments are minimal. At other
times they are larded with the claim to knowledge that I am interested
in here. The editorial's conceptions of the IRA, formal politics and
the ghettos will be briefly looked at.

First, the editorials use recent history, cutting off at apposite points, to create a view of the violence as being both initiated and sustained by the IRA. Protestant violence is seen as a reaction. Apart from the concept of institutionalized Protestant State violence, such a view would not satisfy any Catholic ghetto dweller who experienced the 1969 riots and many of the early bomb attacks in 1970.[9] Consider the following claims (emphases added):

Internment and detention remain politically damaging. Special courts from the standpoint of civil liberties may have little more to commend them but they will probably become inevitable as internment is phased out – *unless violence by a miracle of IRA sanity dies away*. (*Guardian* 28 September 1972)

The reason that N. Ireland has moved from the comparative calm of the Civil Rights campaign in 1968 and 1969 to the bloody struggle with the IRA, *now increasingly bringing in Protestant extremists also*, is that everyone in the province now believes the fight is about Irish Unity. (*Guardian*, 11 October 1972)

Supporters of the Union in Northern Ireland are demoralised by the IRA violence of the last *three or four years*. (*Guardian*, 19 October 1972)

The historical argument is a fruitless one, because every interpretation is open to challenge. What is not open to challenge, yet is too often forgotten, is the consequence of *the IRA campaign in N. Ireland.* . . . Apologists for the IRA will say that they cannot be held responsible for the Protestants, sectarian murders. That view can be accepted only by those who believe that a man is entitled to act without any regard to the probable consequences of his action. (*Guardian*, 1 February 1972)

Only since Operation Motorman in July has the stranglehold of the IRA on the Catholic community begun to slacken. *By that time, of course*, the Protestant extremists were exasperated and the counter-terrorism had been growing in ferocity and spreading to the Republic. (*Guardian*, 3 January 1973)

As with journalism, so the editorials accord a lot of significance to formal politics. As I have said, this can be viewed as an artifact of the ignorance which violent, unofficial politics creates. This leads, understandably, to an exaggerated optimism over the numerous political initiatives (*Guardian*, 11 October 1972):

A clear cut referendum vote for the union with Britain, which is the probable result, would calm the Protestants, steady British opinion, discourage the IRA and force all Northern Ireland parties to look for an internal political settlement probably based on Protestant-Catholic coalition.

The vote accomplished none of these things. The summer 1972 truce was a missed political opportunity (*Guardian*, 26 October 1972):

The SDLP missed that chance, and the IRA willed the truce should not continue and that Irish unity – not later but sooner – should be won with guns and bullets. The SDLP's absence from Darlington [political talks] aggravated the offence. Increased death and destruction stopped the release of internees and began to bring the Protestants on to the streets.

Later the same SDLP is congratulated for attending talks on the White Paper: 'It suggests that – at last – Catholic politicians in the North may be beginning to feel able to take the initiative over from the gunmen' (*Guardian*, 27 November 1972). Even in an editorial (20 February 1973) where it is agreed that violence overshadows non-violent politicians ('while terrorists – on both sides now – hold the population in fear, the role of the non-violent politicians is inevitably made less important'), there is a reversion to optimism ('It will ... have to be clear to the elected politicians that power will come to them gradually as they agree to share it'). But the contradiction is not worked through, except ironically: 'In this atmosphere rumours and eccentricity inevitably thrive'.

Comparable over-simplification and confusion is exhibited in 'knowing' comments on the ghettos, particularly the supposed relationship between the communities, the paramilitary forces and the British Army. For example, after saying that all allegations against the army cannot be dismissed, the editorial writer moves on (*Guardian*, 27 November 1972):

But the Catholic population in Belfast must show good sense just at a time when their lives may be freed from the hell of guerrilla warfare in which they have lived for three years and when their political future seems to be brighter than ever before they would be foolish to be led by the nose into another hostile anti-army campaign.

Following an outbreak of Protestant violence (*Guardian*, 1 February 1973): 'The Newtonards Rd ghetto is a small geographical area. It is easy to blanket it with force and coerce the criminal elements into inactivity.' Or again, in the *Guardian* of 8 February 1973:

The paradox of the situation to outsiders is illuminated by a remark made by the Catholic priest's housekeeper as she recovered from the attack [of a Protestant incursion]: 'The army saved our lives: I am sure we would have been killed.' But there is no real paradox – that woman no more believes the clap-trap which is talked about the Army than do thousands of other Catholics whose only allegiance to the IRA is the allegiance of fear and intimidation.

What these confident assertions exhibit are mere snippets from a complex community debate over shifting allegiances to official and non-official agents of law and order. As such they are conspicuous by their incompleteness.

Articles and editorials are the product of a multitude of contingencies. They are codes which embody a multiplicity of social practices which are not immediately apparent in the words denoted. Preferences, omissions, political machinations and pragmatic constraints are written into the script but they cannot be clearly seen.[10]

Newspaper work is not monolithic either; journalists and sub-editors, at the very least, vary in quality. Accordingly there is frozen in the selections cited above a whole social world. From these materials I have been interested in teasing out just one aspect: the strategies and rules used to mask ignorance in a situation where the access to knowledge is difficult or closed. Taking the line of least resistance, playing the numbers game, using Thomas's dictum, establishing credible respondents and performing the role of the expert are some of the more obvious techniques which attempt to turn ignorance into an air of knowingness. This is not to deny the significance of the occasional scoops when reporters gain access to pockets of information which create exposures and criticism.[11] But it is to point to a predicament of the journalist's relationship with his source material. Because this relationship is for the most part one of dependency, and the material he receives is secondary, the journalist is ill-equipped to analyse the dynamics of how the events he reports were constructed in the context within which they occur. Even before he starts to construct the event he is receiving accounts of it which have already been interpreted. It is this initial process of interpretation and construction which he is unable to evaluate. This is not because of any collective mental disability that journalists share; the structure of their profession makes them outsiders who travel to and report on inside worlds. It could not be any other way. It is this aspect of the outsider receiving accounts of events already filtered by insiders that is at issue here. It might be added this does not absolve the reporter from the type of filtering which *he* practises.

The limits of access to knowledge at this first level by no means incapacitate the creative additions of the journalist as he works with his material. On the contrary, while this predicament necessitates some kind of strategy for the journalist, it does not determine the quality of the journalistic account.

Areas of press limitations: context, construction and connection

What order of knowledge is it that is denied the journalist? I shall argue, in this section on the press, that the reporter has little or no access to the history and context of an event, to the construction of that event and to the consequent connotations attached to the event. These processes take place within the community. This is particularly true of the English press in Northern Ireland, but it is also evident in both Catholic and Protestant newspapers. All three stand on the peripheries of the social worlds which they report, and in varying degrees, each make leaps in the dark. Consequently it is important to emphasize that I am not specifically engaged in a critique of newspaper reportage. News reports have been selected out as one example of decontextualized accounts. News reports are necessarily incomplete and partial. I am interested in analysing these limitations not because they provide a basis from which to evaluate journalism but because they are indications of the theoretical difficulties involved in using decontextualized knowledge in explanation. The inevitably partial nature of press accounting means that, like all decontextualized accounts, they pose serious problems if they are used as the basis of explanatory texts.

A rather lengthy but apt illustration of these difficulties is afforded by a major gun-battle and riot that occurred in Anro. The Friday and Saturday of the weekend in question had seen some violent skirmishes on the fringes of Anro with both soldiers and Protestants. The boys I talked to centered their conversation around the incidents of a petrol bomb being thrown (no longer a frequent occurrence), a man being grazed by a paratrooper's bullet and a Protestant gunman managing to penetrate into one of Anro's streets. In contrast to the daily Catholic/army riots it was the first Catholic/Protestant confrontation for some time. The youngsters considered it something special. On Sunday afternoon a riot started again. It was nothing eventful: a standard army/Catholic stone, bottle and rubber-bullet affair.

A Sinn Féin representative was on the streets broadcasting through a megaphone that an open-air meeting scheduled for that afternoon was starting and she urged attendance. At the meeting people drifted to and fro making the attendance difficult to estimate. Women and children were, by far, the more numerous. Some of the rioters broke away and joined the meeting. The riot fizzled out. A couple of the rioters I knew related the conversation they had just had with Mrs Toal, the Sinn Féin woman: ' "How can we have a meeting if you're rioting", she says; so here's me, "How can we riot if you're meeting".' Mrs Toal spoke first and attempted to generate concern for the interned and sentenced of the district now in Armagh, the Kesh or Crumlin Road jail. She condemned the new detention and tribunals as internment under other names. The next speaker was from the South. He insisted that the Provisional movement was building not just a united Ireland, but a new Ireland, a socialist Ireland. He admired the spirits he had seen in the rioters but he maintained that the British Army could not be defeated with stones. The last speaker, the press officer for Sinn Féin, demanded to know why all the right-wing Catholics were not at this meeting now the church had openly condemned British Army brutality. The message now was that the struggle would be brought into Europe: friends in the EEC countries were carrying the revolution abroad.

Just before the call to internationalism, the young lads broke away and ran up the street to restart their riot. The meeting had little to do with causing the riot. Far from being incited, the boys looked distinctly uninterested. The riot had merely been temporarily postponed; how could one 'meet' and riot at the same time? As the meeting disbanded a lorry packed with someone's worldly goods drove by. Micky, a member of the Relief Committee, told me that the family whose possessions the lorry contained had been intimidated from Newton Street, a lower-middle-class area outside Anro which was still inhabited by a few Catholics. He said that the UDA had given those Catholics until that night to leave. At the riot over 100 youths were stoning and vilifying a riot squad. CESA were trying to stop the riot. Bill, a CESA cadet, told me that he had had enough. CESA had ordered him to instruct CESA cadets to stop rioting, but the Fianna had warned Bill not to intervene.

There was a cry of 'the Orangees' and a large part of the riot moved over towards another Catholic/Protestant boundary. It was based on a false alarm and eventually they returned. Another cry of 'the Orangees' encouraged the whole riot, plus several adult activists, to shift north to an area which was a few streets from Newton Street and opposite solid Protestant territory.

By the time that I had reached the new riot area some shooting had started and I retreated home. Soon the firing became very heavy: some hundreds of rounds must have been released. Gradually our house filled up with several of the young boys who had been rioting and were now sheltering from the gun-fire. The boys were talking constantly about the riot. Its logic emerged both for me and for them. *The* riot did not then exist. There had been many events: rioters had

143

been hit with missiles, other rioters had hit soldiers with missiles, doors had been kicked in to secure an escape and so on, but there was no immediate précis available. Initially the riot appeared as the sum of all the individual rioters' experience. In one sense they had all had their own riot. As the discussion developed, the boys became engaged in conducting a collective synthesis of their experiences. What had happened out there in the streets became organized by the discussion in the house. The running, shouting, throwing, laughter, excitement, fear, hits, near-misses were all talked about. A rough consensus emerged: The Protestant rioters had been engaged, but sniper fire from the Protestants had forced the rioters to retreat into safe houses. For this group of participants the genesis and development of the riot had evolved. For them, the riot had become a reportable phenomenon.

Nearly five hours later the shooting was still very heavy; the riot had given way to a protracted gun-battle. The young rioters who were still trapped in our house became frightened at the scale of the violence. The shooting had now spread all over the district and it appeared that all available weapons were in use. By ten o'clock there was a lull and the boys hurried home. At midnight, two hours after the last shots had been fired, bin lids and whistles started sounding. In turn, the crashing of broken bottles and the booming of rubber-bullet guns indicated that the army was raiding in our street.

At one stage screams and shouts were clearly audible through the back of our house. Immediately after they were followed by a rush of people who were seeking refuge from a 'snatch squad' which was raiding neighbouring houses. The riot continued for an hour. The physical battle was only one element of the confrontation. The rioters shouted that the soldiers' wives were 'in bed with their boyfriends', black soldiers were taunted with racialist slogans; the soldiers matched the abuse. A little further down the road several women demanded to know why the Protestant districts were not being raided because it appeared obvious that a great amount of gun-fire had been directed into Anro. A British Army officer dismissed the argument as nonsense: 'Bollocks, this is where all the shooting came from, madam.'

During the next two days the army put on a massive show of force by constantly patrolling the area in their variety of armoured vehicles (Saracens, Whippets and PIGS). In addition several 'snatch squads' were on the streets. Walking around the devastated streets made me feel limp with fear. On every street corner there were British Army rifles pointed at the pedestrians. The rioting was largely contained by this military saturation of the district. However, on the next day, for the first time in Anro, the IRA fired Russian-made mortar rockets (RPG 7) at the army. One was fired at an observation post; another hit a patrolling Saracen. The effect of these attacks was that the British Army withdrew its constant surveillance and Anro returned to its normal level of confrontation.

The causes, progress and results of this battle dominated the conversation of Anro's residents. The event was compared to the 1969 riots and to other major confrontations. Fears were aroused that if the Protestants were engaging in gun-battles and if the army continued to raid only in Anro, the district would be exposed to a Protestant onslaught. Other residents voiced a scepticism about the number of British Army 'hits' claimed in the newspapers.

Without imposing a neat description on a ragged series of events, some features of the occurrences can be drawn. Normal army/ Catholic rioting had been superseded by the more fundamental Protestant/Catholic confrontation. A three-way army/Catholic/ Protestant gun-battle had resulted and a massive show of force had followed, with the British Army saturating Anro. The participants and non-participants shared experiences which formalized an uneasy sense of what had happened. I am not positing that these experiences were distilled to produce a definition of the confrontation that was monolithic. Anro, as I have argued earlier, is socially heterogeneous enough to sustain multiple interpretations of events. In this particular example, it was my impression that the community did share a broadly 'Republican' view of the weekend. However, what I intend to demonstrate is that news accounts tend to do one of two things. They either fail to penetrate any of the multiple interpretations within the community and thus impose a completely extraneous account, or, alternatively, they tap and embellish one of the interpretations within the community but necessarily neglect the complexity of the internal debate over the significance of events.[12]

Other things happened in Ireland that weekend: principally, Sean Mac Stiofáin, then the IRA Chief of Staff, went on hunger strike. Nevertheless, the *Guardian* gave Anro's battle a minor front page headline underneath the Mac Stiofáin affair: 'Belfast Troops Say Nine Terrorists Wounded'. The text, reprinted in full, reads:

A three sided gun-battle involving Roman Catholics, Protestants and troops broke out last night in the Anro area of Belfast. Several hundred shots were reported to have been fired, and the army claimed to have hit nine gunmen. The battle was still going on last night after the first shot had been fired. The army reported regular outbreaks of shooting at military positions throughout Anro and adjoining areas. The IRA appeared to be doing most of the sniping. In one incident, at an army observation post, three gunmen opened fire from three different positions. The soldiers in the post fired back and later claimed to have hit all three gunmen. The army in this area, the Fifth Battalion of the Light Infantry, said all types of weapons were used – automatic as well as high and low velocity guns. The trouble started after a small peaceful demonstration by Catholics against the MacStiofáin sentence was stoned by Protestants. Shooting began soon after the army had separated rival crowds. Protestants were reportedly firing into the Anro area from the direction of Russell Street which borders the Catholic district. The IRA fired back and also fired at the Benton Road army observation post.

The following day the same reporter added:

There were stoning incidents involving Catholic and Protestant children at the William St end of the Blackstaff Rd near the Anro area. The incidents followed searches of houses in Anro, scene of a battle involving troops and Catholic and Protestant gunmen on Sunday evening.

And on the last day of the affair: 'In Belfast a single rocket was fired at Plunkett school in Anro which houses an army post. The missile penetrated a wall but did not explode.' Limitations of access and news value are combined here to produce an account telling the reader more about newspapers than about the three-day battle in Anro. The dependence on army sources is apparent. The plausibility of the 'Mac Stiofáin' protest meeting leading to the riot is posited. However, Mac Stiofáin was not even mentioned at the meeting and Protestants certainly did not stone the gathering. There is no mention of the saturation of the area by troops and no inkling of the significance of the rocket attack which precipitated the army retreat. The account is noticeable for its lack of contact with the issues of contention in the area – the debate over the fear of being exposed to Protestant onslaughts due to one-sided raiding, the numbers injured, the very genesis of the riot. In addition to patchy description there is nothing to weigh the event against, as it was being weighed within the community against the 1969 riots, internment and other serious confrontations.

The Belfast papers gave, as might be expected, much greater coverage. Their accounts were more detailed. The *Newsletter*, leaning on its sources within the Protestant area and on army statements, produced a different version to the *Guardian*. Its headline was '11 Shot in Gun Battle'.

The army claimed to have hit eleven terrorists during a raging gun-battle in the Anro area of Belfast yesterday. The shooting followed rioting in which at least four Protestant families were forced to flee their homes as a MacStiofáin protest march turned into a riot. The shooting began in the afternoon and lasted for more than six hours. The heavy outbreak of firing was regarded in some quarters as a token of support for Sean MacStiofáin on hunger strike in a Dublin hospital, by Provisional IRA gunmen in the Anro enclave. The protest meeting finished about four p.m. and the mob marched down Tate Street in a belligerent mood armed with sticks, bottles and stones. Residents in the mainly Protestant area became alarmed and frantic calls for help went out to defend their homes. The marchers vented their rage principally on the dining halls of Elmwood school, smashing scores of windows and attacking several homes nearby. Army contingents arrived and got between the contending parties and the crowds thinned out. But it was only temporary. Gunmen from a number of positions let loose with a variety of weapons including automatics and by eight o'clock had fired two hundred shots at the army. The main attacks were on the two observation posts at MacDonagh Street and Mill Street. The army claimed nine hits and they had suffered no casualties. The prolonged exchange of fire and the intimidation by the rampaging mob had terrified some people. A number of families were evacuated and took up refuge in Rosemary Street Primary School, taken over by the area's tenants defence association. An army statement at 8 p.m. said: 'Around 2.30 p.m. there was a peaceful meeting of approximately 150–200 strong in MacDonagh Street. Later there was some stoning and general 'aggro' of the troops. After stoning had been going on quite a while shooting broke out in the Mill St area. There seemed to be little connection between the demonstration, the aggro and the shooting. The shooting became intense in the Mill St area and it seemed mainly to be directed at the observation post at the Tate Street junction and the 'square' – the Sicily Road area. About 200 shots were fired at the army. Fire was returned and three gunmen were hit. It is understood that some Protestant families have left their homes. Shooting is still going on but only very spasmodically. Latest: Army reported about 700 shots fired at them during Anro gun-battle. It was definitely three-sided battle between Protestants, Roman Catholics and soldiers.'

The following day the paper asserted that the army did search two Protestant streets. The reliance upon Protestant sources is interesting because it injected a new element into the riot – the intimidation of Protestant families and the damage done to Protestant property. In Anro only the opposite, the removing of families from Newton

Street, was mentioned. The report until the last 'latest news' obscures the fact that it was a three-way battle. The army statement on the relative independence of the meeting, riot and gun-battle was contradicted in the main text. There is no evidence, either, of the level of army activity in Anro.

The Catholic 'viewspaper',[13] the *Irish News* got closer to some of the opinion voiced in Anro concerning the event. It stressed the three-sided nature of the flare-up, the intensive searches and the seriousness of the army saturation:

> Eleven hits were claimed by the British Army and more than 1,000 shots were fired yesterday during the fiercest gun battle – involving both Protestants and Catholics – in the Anro area of Belfast since the start of the disturbances in 1969.
>
> And early today, when troops started an intensive search of the district as the heavy shooting died down, rioting broke out in protest at what residents described as 'one-sided action by the British Army against the Catholic population'.
>
> In Thomas Street where families reported that soldiers had smashed windows and were 'on the rampage', one woman said: 'The shooting started from the Protestant side but there has been no sign of any raiding there. When the battle was at its height, the gunfire into the Catholic streets was heavier and more concentrated than the shooting from here'.
>
> An Army officer at the scene said: 'It looks as if everyone with a gun hereabouts has come out to shoot'.
>
> More than 700 rounds were fired by gunmen from both Protestant and Catholic districts. No accurate count of Army fire in return was immediately available, but local residents estimated it at 'about 500 rounds'.
>
> Bricks, bottles, and stones were being hurled at the Army in Anro this morning and blast bombs were heard in the district. Several parked cars were reported to have been wrecked when Army vehicles collided with them.

General upheaval

> Men, women and children swarmed into the streets when the Army search operation got under way. Long after the gun battle subsided Anro was in what one resident described as 'a state of general upheaval'.
>
> The start of the gun battle was easily pinpointed – and the first gunfire came from the direction of Protestant streets. Fire was returned from the Catholic section and the British Army was between, caught in cross-fire, but a spokesman

said later that they had suffered no casualties.

There was what an Army officer described as 'a peaceful demo' in Kenton St in the afternoon in protest against the jailing of Mr Sean MacStiofáin and in support of the 25 IRA hunger-strikers in Crumlin Road Jail. Afterwards missiles were thrown at soldiers but an Army spokesman said it was then 'not really serious and no worse than what we have become accustomed to after similar demonstrations'.

But as stones were being thrown at the Army in Kenton St shots were fired from MacDonagh St on the fringe of the Protestant sector, and the Tate St army observation post came under attack by gunmen. People who had attended the Kenton Street demonstration and were on their way home were adamant that the post came under fire from the Protestant area.

Then the shooting pattern became clouded as automatic weapons and small arms were used in a fusilade of gunfire so that it became impossible to say with certainty from what directions it came. An Army officer said troops were fired on from several directions.

Gunmen shot, claim

As the gun battle reached its peak it ranged throughout the whole area from the bus depot at Old Anro through the interlacing streets until it passed the district boundaries, with one incident reported as far away as Pickford St. When the Army observation post came under fire, fire was returned and the Army claimed to have shot a gunman.

During the concentrated gunfire an Army spokesman said it wasn't clear who was shooting at whom, whether troops were under fire from both sides or whether they were caught in the middle of a sectarian flare-up.

Army marksmen went into action as heavy gunfire continued into the night. And army claims of 'hits' mounted during the night. In the wake of the battle, with Anro saturated with soldiers and a massive search under way, it became clear that all the casualties claimed by the military were on the Catholic side.

All Catholics?

Word of this spread through the district, as people ventured out, and feeling in the area was heightened when the search started. There were no reports of any casualties among the protesters in the streets but a woman in Thomas St said early today: 'It is like hell here. The Army have gone mad. They are breaking and wrecking all round them.

'And the people here, under the Army thumb and being abused physically and verbally, are incensed that in the Protestant streets from which heavy gunfire was directed into Catholic streets, they can sit back and laugh now, oil their guns and put them away until another night – maybe to-night – knowing that they are perfectly safe and have nothing to fear from the British Army'.

Falls-style '71 Curfew

At 2 a.m. Anro was still reeling under the battering the district took during the gun battle and in the aftermath when the military search started. 'No one in the whole of Anro is asleep' a young woman in Thomas St said. 'It looks as if this is the start of a Falls-style 1971 curfew. There are as many soldiers to be seen as civilians'.

No arms finds had been reported in the district some time after the troops started moving through the streets. Two men and a woman were reported this morning to have been beaten up by soldiers 'after being dragged from their homes'.

The 'Catholic' newspaper account approximated more closely to views within the community than did the other press renderings. This was because the reporter had access to Catholic respondents whom he was willing to quote. The whole process of selection was geared towards sympathetic treatment. This does not, however, necessarily lead to an appreciation of how the event became viewed as it was. For example, the sense of confusion over the riot and battle which characterized the construction of the event was lost: 'The start of the gun-battle was easily pinpointed – and the first gun-fire came from the direction of Protestant streets.' A whole series of conversations and disagreements are subsumed in that statement. There were those anti-Republicans in Anro who expressed the opinion that the Provos had started the sniping. Conversely, some rioters I talked to thought it was the British Army who had fired the opening shots. As seen, the boys in our house came to agree that, indeed, it was the Protestant paramilitaries who turned the riot into a gun-battle. While the journalist has managed to tune into aspects of this debate he presents it as closed and unproblematic. What has happened is that the journalist has consulted one or two interpretations and has treated them as indicators of a monolithic view. In doing so he 'failed' to appreciate the social distribution of opinion in areas like Anro or the process by which a dominant view emerges.

150

Although the degree of externality varies, the version of events one reads in newspapers is characterized by some distancing from the inner world of a social process. It could not be any other way. At the least news reportage will result in an account which underplays the context, construction and connotations of events in the communities in which they occur.

The allusion to an absence of context means not only the overtly ahistorical nature of reporting. Happenings are recorded precisely because they are new. This concentration on the documentation of the present leaves little space for assessing the importance of the familiar, the old and the commonplace which happen all the time. Time and events take on a discrete quality. 'Context' also implies the cultural frame of reference that may be provided by history. In Anro, for example, oppression is a cumulative phenomenon. The routine nature of screening, raiding or gun-fire may become mundane but it creates a focus for looking at the big, exceptional eruptions of violence. It is a focus which is not shared by those who have not experienced everyday oppression. 'Context' in Anro accordingly refers to a different sense of the commonplace and, therefore, to a different frame of reference for interpreting newsworthy events. Such events as violent deaths and major confrontations will be reported in the daily press. What the papers cannot easily print or portray is the minutiae of the ordinary which give meaning to the events. Without this, the news reporter and his reader will impose a different conception on the event, resulting in a decontextualizing of the initial occurrence. The reporting of the behaviour of the Paratroop Regiment in Anro indicates what is meant here. The following bald initial report gave no idea of the significance of a 'show of strength': 'Paratroopers have now moved into the Anro area, one of the toughest IRA districts in Belfast. They put on a show of strength yesterday afternoon to warn residents of their intentions' (*Guardian*). A month later, after three men had been killed by the Paratroopers, an article in the *Guardian* raised doubts about the regiment's behaviour. It related details of a protest march against them, the shooting dead of one man the reporter felt was an innocent victim, the killing of two IRA men claimed to be unarmed, and of the petty rounds of brutality and intimidation which Anro's residents frequently claimed the troops engaged in. Yet even this mildly critical article failed to capture the sense of terror which these troops created. In particular it failed to specify the *additional* tactics employed by the Paratroopers which exceeded other regiments' activities. If the Paras were producing this response in a community already hardened by nearly three years of British Army confrontation then their activities *had* to be excessive. Judged against what had become the norm in Anro, that is, against its context, Paratroop policies were exceptional. The absence of this context makes it easier for the *Guardian* to revert to the strategies outlined earlier:

> The paratroop officers genuinely believe that they are the victims of a sustained propaganda campaign by the IRA which had gathered its own momentum. They say that because people are afraid of the Paras – and undoubtedly there is real fear in Anro – they expect the worst and tend to see the worst. A harassed soldier pushing people aside to get to an incident becomes a monster indiscriminately beating up women and children. Rumours spread rapidly around the area. Three highly potent ones doing the rounds are that the Paras have been told not to take prisoners, that they are going to kill every wanted man on sight, and that they are determined to beat up the area before they leave. None of these appears to hold any truth, but their power is in the extent to which they are believed. . . . As always the truth in Ulster remains clouded and what is believed is what counts.

Second, within the community's context a construction of events takes place of which the reporter is either ignorant or feels is of no relevance for his own purposes. The distribution of opinion and knowledge within the community assures different perspectives of the same event. Even amongst those who did 'see' the event, there is disagreement over the interpretation to be given to a death, a riot or a beating. Sometimes a dominant view will emerge after the topic has been subjected to discussion. This was evident after the 1969 riots, internment night, and the behaviour of the Paras. But while different allegiances exist within the community, events remain the subject of much dispute and debate. The press, relying on its various sources, tends to neglect this debate. The *Newsletter* refers merely to 'residents say'. The *Guardian*, as I have argued, has its own ground rules for 'getting over' the problem. The *Irish News* tends to take the articulated views of political and community leaders as fully representative of the debate. This was much apparent in the construction of reports which took place after an elderly woman's death in Anro. Though she lived just four doors down from our house and was shot as she turned into her own street, we had no way of knowing what 'exactly' happened. The little girls who were playing in the street at the time said they had seen the woman fall but did not know who had shot her. Frances's mother heard the shots and had remarked to her neighbour, 'Ah, it's those fellas again.' When she heard about the death she blamed it on the IRA. So too did our next door neighbours, members of the SDLP who loathed the Provisionals. Peter, who had just joined CESA, was equally adamant that it was the Provos' fault. The consensus of the anti-Provos people I spoke to at the time agreed that it was the Provos who had done it, unintentionally perhaps, but through neglect. The British Army, in fact, immediately admitted responsibility. A spokesman stated that he deeply regretted the incident but if there had been no terrorists around it would not have happened. The anti-Provo sections concurred; the army had shot her (twice), but it was the Provos who were culpable because they were attempting to operate while innocent people were in the streets. Others, however, who were equally reliant on circumstantial evidence, came to different conclusions. They argued that when the army shot Catholic males they were labelled as 'gunmen'. However, when the victim was a child or woman, the death was called a 'tragic mistake'. They saw this death as another illustration of the army's contempt for the lives of citizens in Anro. An enquiry by the local Sinn Féin took statements from witnesses who agreed that six shots had been fired, probably from more than one British Army foot-patrol. Some witnesses added that a Corporation workman had been in the area at the time and the army might have mistaken him for a gunman because he had been carrying a large broom. Sinn Féin concluded that the soldiers who fired the shots should be immediately relieved of their duties and should stand trial in the ordinary criminal courts, or preferably in the Special Tribunals, set up under the Detention of Terrorists (Northern Ireland) Order, 1972, where it would be easier to get a conviction. The Anro Relief Committee also made enquiries and sent a letter of complaint to the commanding officer of the regiment. Even so, the Provos were out of favour at that particular time and the anti-Provisional viewpoints persisted: the 'fellas' were about to attack a foot-patrol but were fired upon first and an innocent woman died.

The press gave its usual army statement and then the residents' statement. The *Irish News*, however, gave the residents' statements first. The *Guardian* stated: 'Residents claimed that the soldiers opened fire on a group of men without provocation.' The *Newsletter*, characteristically, placed a report about the woman's death in an inconspicuous position on an inside page.[14] It finished its statement: 'A spokesman for the Anro Relief Committee said earlier that he had been told by people in the area that a couple of men had been standing on a corner – not doing anything.' The *Irish News* gave the views of those in Anro who condemned the army's activity, including the army's claim that women in Anro had expressed their sympathy to the soldiers. The Sinn Féin spokesman (Provisional) and the Republican Clubs (Official) were quoted. There was nothing in the accounts to suggest that there had been disagreement about the event within the community. As usual, the residents who were cited were made to appear homogeneous.

News accounts generally gave no indication of the amount of debate and disagreement which contribute to the production of a perspective on an event. Neither do they acknowledge the multiple perspectives that exist within the community.

Finally, news evades the connotations which events have for the community. The process of constructing the reality of an event from a particular frame of reference is also a process of creating meaning. Clearly the significance that is attached to incidents in the troubles is consequential for the continuation or cessation of the war. Newspaper accounts are affected by the social distance that removes them from the community. They have difficulty in portraying the relevance of events that they report. This facet was particularly striking, for me, in the lack of 'feel' captured by the accounts. As I remarked earlier, I experienced a form of culture-shock living in Anro. Living under army rule, in conditions of frequent outbreaks of violence, and generally sharing the experiences of trouble, produced a profound reaction in me. There was a strong feeling that I had little control over how long I lived. There were feelings of loss and misery. There was anger which I could see and share. At other times a feeling of despair was pervasive. It is this affective barrier that the press rarely transcend. That is not surprising as this 'feel' has a transient quality for outsiders. But it is this order of connotative meaning that is important for commitment. It is the profundity of experience that crystallizes opinions and makes radical action possible.

The rage that followed the death of the first man in Anro to be shot by the Paratroop Regiment was only palely reflected in the news reports. The *Guardian*'s account was sympathetic and expressed serious doubts about the army's allegation that the man was a gunman (it gave three good reasons why it was highly unlikely). However, the report gave little indication of the fury that people felt in Anro. It did report that:

> Residents, who held a protest meeting yesterday afternoon,
> believe that the paratroopers who began operations in the area
> at the weekend, are deliberately trying to terrorize them into
> docility. The working-class areas are more afraid of paratroopers
> than any other unit in the army.

Accurate, as far as it goes, this fails to capture the anger and distress of that meeting. Neither can the report relate the conversations of those who knew 'the gunman' or tell of the looks of those who streamed in and out of his house to pay their last respects. Similarly the reality of 'terrorizing them into docility' is left to the imagination of the reader. But there was no one in Anro that I talked to that day who did not feel that they could not easily be the next victim. The

Newsletter demoted the incident to the inside page and to the usual format of 'the army said, residents claim'. The *Irish News* carried several articles over the next few days which argued his innocence. They also reported the attempts to set up an inquiry into his death as well as giving very gruesome details of the actual death. There was close unanimity in the district over this incident in condemning the troops' behaviour. The *Irish News* was, for once, correct in its presentation of a monolithic view.

The connotations attributed to events such as this man's death become community history and contribute to the context in which the next events will be constructed, and, in turn, assigned significance. Context, construction and connotation are the intertwined elements that constitute the process of the contextual determination of mean- ing ·in Anro. I have analysed these elements because they are the dynamics within the community which order the intrusions of the outside world into Anro. As such I consider them the active processes within the Catholic *Weltanschauung* which mediate the wider society. Accordingly they demand the attention of any analysis which seeks to examine the mediated reality of insider accounts. These processes are neglected or underplayed by the most widespread and conse- quential form of accounting of events in the North of Ireland, that of the press. This I have suggested is largely due to the external nature of reporting whose structure imposes limitations of access to knowledge, limitations which have ·definite material effects.[15]

The problem is not exclusive to the press. Rather the press have been analysed because the issues are amenable to study. The problem is in the nature of accounting. An equally valid approach would have been to look at 'authoritative' accounts. Examples of these include the many reports and tribunals that have been set up by the British Government to find out what 'really' happened in Belfast in 1969 or in Derry in January 1972.[16] To close the chapter I want to examine briefly some other political analyses of the troubles, where ultimately all works on Northern Ireland should end.

Limitations to knowledge (2): Aspects of political analyses of the troubles

Proposed solutions to the troubles are as numerous as parties to the problem. There are right-wing settlements which are suggested by Ultra-Loyalist Protestants that seek a return to the previous Protest- ant ascendancy found in the old Stormont. Other similar groups have called for a unilateral declaration of independence in which the Protestant and 'British' nature of the regime would be re-established. There are views from the political centre[17] which seek a reformed democratic Unionist Six Counties with power shared, in some form, by Catholics and Protestants. The SDLP see this as a possible transition to their long-term aspirations of uniting Ireland. The centre groups are backed by the majority of the English and Irish parliamentary political parties.

The diversity of their views is reflected in the variety of policies put forward concerning all the contentious issues in the Province such as policing, detention, schooling and the 'Irish dimension'. There is no shortage of possible solutions or ingenious ideas to implement them, like changes in the voting system, establishing a minimum number of Catholic parliamentary representatives, periodic referenda and so on. What Ireland requires, however, is not the as yet undiscovered solution, but the creation of a political climate in which a possible solution can gain credibility, be it independence, amalgamation, federation or unity with England or the Irish Republic. At present it appears that there can be no solution which is not forced upon some large part of the population. Perhaps, as I think likely, the troubles will end only after a major conventional civil war. There is a lot of history to be undone and a lot of bargaining on non-negotiable issues ('loyalty', 'nationality') to be achieved before any lasting settlement.[18]

As for many others, the attempt to provide an explanation of the intractable nature of the Irish situation has bedevilled radical theorists in England and Ireland. The search among progressive groups for a coherent analysis has produced much interesting material but has largely concentrated on one level of analysis, that of the political economy of the Northern Ireland State. This concentration is entirely justified given the primacy, within Marxist epistemology, of the structural determination of social consciousness.[19] However, the majority of analyses have been exclusively focused at this level. The result has been a proliferation of different interpretations. From the Left a reader can be offered explanations which see the Provisional IRA as either neo-fascists or as true revolutionaries who are to be given critical support. The Protestant working class can be viewed as ultra-conservative and regressive or alternatively, the proletariat of a separate Ulster people, correct in its struggle to remain British. The war can be seen as a genuine national liberation struggle or as a result of the activities of latter-day élitist Fenian dynamiters. The British Government can be seen as the actively repressive agents of imperialism. Other analyses see the British Government as a bourgeois state that has been frustrated in its efforts to democratize Ulster. From this perspective it is argued that Britain's capital and strategic interests will be preserved in a united, peaceful Ireland, or in a reformed Ulster, within the European Economic Community. In some analyses the conditions for socialism will emerge through national liberation, for others they are contingent upon the initial democratization of the North.

This diversity springs, of course, from the varying orthodoxies of the proponents. The analysis and tactics offered by radical commentators originate from the theoretical positions they have adopted on the issues of socialism, nationalism and materialism. I shall argue, though briefly, that such diversity is also *partially* a result of the inadequate theoretical recognition of the significance of the level of mediated reality. Marxist epistemology also recognizes that social consciousness is never an im-mediated artifact. The ideological representations that constitute subjective reality are not mechanistic expressions of the social structure. Consequently, analysis is required to determine exactly how material reality is manifested in the social consciousness of a class or social division. It is required because the social consciousness of subjects is one part of the dialectical interplay between mediated and material reality. It is through the social consciousness that the meaning of events – such as changes in policies and tactics – is contextually determined. Precisely because ideological and political social relations are conjuncturally determined, to restrict theoretical investigation to the level of the structural determinants of a world-view is to neglect the whole arena of mediated reality.

Several 'leftist' attempts to establish a general explanation of the Northern Ireland trouble have, by omitting one level of analysis, produced programmatic and problematic theorizing. The complexity of the problem has been sacrificed to maintain the plausibility of a theoretical position. In this sense, the Left analyses in question differ from press accounts because their theory of description is explicit not implicit, and historical not ahistorical, but they do share one characteristic; that is, both accounts neglect the theoretical autonomy of the contextual determination of meaning.

It is partly true, particularly in England, though not entirely fair, to see the Left as more concerned with the Irish problem as a justification of a view of theory than as a potentially revolutionary situation which demands explanation. Most analyses contain a reference to the 'lessons' to be learnt from Ireland. See O'Connor Lysaght (1973: 40):

> As a problem it is an acid test for anyone claiming to operate
> the Marxist method. . . . The problem about the Protestants of
> Northern Ireland is this: a colonial community bearing certain
> of the stigmata of a nation insists that it has the right to
> adhere to the metropolitan imperial power in defiance of the
> claims of the majority on the island where they both live.

Also Trench (1972: 23):

The problems facing Irish revolutionaries revolve to a large extent around the theoretical and practical attitude to the Protestant (Orange) section of the working class. The problem is to integrate national demands which presently divide the working class into a programme for a Workers Republic which can only be brought about – or maintained by united working class action . . . The argument brings into focus the revolutionary Marxist attitude to the national question.

And Palmer (1972: 15): 'Ireland is an outstanding example of the uneven development of capitalism in a country dominated by a foreign imperialism.'

Radical theorists have concentrated their analyses largely upon the Protestant working class, particularly in assessing the so-called 'two nations' theory. In turn, this has necessarily raised the closely connected debate over the relationship between nationalism and socialism, the 'two stages' theory. In addition, several authors have stressed other issues, such as the need for demonstrating the degree of autonomy that the superstructural institutions of Northern Ireland exhibit over the structurally determinant economic infrastructure, the need for a vanguard party and the need to demonstrate that Republicans have an inadequate theory of the State. Positions derived from such analyses determine the tactical prescriptions of support for the Republican, Loyalist or British factions. I shall concentrate on one area, that of the two nations theory.

Robert Dorn (1973), of the Revolutionary Marxist Group, has argued, for example, that a lesson that emerged from the Fourth International was that socialism could not be limited to the boundaries of states or ethnic groups but must be international. However, the uneven development of capitalism has caused variations in revolutionary struggle. One problem associated with this uneven development has been this: what actually constitutes a nation? National unity, he argues, is a prerequisite for socialism, but occasionally it is unclear which societies actually constitute nations. In such problematic cases, Stalin's (1913) authoritative definition of a nation can be invoked. A nation is 'a historically evolved stable community of language, territory, economic life and psychological make-up, manifested in a community of culture'. In terms of these definitive characteristics, Dorn argues that the Protestant community cannot be considered to be a separate nation. He argues from the grounds that the Protestant community has no separate home market but is economically dependent on the neo-colonial policies of the English market.[20] Consequently, Loyalism and Unionism are the politically regressive doctrines that emanate from the consciousness of a labour aristocracy and the consequent social division, not from a separate proletariat. Thus, support should be given to the national liberation struggle because it is primarily anti-imperialist. Moreover, not to support the nationalists would be to leave an objectively revolutionary situation in the hands of 'petty-bourgeois' Republicans. The task for Irish socialists is to replace the two IRAs with a vanguard party, complete with an armed wing, in an effort to mobilize the southern Irish workers.

In contradistinction the British and Irish Communist Organization (BICO) (1972, 1973) maintain that the Protestant people do constitute a separate nation and have a right to their own self-determination. Catholic Nationalism wrongly denies this right. What they consider to be a pseudo-national liberation campaign led by petty bourgeois Republicans has no hope of developing into a socialist struggle. Moreover, they argue that it is in Britain's economic and political interest to see the country united. Any revolutionary potential in the North of Ireland rests in the Protestant workers. They are the independent proletariat of a separate nation and state, which the uneven development of capitalism has produced. Partition, BICO argues, was economically inevitable and was also in the interests of the Ulster working class. Such a situation is equally true at present. This group is aware of the potential persuasiveness of this position (BICO, 1972: 3):

> The fact is that when the Northern situation erupted in July and August last year, the bourgeois left found that it had nothing even with a remote resemblance to reason to say about it. That was a sad state of affairs because the bourgeois left dearly love to comment knowingly on the world as it happens. . . . Then at the height of its desperation the left-wing scene discovered 'The Economics of Partition' and there was nothing for it but to read it, Stalinist though it might be, in order to be able to resume commentary.

Brian Trench (1972) agrees with BICO that by the Stalinist definition Ulster is a separate nation, but: 'Nothing could have less to do with the Marxist method. The analysis is static and arbitrary' (Trench: 1972: 23). What matters, he argues, is the role that historically the Protestant workers have played in the fight for socialism. Their record is exposed and found to be, again, regressive. However, support for the Nationalist movements is tempered: 'the central problem of the Irish revolution at the present time [is] the struggle for socialist leadership of the anti-Imperialist movement and the building of a revolutionary party' (Trench, 1972: 24). The two nation theorists, he argues, digress from such a strategy because they mistake the Unionists' Loyalism for nationalism. This mistake arises because BICO underestimates the relative autonomy that superstructural forms can situationally develop (Trench, 1972: 28):

> Northern Ireland demonstrates the possibilities of contradiction
> between base and superstructure, the different rate of change
> of economic and ideological structures. It is this 'relative
> autonomy' of ideology, and the non-completion of the national
> revolution, which means that simple class-versus-class first
> principle programmes offer less chance of intervention in the
> class struggle in Ireland than elsewhere. It is also this 'relative
> autonomy' of ideology which has misled certain people to
> deduce from the strength of loyalist consciousness, with
> certain traits of a national consciousness, the existence and the
> legitimate right of a Protestant nation.

Trench's analysis leads him to support the struggle in the North and
to support the secularizing, organizing and radicalizing of the
southern proletariat as the only way to create a socialist Ireland.

Anders Boserup (1972),[21] however, agrees totally with BICO
that the Protestants are a separate nation and with Trench that there
is considerable autonomy of the superstructure. For this author the
revolution in Ireland is the revolution to dismantle the Orange
discriminatory regime. Effectively, this involves the 'revolution' from
clientilist capitalism to twentieth-century managerial capitalism:
the welfare state society. Thus he states (Boserup, 1972: 27):

> This means that a revolutionary strategy does not at this
> juncture consist of producing the socialist revolution itself,
> but in producing its ideological pre-conditions. . . . Instead of
> fighting their little battles on the side in the hopeless endeavour
> to turn a Catholic Nationalist wave into a force for socialism,
> Irish socialists would . . . be better advised to engage directly
> in the main struggle . . . the destruction of the Orange system
> and its replacement by the 'welfare state' of managerial
> capitalism [which] is historically necessary and historically
> progressive.

This analysis demands for socialists a complete disassociation from
Republicanism and a working alignment with the forward-looking
sections of the Protestant proletariat (Boserup, 1972: 29):

> There is no surer way of perpetuating religious divisions than
> to impose Irish unity against the will of almost a quarter of its
> population, and a state so created would be socialist in name
> only, if at all. The unity of Ireland will come after the feudal
> and colonial remnants in the North have been swept away
> and after the South has given up its demands.

In this discussion concerning the two nations theory, conflicts have emerged over: the different theoretical significance attached to the uneven development of capitalism, Stalin's definition of a nation, the relative autonomy of the superstructure and the Marxist method. Such differences are crucial in determining support from socialists for Protestant or Catholic movements. Either position in this debate is unsatisfactory. Supporting the Republican movement effectively excludes the Protestants from Ireland unless their political aspirations and consciousness changes. On this point there is a remarked absence of debate. I have not read a pro-Republican position which analyses the problem of Protestant resistance: how can a million people be forced to do anything? How would Protestant guerrillas be contained after an enforced unity? How would a slaughter of the Catholics in the further northeast counties be prevented during the revolution? In an informative pamphlet Bob Purdie[22] (1972) at least works through the logic of critical support for the Nationalists (Purdie, 1972: 37, 68):

> No revolutionary movement can cut itself off from this tradition
> [Republicanism] and no new revolutionary movement can be
> built in abstraction from it. . . . To fight the Irish revolution
> in the face of the hostility of those workers (i.e. the Protestants)
> would be terrible and costly but it may be necessary; and it
> could be weighed against the implication of allowing the Six
> County State to go on for another fifty years.

Similarly those who argue that the Protestants have a valid national claim deny it of the Catholics. This logic leads to supporting the defeat of the IRA and often by the British Army's methods. It also entails the optimistic presupposition that a Six-County government is capable of producing a non-sectarian or even socialist state.

This type of difficulty, where a viewpoint unwarrantedly leaves massive problems aside, is found again and again in 'left-wing' analyses.[23] When a leftist pamphleteer analyses a political situation he is also engaged in political practice. Consequently the political positions contained in such accounts are also to be read as exhortations of support not as mere analysis. However, allowing for this, the reader in search of a persuasive explanation will be presented with a good deal of complexity that appears to be unhappily suppressed into an inadequately theorized framework. One result is a seeming reluctance to analyse the glaring omissions and oversimplifications that subsequently arise. For all its faults – of party political point scoring, self-imposed censorship, arrogant omniscience and unabashed swapping of personal feeling for analysis – Conor Cruise O'Brien's *States of Ireland* (1974) at least has the merit of facing the great problems.[24] He draws scenarios, for example of the

161

possible outcome of British withdrawal; he probes the Protestant's consciousness and he questions the *likely* political character of both a redrawn North and South following a major civil war.

Apart from the omissions, the lemon-squeezing also results in the formation of questionable policies and tactics. What, for example, is the likelihood of building a socialist vanguard party which several of the groups call for in Ireland, North or South? My own work would suggest a great pessimism regarding such a party's appeal amongst the Northern Irish Catholics. I have argued that the Catholic social consciousness is permeated by the much stronger ideological patterns of 'sectarianism' and 'Republicanism'. On this ground alone, for example, the often sophisticated and frequently knowledgeable analyses of Eamonn McCann, who persistently calls for the building of a vanguard Marxist party, would seem to be working against very deeply rooted opposing forces. This, together with the violent disagreement between the various Republican-Socialist groups, accounts for the limited appeal of the Irish Republican Socialist Party, the so-called 'super-sticks'. Political struggle, of course, need not concern a dedicated politician; working totally against history should. At the very least a reappraisal of tactics should follow a realization that the politics of one's group is, literally, out of time.[25]

Conclusion

The central concern of this chapter has been to examine some of the difficulties that are involved in the construction of a general explanation of the Irish troubles. General explanations are necessarily external accounts. They must transcend the relativity of perspectives. As such they should seek to subsume all inside the partial perspectives into their explanatory framework. Press accounts which are external and aspire to generality, I have argued, are characterized by serious limitations. Primarily they demonstrate a limitation of access to knowledge which results in theoretically inadequate accounts of insider perspectives, such as those held in Anro. Certain left-wing analyses have a serious commitment to generality but appear to be hampered by over-formalist and non-conjunctural readings. In particular even those who recognize the materiality of ideological formations tend to excise the consequences of this recognition from tactical and policy recommendations. Consequently both sets of accounts can result in confusion, omission and programmatic statements.

I am not suggesting that there is a general explanation to be discovered. There will be as many general explanations as there are theoretical positions.[26] What I am arguing is that there are preconditions for any one general account. An inclusive explanation must, at the least, contain structural analyses of the various groups which are party to the troubles: English, Irish, Catholic/Protestant Northern Irish. It must also contain a level of analysis that demonstrates how the material reality of the Northern Irish society is evidenced within the social consciousness of that society. Any general explanation must be able to locate the level of mediated reality into its framework because it is that social consciousness which is the active process in the contextual determination of ideological and political struggle. I have examined certain press and leftist accounts of the troubles in an attempt to illustrate the problems that arise in the absence of such a theory of mediation. In this work, I have argued that the politicized violence of Republicanism can be explained precisely in terms of the articulation of the dominant elements of the Catholic social consciousness into a political practice. Such an argument has been developed from documenting and analysing the Catholic world-view and its relationship to IRA ideology. This does not constitute a general explanation but I believe it does contribute to the understanding of an extraordinarily complex political situation, as well as illustrating the considerable epistemological and theoretical problems involved in the explanation of any social phenomena.

Appendix 1 Theory and methodology in participant observation

Methodological appendices in participant observation are strange phenomena. Their arguments should be locked into the body of the text. Instead they are used as supplements, though often readers are exhorted in the preface to read them first of all. Ideally they should not be necessary. It is a sociological cliché that the theory and method a researcher uses influences the particular transposition of social reality that is produced in the research monograph. If more than lip-service were paid to this fundamental proposition the sociologist would have his theoretical problems and methodological predilections explicitly intertwined with his substantive text. The 'why' and 'how' of a thesis would be openly enmeshed in the production of the 'what'. Committed as an author might be to this position of theoretical and methodological immanence, there are numerous problems involved in moving beyond the level of good intentions to achieve such a formulation. In this appendix I want to resurrect some of the immanence in my own work. I shall attempt to address the relationship between theory, method and substantive claims in participant observation, and to pose how that inter-relationship was ordered in this book.

This research was orientated to a theoretical interest in the nature of politicized violence. The particular focus concerned both the explication and explanation of an ideology that sanctioned militant political activity. In the empirical example chosen, the social consciousness of Catholicism in Northern Ireland was investigated in terms of its relevance in creating and sustaining such an ideology. The theoretical concern at this level of analysis led to the adoption of participant observation as an empirical method to supplement theoretical and historical inquiry. As in anthropological studies there was a *prima facie* argument for the method employed. It is just not feasible to survey or formally interview those who are secretive, hostile, wary or underground. The object of the study was to investigate the relevance of the Catholic world-view to political violence. As such it involved an interest in a community containing a number of people actively engaged in political violence. These people are not known for their high response rate to questionnaires.

However, the justification for qualitative methods runs deeper than this 'special method for special conditions' approach. Participant observation was chosen because it accorded with the theoretical persuasions of the author concerning the nature of social reality and sociological abstraction. I would argue that it is a method particularly conducive to analysing mediated social reality. At this level I take the sociological enterprise to consist of abstraction based upon the already structured world of actors and groups in society. In this context, there is an empirical task. It is to tease out and to document the structures of meaning that constitute the social consciousness of any particular social world. The second task is to abstract. It is to embark upon explanatory accounts of these particular social worlds and to theorize about the general properties of any social world. Participant observation – the empathetic and analytic immersion into a social world – is suited to the fulfilment of the first task: the documentation of the patterns of meaning which constitute the basis of a social consciousness. Having documented this basis, *itself a theoretical decision*, the theoretical work can continue. In this account the social consciousness of Catholicism in the Six Counties has been viewed as a mediation of the structures of the Northern Irish society. This mediated reality has been considered as categories of thought and practice which sustain a consciousness that has relevance for the appeal of political violence. I have argued that communalism, sectarianism and republicanism are the dominant elements of the Catholic *Weltanschauung*. These elements constitute a total ideology that is isomorphically reproduced in the articulated practice of the IRA's particular ideology.

Two reasons, the problem under study and the level of analysis adopted, thus account for the method being used. The problems inherent in the technique have received lengthy documentation. More recently there have been attempts to establish participant observation as a serious alternative methodology, modifying its reputation of being able to produce rich, ideographic monographs but falling short in some sense of explanatory power and analytic rigour.[1] This appendix will only briefly mention the issues involved in the debate. I shall argue that the method-biases cluster around what I consider to be the central methodological problem in participant observation: the stages and process of becoming an insider.

First some preliminary details about the setting of the research. My eight-month stay in Anro was spent in a house in the 'new' part of the district. The house had been used over the summer of 1972 as a residence for student play leaders. Two of these play leaders, Roseleen and David, both English, had stayed in Anro after that summer to continue their work. We all had mutual friends in England and had met each other once or twice. Roseleen and David agreed to let me share the house they were renting and so effectively made the research possible. This couple had already worked for three months in Anro by the time I had arrived. They were well known and liked in the area and this fact cushioned me from the potentially very difficult problems of entry into Anro. People immediately designated me as 'one of the students' from the 'students' house'. This was a role I gladly embraced as it involved no pretence: I was a student. Moreover, the status 'students' satisfied a lot of curiosity in the district. Students were a phenomenon of the troubles. They came to run play schemes, to take children on holidays or just to see the political situation.

The house became a research haven. This was largely due to the engaging personalities of David and Roseleen. The house was never free from visitors. Children used it as a play centre most of the day. Adolescents, particularly boys, were daily callers. These lads provided me with a lively introduction to Anro. They were totally enthralled by the troubles and were willing to talk at great length about their experiences of the conflict. They seemed to enjoy being in our house. It was, after all, something of a novelty. There were no parents, or holy pictures; instead they found the 'weird talk' and 'funny foods' of the 'students' interesting. Moreover, there were very few places that friends could meet, talk and frequently share a cup of tea as well. The house was a shelter from the street corners and entries where many adolescents spent most of their spare time. Some of these youths told me later that their presence in the house was initially also to report our movements and opinions to the IRA. We were all aware that a polite vetting process was going on. I was not, as it happened, the only one with a microscope.

In the evenings a number of adult callers would drop by for a talk or a drink. As time went on the number of callers to the house increased. The house, as a mini-community centre, constituted an arena where different sections of the community could meet and talk. This made living in Anro a particularly rewarding experience. Methodologically, this meant that most of the information I received came through general discussions between conversationalists in the house. This was especially productive when different views were being aired. On these occasions the various issues within the district were raised by their exponents. Frequently the very questions I would like to have asked, but felt it imprudent to do so, were brought up by someone in the house whose claims to enquire were not in doubt. Because of the relationships that were established in the house we were introduced into the community through the clubs and through people's homes. This enabled me to see which groups in the community I had little contact with and those with whom I was well acquainted.

Traditional problems associated with participant observation

At this juncture I shall return to the conventional problems associated with participant observation. This will lead to a discussion of how these problems were attended to in this work. The major points of contention in the method centre around three concerns. First there is the issue of the so-called 'personal equation', second the matter of the social process the observation activates, and finally the difficulties involved in *post factum* explanation. After outlining these problems I shall argue that they can be subsumed into the one problem, that of the stages and process of becoming an insider.

The personal equation

The 'personal equation' suggests that the perceptions and interpretations of the research will be contingent on the values of the researcher. It is argued that the emotional and intellectual make-up of the sociologist will determine the type of moral judgment that is attached to events. Fear, anger and disgust as well as romanticism, compassion and concern are thought to create a moral veil which filters the emphases the report makes. Stated at its worst: What relationship does the 'data' bear to the actors' reality after a researcher, with a certain emotional outlook and with certain psychological needs, who might be culturally blinkered and class biased, and who has a particular ideological outlook and intellectual persuasion, has digested a series of realities and called them 'findings'? The numerous authors who have raised this familiar problem of fact and value see it partially resolved by treating the author as a variable.[2] Such a formulation usually involves a laying out of one's self in the methodological appendix to let the reader know that the researcher was a socialist, or a symbolic interactionist, or an atheist and so on. Some authors take this to heart and let the reader know they cried twice, made love fifteen times and changed their socks once a week while in 'the field' (e.g. Johnson, 1976). Everything might be relevant to someone. Treating preconceptions as variables, letting the reader see the researcher's dirty linen, however honourable an intention, appears to me as somewhat naive. In the first instance, who defines what elements of a researcher's personality are relevant? Second, all the sincerity in the world does not remove the possibility of the theorist's operating with 'biases' he is unaware of. We rarely do see ourselves as others see us. But the most important objection is that the mere stating of one's 'position' is an entirely different matter to weighting the effect that an individual's biography has on the monograph he produces. A problem is not resolved by admitting it exists.

Observer presence

The second salient problem associated with the method is the effect the observer's presence has on the setting being studied. As Vidich (1955) makes clear, the researcher by joining a social situation disturbs a scene he would like to hold constant. This problem varies according to the degree of participation in the researcher's role.[3] Rarely will a researcher be a fly on the wall observer. His observational work will be interlaced with periods of participation. Nor is the problem solved through covert participation. Whatever the role the researcher is assigned or carves out for himself, it will affect the quality of the social interaction he has with his respondents. Whatever he or she does the situation has changed. This is true whether the researcher is known as a researcher or whether he is not. If the role he takes on makes him aloof then there is a danger of missing much of what he is interested in finding out. If he 'goes native' there is, apparently, a danger of romanticizing his actors or never bothering to report his study. Somewhere in the middleground loom two other problems. The researcher may develop interests and acquaintances which effectively exclude his acceptance with other respondents. But, alternatively, if he tries to be a marginal man, with a foot in all the different social worlds of the milieu he is studying, there is a danger of becoming a social eunuch. The social eunuch does not dare to have views or opinions lest he 'spoils' his research by alienating his respondents. This problem, commonly referred to as 'rapport', is not restricted to sociologists. Rapport refers to the quality of any relationship. For example, I was rarely able to document how my relationships differed from Roseleen's and David's relationships with the same people, or indeed how any of these differences were due to my being a researcher. Initially people may have been a little reticent because I was a researcher, but as relationships developed this problem receded. The quality of a relationship becomes dependent on the same factors as any relationship: personality, time, situation and so on. I would argue this by pointing to those individuals in Anro who were precisely those to comment, often bitterly accurately, on my role as researcher:

'I hope you're not one of those making
sociological capital out of our plight'.
'Hey Frank, you're good at picking people's

brains, what do you makes of this?'
'Look at him, you can just see him mentally
taking notes'.
'We did participant observation last night in
sociology; I thought of you'.
'Now this [piece of information] is for you,
not your research.'
'This is Frank, he's experimenting on us.'

Such remarks made me want to creep into the nearest hole and
bury myself. However, the point that I am making is that all the
people who made the above remarks later talked freely to me, or
in my company, about a whole range of issues. This was because,
apart from the building of trust, participant observation's efficacy
lies in the inability of respondents to be constantly aware that they
are in the presence of a researcher.

The method breaks an elementary rule of social life by documenting for posterity what was said, within a tacit convention, for the
moment. Conversationalists do not operate with the idea that what
they say will find its way into someone's notes. The building of trust
and familiarity creates a situation where people become even less
reticent. The observer can use the subsequent openness to his
advantage. This can leave a bad taste in the researcher's mouth. At
this level the distinction between overt and covert participation
becomes blurred. Respondents who are aware of the researcher's
interests do not constantly hold that awareness in mind. During
such times the researcher is a covert observationist. The formation
of a relationship increases the likelihood of 'covert' observation.
Respondents at this stage interact with a researcher as a person like
anyone else. As Whyte (1955) said long ago, what type of information an individual sociologist receives is, in this sense, contingent on
what type of individual he is.

Consequently playing the social eunuch is misconceived. People
will soon realize that this particular front is a sham and being
labelled a 'phoney' is not particularly conducive to gaining access
to information. Though 'being yourself' might lead one to upsetting
some people it can equally endear one to others. In Anro I found
telling people my own views on various topics always generated a
discussion, and in one or two cases created close respondents from
previously lukewarm acquaintances. I would suggest, then, that the
social skills needed to weave one's way through the labyrinth of
social research cannot be learnt from methods texts. In the absence
of a prescription for ground rules of tact, diplomacy and political
nous the researcher would be better to 'be himself' than play the role
of a sociological Henry Kissinger.

The issue of rapport is confused. Rather than concentrating on evaluating the degree of intrusion the researcher makes on the social setting he studies (how good his rapport is), effort should be directed to justifying why the comments a researcher makes on that setting are the ones they are. It is the researcher's 'findings' that need justification, not his rapport.

Post-factum explanation

The third problem hinges around the potential abuse in after-the-fact explanation. This can involve waiving or forgetting material which does not fit in with a desire for conceptually tight reporting. The accounts produced by participant observation, like any others, do not just emerge. They are shaped. Whyte's work fell into patterns, he assures us, when he had to write it up to get his grant renewed. Similarly Malinowski (1922: chapter 18) has remarked of his kula ring: 'In fact I have written up an outline of the kula institution at least half a dozen times while in the field and in the intervals between my expeditions. Each time new problems and difficulties presented themselves.' The issue of partial selection arises principally at two stages. The note-taking or tape-recording of fieldwork is usually done after the event. Consequently a degree of selective retention may set in which the dating of data (Becker, 1958) cannot erase. Second, when the report comes to be written a process of massive selection ensues. This selection is not just from the field diary. The researcher's report relies very heavily on the store of knowledge, feelings and experiences that are not documented at all, but are carried in the author's mind. Consequently the interplay between mind and notes can justify an interpretation in the text on the grounds that the written words are put into context by the unwritten mental information of the researcher. Patterns that 'emerge' could consequently be argued not as machinations but due to the result of the tension between mind and notes. Much will be left out that is in the notes and some will be put in which is not there. A natural history of the actual field notes, or indeed their total publication, would not entirely resolve the possibility of the conscious or unconscious slanting of the material. Just as everything documented cannot be published everything perceived cannot be documented. Those authors who urge fieldworkers to replicate in their diaries the complete interactional process inherent in the reception of information fail to grasp this point.[4] To pose the solution to this problem in terms of documenting and 'publicating' (Johnson, 1976) the nuances, gestures, graces, overtones and ellipticalities of social interaction as a form of validating one's *post factum* interpretation is to commit a reproductive fallacy. The task of justifying the particular view of reality presented in a research report cannot be achieved by attempting to reproduce that reality *in toto*. I shall argue below that the effort is also misguided on other grounds.

Towards a theory of data

The three issues discussed raise aspects of the same problem. All are concerned with why interpretations and meanings in the study are the ones stated. Are these inferences drawn because of personal 'bias', because of the role assigned to the researcher or because of selective presentation in after-the-fact explanation? These thorny matters were addressed in the present work by attempting a theory of data.[5] This theory of data can be treated as the stages and process by which the researcher became cognizant with the social worlds that he is studying. A documentation of the passage of becoming an insider correctly conflates theory and methodology. It attempts to link explanatory claims with the process by which they were arrived at. Methodologically the theory of data is an account of the author's socialization into his respondents' society. Reconstructing the socialization process – the actors' view of their worlds – allows the researcher to give reasons why he interpreted and explained behaviour in the manner he reported. By establishing an account of his introduction into the worlds of his actors, the researcher attempts to minimize the translation problem involved in abstraction.

Cicourel puts this translation problem in perspective by emphasizing Schutz's contention that social life is pre-interpreted and prearranged before the sociologist comes to his 'facts'; in other words, that there are ideological configurations. The researcher's task is to grasp the structures of meanings in the pre-interpreted world and then to analyse them by establishing them within a theoretical construction.[6] Problems that have been discussed here as methodbiases arise because the sociologist-as-man has his own set of pretheoretic meanings. Methodological problems concern the possibility that the actors' 'meaning-structures' only become once translated into the world of the sociologist-as-man and not into explicit theoretical categories. It is a similar debate to quantitative sociology's difficulty of ascertaining whether its empirical indices are of the same equivalence class (that is, are valid and reliable indicators) as its theoretical concepts. The statement of how an author becomes socialized into the world that he is studying requires a theory of the translation problem, a theory of data.

Yet this socialization process is exactly the theoretical purpose of the study. Theoretically the author is interested in the model of the actors' world (the social consciousness). A view of the actors' world is the basis of a systematic appreciation of the actors' categories of thought, and the rules and meanings such categories of the social consciousness create. By explicating the grammar and syntax of the actors' social world the researcher is stipulating both the content of that world (the theoretical base) and *how* that world presented itself to the researcher (the methodological problem).

An example of the coincidence of theory and method is the phenomenon of telling outlined in chapter 2. Methodologically I was confronted, as an outsider, with remarks and situations that required interpretation. Those situations where colour, face, dress, language or territory were used to 'tell' were offered to the reader. Taken together I have suggested that they constitute a social phenomenon, that of 'telling'. This phenomenon was then used analytically to illustrate the significance of sectarianism as a category of thought and practice which orders a sectarian social division.

Similarly the meaning of Republicanism were presented to the reader in terms of the plethora of argument and counter-argument about the IRA Provisionals within Anro. In both cases my own socialization into these phenomena was explicated. This is not to deny that my theoretical concerns and persuasions influenced what I was interested in with Anro. That *must* and *should* be true of any perspective. But it is to emphasize that my view of Anro is attached to an empirical reality. What is presented in this book is necessarily composed of selections: selections which are documented because they are of theoretical interest. But these selections are located in an empirical setting. It is the interplay, between the ordering of the empirical world through theory and the emphasis that the theory is explanatory of the empirical world, that constitutes a theory of data.

Cicourel (1964) suggests that the construction of a 'typical course-of-action pattern' captures a view of social reality while simultaneously demonstrating that the view is located in a social world rather than in a theorist's imagination. The 'typical course-of-action pattern' involves hypothesizing a model of the basic interactional rules that actors follow. It is somewhat similar to Schutz's programmatic ideal-typical 'humunculi'. By showing how the view of the actors' world is constructed, the translation problem is confronted. Cicourel offers Goffman's work as instructive in documenting this model of the actor.[7] Certainly Goffman's insights into the information-seeking processes of social interactions, or his analyses of 'front' management are helpful. I would stress, however, that Goffman's work concerns action in general. He is interested in the sociological bases of *all* communication. The model of the actor that should be stipulated in participant observation will, by definition, contain those dynamics. But in an empirical study it is the particular content of the model of the actors' world that is of prime interest.

The investigation of the general properties of all social consciousnesses is a legitimate theoretical interest. It should not be confused, however, with the theoretical discussion of the differential content of social consciousnesses and the social worlds they structure. This distinction should be understood as it is at the root of the reproductive fallacy which attempts to stipulate the general features of how all events are interpreted in fieldwork. Johnson (1976), for example, gives lengthy and detailed accounts of the strategies that he used to gain entry and to maintain rapport in his research setting. His rationale for the long discussion of the ploys be used is that publication (the making public) of these processes provides the reader with knowledge that can assess the 'truth-claims' he makes. Johnson's interest is, ostensibly, the social world of welfare workers, but his methodological energies are diverted to eliciting the universal properties of interaction. Instead of the documentation of how he became cognizant of the 'natural attitude' of social workers, we have a phenomenological treatise on the origin and maintenance of any relationship. This is entirely divorced from his substantive interest yet is supposedly the epistemological basis for making substantive claims. I would argue that the theory of data in participant observation should be governed by the theoretical interest of the research. If the research is interested in the general properties of communication then its focus would be on the *structure* of the 'natural attitude'. If, however, as here, and as apparently in Johnson's work, there is a theoretical interest in a substantive area, the model of the actor depicted should consist of the content of that 'natural attitude' which is not shared by actors in other social worlds. The purpose of empirical work at this level is to capture and explain the distinctive qualities of various social worlds just as much as it is to discover the analytic structure of all social worlds. In my view confusing the two issues produces the paralysis inherent in the reproductive fallacy.[8]

The stages and processes involved in a theory of data

Heuristically, the content of a social world under study can be presented by delineating the stages and process by which the researcher becomes aware of the social meanings in that world. The point can be drawn by a brief sketch of what the stages and process would look like if I documented a social world in Anro that I have not included in the text.

What I refer to as the stages can be seen in the progression of my knowledge into the world of the 'adolescent youths who were frequent visitors to our house. It was likely that some of these lads were members of Na Fianna Éireann, a formally secret organization of the boys' IRA. As we got to know each other these youths began to refer occasionally to their Fianna involvement. The move from my ignorance to partial knowledge about that organization marks the passage into the social worlds of Na Fianna Éireann. Some three weeks after I had known them, which in terms of social time was considerable, as we had met during most days, an adult friend, Jimmy, brought the subject of the Fianna into a conversation that I was having with these boys. He told Henry to tell Michael to make sure he did his Fianna duty because if he stopped doing it, it would reflect badly on the 'students'. Some, he continued, might erroneously think that the students had turned him against the Provos. This was a complicated interaction as it involved Jimmy pretending to be involved in the campaign, perhaps trying to impress us, or perhaps trying to lend authority to his concern for us. Either way, Henry looked distinctly uneasy and I too felt awkward as it marked the first time the topic had been brought up. Henry, who, in fact, I found out later, was not a Fian, agreed that Michael was in some kind of trouble over this and he would tell him what had been said.

A few days later John slumped onto the sofa and announced that he was tired after all the work he had been doing. The remark seemed to be addressed to no one in particular and so I did not ask him what work he was referring to. I knew, however, that he was alluding to what was probably a Fianna duty which Roseleen had seen him carrying out. This was clearing furniture out of a house. The occasional mention and the casual allusion marked the first stage in getting to know what Na Fianna Éireann consisted of.

Next came a *faux pas* when I naively asked Michael whether the person he had just acknowledged, as we walked down the street, was on vigilante duty. This duty involves looking out for the 'Brits' and is a major Fianna task. Michael became agitated and advised me, 'You'd get a good hiding if anyone heard you say that: don't say it again.' He spoke with a degree of melodrama that these boys had become adept at expressing. But the remark clearly suggested I was not yet classified as one who could say such things. A month later, Joe, another Fian, stoically commented after a British army raid, 'There's hardly any fellas left now.' John took him up on this: 'Ah, get away; there's a brave few left yet.' Joe's reply was: 'I'm not talking about the wee lads [Fianna], but the big men.' These remarks raised no eyebrows though they marked the first time the 'fellas' had been talked about openly in my presence by Fians. I had reached a stage where I expected such talk, a sort of anticipatory socialization.

The next recorded incident took place during a gun-battle. Apparently a youth passing through our house had mentioned to others, sheltering in the house, the name of an IRA man who had been shot in the battle. This contravened part of the district's secrecy code and the boys held court in the house to determine the individual's guilt and the consequent punishment that the youth would receive. The significance of this was that minor Fianna activity had taken place with our obvious knowledge.

Between this stage and the next I came to know several adult activists. I was talking to one of them in a club when a Fianna scout came to tell him that the Brits had raided another club and had arrested ten people. The man, Gerry, asked the Fian if any of the fellas had been lifted. Kevin, whom I know quite well but had never talked with about the IRA, said that a couple of IRA men had been 'lifted'. Gerry asked who they were. Kevin, looking at me, reluctantly gave their names. Gerry said at least they did not get John and Paddy and went out. Kevin stayed for a while and bemoaned the fact that Gerry talked too much and suggested it was 'blabbermouths' like him who put the IRA in danger.

After these early stages events began to accelerate. For example, two Fians asked me to attract the attention of two non-Fians in order that they would go to a Fianna meeting unnoticed. I witnessed a discussion between two Fians and an IRA man on the structure of Republican organizations including their own. A small riot was temporarily halted by some Fians to allow us to get to a place of safety. I attended a Fianna education lecture. A boy who derogatorily called us 'them English' was punished by two Fians and so on.

The level of social intimacy with several Fians had developed extensively. With others the degree of confidence remained minimal. That I was only a partial insider was evident from the fact that Fianna activity was never an entirely open topic of conversation. But enough had been shown to me to enable me to assess the significance of Fianna membership and to be seriously impressed by the militancy of these adolescents. I came to realize that the length of the war in Ireland has created potential cadres of youth who are able to assume IRA status when their age allows it.

One way of knowing that I was still only an outsider with some inside knowledge was when I was engaged in a conversation that alluded to an incident I was familiar with. The event in question had been described to me by the individuals involved and consequently I knew a great deal about the affair. I would have thought the matter, a punishment inflicted upon a Fian, would have been discussed openly with me by the conversationalists as I valued them as my closest Fianna respondents. Instead, during the conversation the boys merely alluded to elliptical innuendoes and vague asides which the non-initiated would not have appreciated. I learnt then that instances where I knew more than others thought I did were poignant measures of my social exclusion. 'Becoming an insider' is necessarily an overstatement.

Similar stages could be documented for other groups the researcher came across. Becoming an insider, in this context, involves progressing into the division of the community so that after a while the researcher can reflect and assess what groups he has not got to know and those to which in varying degrees he has. This should restrict his analyses to those areas he knows about and which he can methodologically justify. The strategy of becoming an insider attempts to resolve the methodological problem not by justifying the selections made from the social worlds under investigation (that is a theoretical choice), but through the demonstration that these selections are rooted in that empirical world.

The stages in this passage are easier to document than what I have called the process. The extremity of the stages are very clear. In Anro at the end of my stay the young men on the street corners no longer seemed menacing. Similarly, going into the clubs no longer filled me with apprehension. I became less susceptible to the scare-mongering rumours. I felt less English at the outdoor meetings which poured scorn and acrimony on the English. What is harder to document is the process of these changes, the interactional scenes that effect role changes.

The process involves becoming familiar with what is socially relevant and using the information to become more familiar. Some of these relevances are universal. With others – the ones under study – rules and meanings have to be collated. The meanings of words, views and values need to be learnt. Their distribution, cues and associations need to be mapped. A grunt of disagreement, for example, when '*UI*' (the *United Irishman*, the newspaper of Official IRA) was mentioned allowed me to know the 'grunters' were 'Sticky' antagonists and therefore possibly Provo supporters. An interactional stock is built up and constantly adjusted. By explicating and using the generally held views (on Faulkner, on getting on dangerous buses), the community values (the role of women, attitudes to drink), and forms of deviance (informing, drug-taking), social interactions become progressively smoother. As these skills become apparent to co-conversationalists they may even be congratulated: 'You're just like an Anro lad now'; or again, 'I don't care if you are an army spy, I like you'. The process involves studying and employing the social rules which order the contextual determination of meaning.

For example, territory, as I have argued, is rule-bound. As Anro's boundaries are approached stricter rules of safety come into play. Passing cars on the perimeter roads are potential assassin carriers. Passengers are thus scrutinized to see if they are pointing a gun at you. At night in the darkened streets of Anro when the headlights of a car illuminate pedestrians, the fear is greater. Passengers cannot be seen until the car is overtaking. Consequently it may be safer to step into someone's garden. Again certain streets are to be avoided during trouble as they constitute the usual firing ranges. Alternatively other streets are cherished as blindspots from the British Army and Protestant observation posts.

The attempt to document such rules as they become apparent to the researcher is helped when the rules are inadvertently broken, during situations of trouble, and in what can be called 'natural experiments'. A researcher knows a rule has been broken because its breach is frequently accompanied with a response of fear, embarrassment, silence or confusion (Garfinkel, 1967). Tom, the loquacious volunteer, for example, illustrated the secrecy/prestige rules by flagrantly breaching them. Michael, an irate Fian, rebuked me for talking directly about Fians doing vigilante duty. Again I found that generally people felt foolish when they assumed their partner in conversation was a Catholic when in fact he was a Protestant and vice versa.

Trouble situations are equally helpful. Trouble forcibly compresses a lot of social activity into a small period of time. It requires people to respond in front of others in a manner that they might not ordinarily choose to. It therefore tends to break the level of conversation that a researcher may have settled upon with a respondent. It intensifies sociability. Being hemmed into a house with wanted men as the British Army raid neighbouring houses creates an awareness of the significance of being on the run. Witnessing the Provo/'Sticky' or the Republican/church confrontations in our house produced insights into the multiple positions contained within a seemingly homogeneous community.

Once the potential significance of a phenomenon has been raised confirmatory examples of it may be found in 'natural experiments'. One example of these natural experiments was the animated discussion on the efficacy of telling that I heard in our house. Another was when I watched a youth rioting and then compared it to his account of his part in the riot. A further example was occasioned during a time when there was widespread violence throughout Belfast but Anro was quiet. This provided an opportunity to assess what is involved when one is totally reliant on the mass media for information about the troubles. A further particularly vivid example of a natural experiment concerned a bus journey with a Legion of Mary woman into Belfast which I partly related in chapter 2. The bus went through a Protestant area. The attention of the Protestant passengers was aroused not only by her Catholic ejaculations like 'Oh, sweet Jesus!' as the bus went over a ramp, but also when I said 'I see they lifted a wee girl last night'. This referred to the fact that the first woman to be interned had been arrested the previous night.

Frances replied, 'Ay, she lives near my Rose.' The internment was received in Belfast with a lot of publicity and it was consequently widespread knowledge that the woman was from Andersonstown. The heads that again turned round to see who was having such a conversation had been triggered by two of the cues in the telling syndrome: 'Oh, sweet Jesus' and 'She lives near my Rose'. Everyone on that bus knew what type of an area Andersonstown was and *ipso facto* that anyone with relatives there must be Catholic.

Part of the 'process' also involves documenting the affective content of the social meanings that such rules structure. The rules become meaningful when the researcher has experienced or sympathetically intuited their affective background. Chapters 1 and 4 were partially designed to portray this theme. As seen there, the conditions that these rules attempt to structure concern the pervasive threat of trouble. The fear, for example, of walking into trouble is greater than the normal interactional prohibition of talking to strangers. Consequently people I did not know would stop and ask me if it were quiet at 'the top of the road'. Similarly, a battle or a raid produced spontaneous interaction between casual acquaintances and among strangers. To these simple illustrations can be added those already alluded to in the text over incidents of death, internments and riots. The researcher will not be able to, and should not intend to, relive the life of the people he studies, but he can gain insights and experiences of the affective background of his respondents' social world. The explication of this is important as it constitutes the insider experience that welds insiders together. Grasping this captures the process of becoming an insider because it documents the predominant features within the social consciousness under study.

The stages and process of the researcher's entry into the worlds he studies help him to document the content of that world. With some respondents, who become friends, an interactional *impasse* sets in where the researcher may no longer sustain his dualistic stance. At this stage, probably towards the end of his research, the sociologist will still be meeting strangers. These strangers are particularly helpful at the end of the fieldwork. Because they treat the researcher as ignorant he is able to catch glimpses of how insiders treat outsiders and how what they say presupposes insider knowledge.

Conclusion

I have argued that the passage of becoming cognizant of the social worlds under study can be methodologically approached in terms of the stages and process of becoming an insider. Such a formulation involves linking theory and method through the documentation of the content of a group's social consciousness together with an account of how this content was arrived at. This theory of data has been used in this text to help order the relationship between theory, method and substantive claims. Participant observation as a method should be intertwined in the text with these theoretical issues and substantive claims. As a method its strength lies in its ability to grasp meanings in context. Alone, however, that is never sufficient. These meanings have to be located within the wider social structure that they have mediated and within the theoretical discourse that attempts to explain that structure. In this thesis the method was used to document and analyse the mediations of the social structure of Northern Ireland society as they were evidenced within the Catholic *Weltanschauung*. These mediations were not treated *a priori*. The ideological configurations of Catholicism in Northern Ireland were used analytically to argue their relevance for political violence. This intertwining of theory, method and substantive claim is precisely the argument for the methodological immanence inherent in a theory of data.

Appendix 2 Some residents' drawings of Anro's mythological figures

1 Edward Heath, then Prime Minister of England, surrounded by Galloper Thompson, 'the Big Man of Arden Street', and the IRA man in a bucket. This cartoon was drawn in response to the Prime Minister's visit to an army barracks within Anro.

2   The 'Big Man of Arden Street', together with some Banshees.

References

Introduction   The problem and the approach

1 These range from counter-insurgency texts, anti-terrorist legislation, international conferences on terrorism through to newspaper-initiated 'Beat the Bomb' campaigns.
2 A classic example of this anthropological commonplace remains E. E. Evans-Pritchard's *The Nuer* (1947). See Suttles (1968) for an interesting application of Evans-Pritchard's work to a Chicago community.
3 See Rose (1971), especially chapter 10 and table 10.2, p. 307 for some factual data on some of these issues.
4 As with the first, and as will be seen with the third, this second element of the Catholic world-view can only be appreciated in the context of the existence of the Protestant community.
5 Rose, for example, in a survey of 1,291 Protestants and Catholics reports how 76 per cent of Catholics thought of themselves as Irish, rather than British or Ulster (20 per cent of Protestants thought themselves Irish) and 56 per cent of Catholics wanted the border abolished (Rose, 1971: 477, 213).

Chapter 1   Ethnographic snapshots: the radical Gemeinschaft

1 I constructed a survey to get an accurate picture of employment, unemployment and under-employment in Anro. The administering of the survey proved to be politically unacceptable.
2 Anro is actually in two parishes, one small part of Old Anro being in the neighbouring ecclesiastical area. Being unaware of any social significance attached to this I will not attach importance to it.
3 Taken from the parish history written on the occasion of the church's centenary in 1968, published by the parish.
4 All names used throughout the text are pseudonyms of respondents.
5 This, together with the veto on the unemployment survey constitute the two occasions on which I was prevented from gathering information by people within Anro. I have left the general discussion of 'rapport', which these issues raise, to appendix 1.

6 The use of these public condolences as a valid and reliable indicator of the kinship network presupposes it is a total social custom, not too great an assumption: 'Be my Valentine, you can't refuse or you'll read about my death in the *Irish News*'. It is also assumed that it is representative and that kinship terms are stated: it necessarily omits those who have no one; that people give their addresses; that deaths are equally treated (which they are not as assassinations and military deaths elicit more response from the kinship web) and so on.

7 It also brought 46 condolences from émigrés (usually UK, USA or Commonwealth) 94 from other parts of Northern Ireland and 36 unspecified. The months were January–August 1972 and January–February 1973.

8 The Anro song, written in 1969, recalled the experiences the community underwent in the riots of August that year.

9 This theme is expanded in chapter 2.

10 The 'B' Specials were a part-time auxiliary armed police force who were called upon, when required, to assist the Royal Ulster Constabulary. This overwhelmingly Protestant force had a notorious reputation amongst the Catholic population. See Scarman (1972), Cameron (1969) and Hunt (1969) for official criticism of the Specials' part in the 1969 riots. See also Hezlet (1972).

11 The Ulster Volunteer Force first originated as the organized paramilitary resistance to the Home Rule movement in 1912. The organization carries something of the equivalent significance of the IRA, only within Protestant communities. See Boulton (1973).

12 Screening is the lifting of individuals who are then taken to barracks, questioned, photographed, seen if wanted and detained or released. Over the last six years the British Army have amassed an extensive dossier on thousands of people living in the Six Counties. Much of this material is now computerized, making the screening process more efficient.

13 Internment and detention without trial have now ceased (1976). The increased number of sentenced prisoners, however, makes the above comments still relevant.

14 On this issue see Fields (1973).

15 This is developed in chapter 3.

16 This theme where religious symbols are extended to incorporate new significance, like the meaning of Friday abstinence for the Irish émigré in London, is one of the many extremely relevant issues discussed by M. Douglas (1973).

17 Fians are members of Na Fianna Éireann, the IRA youth wing.

18 See the drawings in appendix 2. None of these tales seemed, in the Lévi-Strauss manner, to reflect the major binary opposition of thought in Belfast, that of Protestant/Catholic.

19 These essays were written at school after the subject of 'the Black Man' had been discussed. Several of the extracts are by boys I knew well and who were frequently in and out of our house.

20 A street in Anro.

21 A street in Anro.

22 See *Intimidation in Housing* (NICRC, 1974) for a history of such intimidation, 1968–74.
23 The Anro Redevelopment Association instigated the rebuilding programme of the houses destroyed during the first internment raid.
24 Examples of this are to be found in chapter 4.
25 See chapters 3 and 4 for details.

Chapter 2   Sectarianism: a category of ideological thought and form of practice in Northern Ireland

1 For an excellent collection of these old themes found most clearly expressed in Marx and Durkheim, see M. Douglas (1973), *Rules and Meanings*.
2 For examples of how these categories of thought are evidenced in forms of ideological practice (sectarian policies), see Cameron (1969), de Paor (1970), McCann (1974).
3 He also found Catholics could tell slightly more accurately but does not wish to generalize from his sample. Telling is not just achieved by face: it involves a system with multiple signs and consequently Ross is attempting to isolate only one element from this system of signs.
4 Cooper's 'phenomenological' thinking seems to have little impact on his methodology as broadly similar stimulus/response testing is used. The methodology used here to elicit sectarianism as a category of thought is based on how members manifested these rules in their routine activities.
5 See Himmelfarb (1966).
6 See also Bayley and Loizos (1969) and many other commentators, particularly Russell (1972) and Edwards (1970).
7 A reading of any of the nineteenth-century Commissioners' Reports in Belfast's riots followed by a reading of the Cameron, Hunt and Scarman Tribunals into the recent troubles will make this point.
8 This section draws from the following texts: Budge and O'Leary (1973), Beckett and Glassock (1967), Moody and Martin (1967) and Beckett (1969). See Gibbon (1975), however, for a considerably more analytic and provocative text.
9 See Gibbon (1975) for the significance of the colonist's small commodity farming and weaving tradition which provided, in the Northeast, the capital accumulation for the transition to capitalist forms of production. This had overwhelming significance for the subsequent development of the two economies, North and South, in Ireland.
10 See also Pakenham (1969: 185). Gibbon (1975) shows how United Irishman support came from the tenant farmers and independent artisans, whereas Orange support was to be found where the linen trade was well advanced. The end-of-century clashes were inextricably connected with the threat to the monopoly of Protestant labour which the boom in the linen industry created at that time.
11 These riots were not, however, of equal significance. The pre-1864 riots differed to the post 1864 both in the ideology espoused and the social composition of the participants (Gibbon, 1975: 67–86).

12 In 1851 there were 35 lodges and 1,325 members in the Orange Order in Belfast; by 1870 there were over 4,000 members (Budge and O'Leary, 1973: 92–3).

13 He defined Evangelical fundamentalism as the doctrine of being saved by faith alone together with believing the Bible to be the word of God (Wright, 1973).

14 See the Reports to Commissioners on Belfast Riots, 1857–8 (Parliamentary Papers, 1857: XXVI); 1864 (P.P. 1865: XVIII), and 1887 (P.P. 1887: XVIII).

15 The same (1974) effected the collapse of the traditional Unionist party by voting out its leader, Faulkner.

16 See Fox (1957) for an account of an earlier clash with British troops in the 1908 riot.

17 Proportional representation was no longer used after 1929.

18 See O'Farrell (1976) who provides the fullest account of the history of the Northern State.

19 Rose sees him as 'even a revolutionary' (1971: 97).

20 There were other indicators such as the decline in emigration, the increased house building programme (Rose, 1971: 97).

21 'Castle Catholics' is the term used to describe those Catholics who were willing to support and partake in the affairs of Stormont Castle, the old Northern Ireland Parliament and civil service. Its somewhat derogatory overtones have been extended to all those Catholics who support the union with Great Britain.

22 All of these developments are well documented. For a purely chronological account see Deutsch and Magowan (1974). For official accounts see Cameron (1969) and Scarman (1972). See also McCann (1974) and Callaghan (1973).

23 The main paramilitary organizations of the Protestant community are the Ulster Defence Association and the Ulster Volunteer Force. A crop of other groupings, either splinter or front organizations, are constantly emerging, such as the Ulster Freedom Fighters.

24 These views represent my reading of the history of the North since partition. The Protestant apologist thesis for these practices hinges on the non-bargainable concept of Loyalty – Catholics systematically excluded themselves by not being trustworthy in the elementary matter of giving legitimacy to the State and therefore were not entitled to even the menial jobs and services which the State could directly control. Such reasoning is by no means the preserve of Northern Protestants; consider the following quote from Anselm Strauss (1959: 174) ' "and why do you not draw on us Croats for officials?" asked Valetta. . . . "But how can we let you Croats be officials?" spluttered Constantine [a Serbian], "You are not loyal!" "And how", asked Valetta, white to the lips, "can we be expected to be loyal if you always treat us like this?" "But I am telling you," growled Constantine, "how can we treat you differently till you are loyal?" ' See McCann (1974: 183–9) for the Boundary Commission's interpretation of electoral wards in 1924–5.

25 McCann (1974: 203), in a good analysis of the southern State, makes the point that the revolution in the South failed to produce anything but a mirror image of Protestant ascendancy (in Catholic Nationalism) and consequently provided no alternative to offer the unrest of the North in the 1920s and 1930s: 'W. T. Cosgrave and Eamon de Valera were the crutches on which the Unionist Party staggered through the twenties and thirties.' See also BICO (British and Irish Communist Organization) (1969) for a view that stresses the economic rationality of partition for the proletariat of Northern Ireland at the time of partition.

26 Allport's definitions (Allport, 1954) are 'pandiacritic', everyone is recognizable; 'mesodiacritic', 30–80 per cent are visible; and 'microdiacritic', less than 30 per cent are visible. I am using only the idea behind this, not its statistical range.

27 See Braidwood (1964: 34): 'The fact that many Ulster Protestants bear distinctively southern surnames has been attributed in part, at least, to the custom of the charter schools sending the children of southern Catholics to schools in Ulster to prevent the parents from stopping them being brought up Protestants.' See also McLysaght (1975) which unveils the Gaelic origin of many Anglicized surnames. In Anro there were 754 conversions (Protestant to Catholic), 1869–1952.

28 The Belfast Directory, a catalogue of street occupants, is somewhat dated because of its inability to keep pace with the massive population shifts and consequent squatting. However, the point can be made by looking at traditionally homogeneous areas – Shankill, Falls. The Parliamentary Papers (1865, XXVIII, appendix B) lists the names and religions of the City of Belfast's 160 policemen, which makes interesting reading. There are no 'Gaelic' Christian names amongst the Protestant police; of the five Catholic names three are distinctively un-Irish: James Walker, John Rodgers and William Harbinson; while the other two are more 'Catholic' sounding, Thomas Murphy and Patrick Heney.

29 I was working with Joseph in a job that eventually required asking an individual's religion, and so was in a position to see his ability in practice, an ability which he claimed enabled him to tell Protestants in Donegal in the Irish Republic, a county overwhelmingly Catholic in population.

30 Which differed from lay members' experience, if for no other reason than because of my overt attempt to analyse and reflect upon, as well as learn, the content of the socialization experience. See appendix 1.

31 The 'sample' in this incident was solidly working-class, in working clothes, of mixed sexes and of working age.

32 I do not wish to be offensive to Protestant working-class women by calling their appearance 'brassy' or 'ostentatious', which are clearly evaluative terms. The point is that it is held by some, and I have seen evidence of this at mixed public meetings, that working-class Protestant and Catholic women may well present different types of dress and decoration, to which both attach a moral significance.

33 This might well have been because of my crudely adjusted eye for these matters.

34 I am indebted to Budge and O'Leary's passing reference to Black for this material coming to my notice, which documents the very rules I had come across in contemporary Belfast, nearly 110 years later.

35 It seems that Dowse might have meant, apart from looking at their size, 'Do you look into their backgrounds [and consequently determine their religion]?' whereas Black, thinking in terms of the sectarian consciousness, took the remark to mean: 'Can you tell by looking?'

36 Over 80 per cent of intimidation was suffered by the Catholic population from Protestants and the British Army (Community Relations Commission, 1974). This work was withheld from publication for some time; one imagines such 'censorship' is supposed to be harmonious for community relations.

37 See Braidwood (1964) for the initial geographic settlement of Episcopalian and Presbyterian people in Belfast.

38 This last example may sound a little paranoid but in the climate of daily sectarian assassinations and with all my cues suggesting the porter to be Protestant, I could not help responding with a modicum of fear at his interest in my 'Catholic' address.

39 Taxis in Belfast have taken over, in both Catholic and Protestant communities, a supplementary bus function. They are cheap and numerous and minimize risk. Their presence is indicative of what happens on buses.

40 F. Boal's work on the social geography of Belfast confirms folk knowledge about the importance of an area. See Boal (1969) where, in looking at the Catholic (98 per cent so) Clonard and neighbouring Protestant (99 per cent) Shankill, he shows all but one child going to the 'wrong' schools. Similarly in 450 social visits only one was across the divide. See also Boal (1972) and Jones (1960).

41 A linguist at Queens University, Belfast, assured me of the quite real possibilities in this line of inquiry. Social linguists have already achieved sophisticated documentation of both linguistic and phonetic variation and change (Labov, 1973). See also Fraser (1973: 116).

42 This obviously involves an element of interpretation and imputation of motives to our fellow passengers. The phrase was not said loudly and I do not think it involved the natural curiosity to see if someone was falling out of their seat – a quite frequent phenomenon. There is no way of knowing 'for sure', most certainly it was my immediate interpretation of the situation.

43 R. Moore (1971) sees what I call 'telling' as an indication that the Northern Irish situation is therefore a problem in race relations which accordingly requires a non-liberal solution. The merits of this analysis, concerning non-liberal solutions, I would argue can be reached more persuasively through other paths. Looking at the economic and political history of Ulster since the plantation it is instructive to see how 'race' has been created to maintain political hegemony.

44 See Dillon and Lehane (1974). Take, for example, the case of the Quaker social worker who presumably could not explain away his

Catholic Unity Flats address on an envelope he was carrying and became a victim of a sectarian assassination.

45 See Douglas (1966: 18, 188). 'Ideas about separating, purifying, demarcating and punishing transgression have as their main function to impose system on an inherently untidy experience. It is only by exaggerating the difference between within and without, above and below, male and female, with and against, that a sense of order is created'; 'powers are attributed to any structure of ideas and rules of evidence make a visible public recognition of its boundaries'. See also Douglas (1970).

Chapter 3 Republicanism: the IRA and the community

1 The following relies heavily on the two authoritative histories of the IRA: Bowyer-Bell (1970) and Coogan (1970).

2 The stages theory assumes that a democratic Six Counties must precede a National Liberation struggle which will then lead to socialism.

3 'A group of intellectuals, tradesmen, clerks, students, professionals and the like – above all, of women – capable of promoting funds, circulating petitions, organizing boycotts, raising popular demonstrations, informing friendly journalists, spreading rumours, and in every conceivable way waging a massive propaganda campaign' (Taber, 1970: 32).

4 'Stickies' is the widespread term used to designate the Official IRA/Sinn Féin. I heard two accounts of the origin of the term and both were somewhat apocryphal. One referred to the fact that the Official IRA 'stuck' to the existing organization whereas the Provisionals broke away. The other explained the name by referring to the fact that the Provisional IRA Easter Lilies were pinned to their supporters' clothes whereas the Officials had theirs stuck on.

5 The British Army capitalized, when it could, on such antagonisms. For example, a number of men arrested simultaneously would be held if they were Provisional and released if Official, creating an impression that the 'Stickies' had co-operated with the army.

6 For the Provisionals' position on the split, see *Where Sinn Féin Stands Now* (Sinn Féin, c. 1970).

7 For example, 11 October 1969 riots on Shankill, 3 deaths; 23–7 January 1970, four nights of rioting on the Shankill; 2 June 1970, Protestant/Army riots near Ardoyne; 26 September 1970, weekend riots on Shankill.

8 For example 31 October 1969 at Bodenstown; 10 February 1970 at Crumlin Road Jail; 18 February 1970 at Belfast Assizes, and 7 March 1970 at Austin Currie's home.

9 The overall death toll for 1972 was 467 compared with 13 in 1969, 25 in 1970 and 173 in 1971 (Deutsch and Magowan, 1974: 379).

10 They in no circumstances constitute enough information to appraise the rise of the Provisionals. See Deutsch and Magowan (1973) for an appreciation of the complexity facing a competent historical analysis of this issue.

11 For example, Belfast was kept out of the 1956–62 campaign, as bringing the war to Belfast would have only brought a wave of sectarianism on to the streets.

12 The IRA might be better termed 'terrorists' than guerrillas in that they do not seek to build up a military force which eventually confronts the reigning militia in conventional fashion, as, say, in Vietnam. Rather it wishes to inflict political defeats by acts of violence which wear a government down. The terrorists can afford to be sacrificed in a way the guerrillas cannot. However, the IRA Army Council is not committed to complete terrorism and forbids IRA men taking kamikaze missions and places limits on the use of bombs. I use the word guerrilla because of the moral connotations associated with terrorist, while 'freedom-fighter' is perhaps accepting connotations of a different sort.

13 This paradox is very similar to what Martin Oppenheimer has called the liberal solution of dealing with urban terrorism, the so-called two-war strategy. Here the establishment moves to implement 'radical' reforms which cut off the basis of support for the terrorist. Simultaneously the military moves against the guerrilla. The inconsistency is that in performing the latter task the military injure the innocent giving the terrorist more support and undermining the reform pro-gramme. In addition, the two-war strategy might spark off an ultra-right revolt by those threatened by the reforms – the parallels in Northern Ireland are obvious (Oppenheimer, 1970).

14 'Croppies' were those Irish rebels of the 1798 rising who cut their hair short in the manner of the French Revolutionaries. 'Croppies lying down' consequently refers in general to defeated rebels and by extension to passive, quiescent Catholics.

15 The polarity posed here is over-simplified. The campaign morality of the Provos does become expressed in personal morality terms – 'the fight continues for our dead comrades, our fellow volunteers imprisoned'. Disagreement over the continuation of the war can more accurately be described here as due to the clashing and lack of overlap among spheres of personal morality.

16 For a general appraisal of this issue, see Dillon and Lehane (1973).

17 See *Republican News*, vol. 2, no. 65, 15 December 1972, for an example of a contemporary 'Provo priest'.

18 Extracts from the *Irish News* (Belfast morning newspaper) interview with the priest reported in the parish bulletin.

19 This and the following quotes are from the *Irish News*. Details available from the author.

20 This is not to imply that the IRA had complete control over the children. It did not.

21 I had a similar experience running down some stairs out of a building in which a bomb alarm had gone off. I found myself saying: 'Don't let it go off yet, not yet, please.' The building was a wreck ten minutes later. On reflection my pleas can be considered as prayers. The ghost of my own Catholic upbringing, it seems, had not been finally laid, despite several years as an avowed atheist.

22 On two occasions he played 'jokes' on me which if discovered would, I imagine, have had him severely reprimanded. I awoke one morning to see him in my bedroom pointing what looked like a primitive ray-gun at me (apparently it was a Thompson submachine gun). 'Right,' he said, 'you're a Four-Square laundry job.' This was an allusion to being an army spy. Before I had chance to have a heart-attack his face cracked and he laughed and went out. Another time he tapped me on the shoulder and I turned round to see a hooded man holding a pistol. He took the hood off and astutely remarked: 'You nearly died off!' (that is, nearly died of fright).

23 Public humiliation would take the form, for example, of a man tied to a lamppost, trouserless with 'I am a thief' pinned on him. Severe corporal punishment might be carried out by a volunteer from another company.

24 For examples of men being interned after being acquitted by the ordinary courts, being kept on remand for several months and being subject to the spurious detention tribunals, see McGuffin (1973: 194, footnote 15; 184, footnote 16; 212, appendix 3).

25 See McGuffin (1973: appendix 2) for the retrospective legislation that was rushed through the Westminster Parliament when it was found to be illegal to arrest men in the fashion the British soldiers had been doing.

26 For the documentation of these allegations see: Association of Legal Justice (Belfast organization's files), Kennally and Preston (1971), Faul and Murray (1972), Parker Report (1972), Compton Report (1971), McGuffin (1973, 1974). In addition several respondents in Anro recounted in great detail some of the British Army's excesses, which I occasionally also witnessed.

27 The circular nature of the causality involved in such arguments does not mitigate the consequence of the claim.

28 The impossible position of the British Army if attacked from both communities seemed to be recognized by the British Army during the Loyalists' Ulster Workers' Council strike in May 1974. There was no attempt to move against the strikers. Should the confrontation come about, however, it is unlikely that the British Army would be any less severe in its approach. The paratroopers, for example, have shown on the Shankill and in East Belfast that they do not seem to mind whom they attack.

29 A Belfast Protestant QC, Desmond Boal, has made the same point concerning 'would-be' Protestant UDA men and the tribunals.

30 Tim Pat Coogan reports something similar in his friend's biography: 'While I was too cowardly – rather than too prudent – to involve myself with the IRA I was like many others delighted to sniff the powder and vicariously enjoy the actions of others who were deeply involved, delighted to hang around the fringes of the movement and know people who were involved' (Coogan, 1970: 117–18).

31 More IRA volunteers have died through their own bombs than have been shot by the British Army (Provisional IRA, 1973: 99–101).

32 Governments do have images which can be dirtied. The behaviour of the Parachute Regiment in Northern Ireland from Bloody Sunday onwards has seriously undermined the credibility of the British Government's claims of good intentions.

33 I am aware that the conditions outlined here – fear, danger, excitement, boredom, grief – are also experienced by the British Army.

34 See Coogan (1970: 236) for an example of the young volunteers in the 1940. As in most armies, the British included, a lot of soldiers are very young. At present you have to be eighteen to serve in Northern Ireland on the British Army's side.

35 Kitson seems to take his model of the civilian population from the model of the 'men' in the British Army. Here the hierarchical control of men does make them more amenable to manipulation, propaganda and conditioning. Brigadier Kitson of the British Army has served in Northern Ireland.

36 The toll of civilian deaths includes: (a) several hundred shot by the British Army, including dead IRA men, (b) several hundred assassinated by Protestant paramilitary forces as well as (c) those hundreds who have died by IRA activity. Clutterbuck is intimating that all three categories belong to IRA activity, an absurdity. Most informing is done through the telephone: can the IRA intimidate that much to stop an anonymous telephone call from a public call box in central Belfast?

37 'Moreover, the almost universal reaction of British soldiers when they asserted or captured known senior officers of the Provisional IRA was astonishment at their low standard of intelligence . . . their organization was not remotely up to that normally found in successful urban guerrilla movements' (Clutterbuck, 1973: 105). I detect tinges of both racialism and propaganda here that make me want to leave the statement to speak for itself. I might add (a) this generalization runs directly counter to my own experience of a number of IRA men; (b) it does not tally with the military 'success' the organization has had, or its sheer persistence in the face of one of the best-equipped militia in the world; (c) it is not a particularly flattering comment on the ability of British Army officers, whose success has been so minimal.

38 A view, for example, that sees all theft as a redistribution of wealth, if from a capitalist source to a working-class thief, may have a semblance of truth as regards effect. It would, however, be highly misleading as an indication of the political consciousness of most thieves' intent. Walton (1973) has directly addressed himself to a theoretical analysis of political deviance. While there is much in his paper that is persuasive, it fails to resolve satisfactorily this problem of intent and effect. He criticizes transactionalist theory for not being able to cope with an actively conscious political violator of the law because its approach sees deviance as a quality of the labeller. He suggests that in seeing deviance as a quality of the act the deviant becomes 'a decision maker who actively violates the moral and legal codes of society. This is obviously of the utmost importance in the case of political deviancy, for our theory must allow of a creative but purposeful deviant who

consciously decides to transgress law and order' (Walton, 1973: 163). However, in his attempt to put 'a political sociology of the state' (Walton, 1973: 165) into the labelling perspective his purposeful actor is crushed: 'structured inequalities, preserved and protected by the powerful, act as causal forces preventing actors from pursuing their interests except via deviant means. It is my contention here that much deviancy both "political" and "non-political" – must be viewed as a struggle or reaction to normalized repression' (the moral climate the powerful create – F.B.) (Walton, 1973: 163). In this statement the intentionality of the non-political deviant goes by the board, he *'must'* be viewed as struggling or reacting against normalized repression. It is hard to see why he bothered creating his purposeful deviant if he is only to be prevented by causal forces in getting what he wants other than by deviant means; that is very reminiscent of Merton's theorizing. The statement is made with the political deviant in mind and *his* intentionality does fit the analysis. The non-political deviant is, however, made to fit in as best he can be by pointing at the possible effect of his action as perceived by the author. This contradiction is tempered but not eradicated when he says: 'Whether or not deviants merely neutralize the moral code in order to justify their breakthrough, or whether they develop an ideological opposition to the code will, of course, be an important feature in any explanation or classification of deviancy' (Walton, 1973: 164). See also Taylor, Walton and Young (1974).

39 Clutterbuck (1973) suggests over half the world's governments are based on violent accession. This should underline the point that my use of the phrase 'politicized deviant' does not imply that the activity is abnormal, immoral or that there is anything 'deviant' about the politics. The phrase refers merely to the means being illegal. The term is used to locate any insights the sociology of deviant behaviour may have for illegal political activity and how the theories of the former need modification to appreciate the latter.

40 In this respect 'felon-setting' has reached national proportions in England with the crop of jokes emphasizing stereotypical conceptions of Irishness. The connotations are not so much that the 'Irish' (there is a failure to distinguish Irish/Northern Irish, Catholic/Protestant) are 'bad' or 'mad', but stupid. The phenomenon can be seen in the same manner, however, as a denial of political relevance, or *ipso facto*, that the Irish problem is itself a joke.

41 See British Society for the Social Responsibility of Science (1974) for a full account of the community punishments.

42 For a cogent appreciation of this theory, which does justice to its sophistication while pointing to its limitations, see Box (1971).

43 For criticisms of labelling theory from this perspective see Taylor, Walton, Young (1974); Walton (1973); Schervish (1975).

44 The clearly terrorist bombs in England in 1974 and later (Tower of London, Birmingham) might also suggest that some volunteers reason that if they are universally condemned as terrorists in England they have nothing to lose in acting as terrorists. Planting bombs

without warning, of an anti-personnel make-up (that is, designed to cause maximum physical injury) and in crowded public places, would very soon freeze the Provos out of the Catholic communities in Ireland. 'Across the water' is another matter. This is highly speculative as I have no knowledge if the Provisional IRA are responsible or if it is their policy.

45 An excellent discussion of the general relationship between violence and politics is Oppenheimer (1970).

Chapter 4 Leaps into the dark: views into and from the inside

1 In these terms, the particular ideology is a political activation of the possible (Goldman, 1975) or imputed (Lukács, 1971) consciousness that characterizes a group's collective or social consciousness.

2 See, for example, P. Foot's letter to the *Guardian*, 10 September 1971; McCann (1971: 24).

3 See, for example, McCann (1971: 24–5): 'the Press is not an independent institution. There is no "free press"... Every British national newspaper is either directly or through its major shareholders, linked to other big business, inextricably enmeshed in the capitalist system. The Daily Mail and General Trust Limited ... through Associated Newspapers ... is involved in ... fifty subsidiary enterprises.... The International Publishing Co. (Reed Group) ... has four hundred associated and subsidiary companies.... The Thompson organization has one hundred and ninety-two subsidiary and associated companies', etc.

4 See Hall (1973) for an interesting example of this in regard to press photographs.

5 See Part 1, Cohen and Young (1973); also Chibnall (1975).

6 All dates and names of the publications quoted, where omitted, are available from the author.

7 What 'responsible' means in practice is a close agreement with British Government policy – on reforms for Catholics, introducing internment, beating the IRA, phasing out internment, the Assembly, the Convention, etc.

8 A noted example of this is when a *Guardian* reporter presumed the death of a man resulted because he had been engaged in petrol bombing and was accordingly shot by the British Army. When justifying the status of the dead man as a petrol bomber to Bernadette Devlin his reasoning was such that if the army shot him he must be a petrol bomber as otherwise it would not have happened: 'a soldier cannot legally shoot "a rioter" ... he has to wait until a man has committed one of a number of specific offences, of which throwing petrol bombs is one. I accepted at the time that this is what Mr —— must have done, and this I duly reported' (McCann, 1971: 18–19).

9 See Deutsch and Magowan (1973) for a chronological account of such early bombs.

10 The *Guardian* editorial on the Niesewand case (7 April 1973) brings a lot of these processes into the open. Entitled 'A Sample of Savagery', the editorial is indignant over the sentencing of their Rhodesian journal-

ist by a special court in Rhodesia: 'His trial was held in secret so that neither we nor anyone else without access to him can have any knowledge of the detailed charge or evidence.' (This is the same position as the detention process in Northern Ireland which it supports. See Boyle, *et al.* (1975) for a detailed appraisal of internment and detention.) 'How Mr Smith can square the plainly political attempt to stifle Niesewand with his professional desire for talks with Britain . . . is hard to fathom.' (At exactly this time paratroopers were taking Anro apart while the British Government was urging the peace and politics of the White Paper.) 'During this separation and his own solitary confinement, Mr. Niesewand has evidently conceived fantasies about his wife's health.' (See McGuffin [1974] for an account of experimental sensory deprivation on selected internees.) This brutality was slow to be recognized by the *Guardian*: 'The *Guardian* has been criticized for treating such allegations with caution. But the sad fact is that propaganda is an integral part of the war in Ulster' (*Guardian*, 19 September 1971).

11 See the *Guardian*, 16 October 1972, on the UDA/British Army liaison; see the *Guardian*, 8 November 1972, on the riots in Lenadoon; see 13 January 1973 on the tribunals for the detained; see 4 March 1973 on civilian deaths by soldiers.

12 Thus, like the counter-insurgency theorists, journalists underplay the significance of the total mediating context.

13 See Morris Fraser (1973: 42) for some examples of Belfast papers reflecting the prejudices of their readers. He uses this term.

14 The paper seems to have a tendency to put those Catholic deaths that are admitted to be 'mistakes' by the army off the front page. A few weeks previous to this incident, a workman was shot dead by troops in Anro. They had mistaken him for a gunman. The headlines on the front page underlined the tragedy and a long statement by a Unionist MP, an ex-captain, praised the work of the troops and emphasized how infrequently mistakes like this happened.

15 Thus I might stress again that this does not demote the problems of press coverage merely to a problem of access to knowledge.

16 See Burton and Carlen (1977) for an analysis of the structures of argument realized in official discourses.

17 Such as the Protestant Faulkner Unionists, the Alliance Party, the Northern Ireland Labour Party and the Social Democratic and Labour Party.

18 Rose, rightly in my view, set the tone of the pessimism in his book *Governing Without Consensus* (1971) some five years ago. He particularly emphasized the non-bargainable issues of sovereignty and nationality.

19 'Just as our opinion of an individual is not based on what he thinks of himself, so can we not judge of such a period of transformation by its own consciousness; on the contrary, this consciousness must be explained rather from the contradiction of material life, from the existing conflict between social productive forces and the relations of production' (Marx and Engels, 1968 edn.: 183).

20 Padraig O'Snodaigh (1972) has written an erudite pamphlet rebutting the two nations theory on cultural grounds. He emphasizes that the Irish language is an integral part of the heritage of the Ulster Protestant because a lot of the settlers moved 'within what had been part of a single culture' (1972: 4), Gaelic, for example, being their native language. The pamphlet has much fascinating material, including evidence of a Gaelic-inscribed Orange Order banner.

21 This author represents the most sophisticated exponent of the two nation, two stages theories.

22 See chapter 6 in Purdie (1972) for a profile of the major left-wing groups involved in Ireland.

23 Particularly the related stages theory which the Official IRA is said to adhere to. This view is considered Stalinist and a justification of reformism by the more Leninist and Trotskyist groups, plus the Provisionals. See particularly McCann (1972a), Foley (1972), Redmond (1973), *United Irishman* (October 1971), Purdie (1972), Brennan (1975), Revolutionary Communist Group (1976).

24 Though this book has this merit of grappling with what I take to be the issues, I think he is wrong on several points. In particular his views on the Provisional IRA are clearly Dublin-based.

25 What these changed tactics might be, is another, difficult, question. The Republican movement (Provisional Sinn Féin) would seem, for example, to be more amenable to inside reform than external competition. The same may or may not be true of the Loyalist groups. Either way I hope to have shown, particularly in chapter 3, that McCann's thesis, that the lack of a socialist alternative created the Provisionals, is untenable. More important is that there was no hope of socialism, except in its Republican form, in the Northern Irish Catholic consciousness which was saturated with a mixture of civil rights and liberation ideologies. See McCann (1974: 243).

26 Looking for a socialist solution to the troubles will, of course, produce a different theory and explanation than a 'liberal' or Loyalist or Republican approach.

Appendix 1 Theory and methodology in participant observation

1 See Johnson (1976), Douglas (1972), Cicourel (1964). All these authors question the relevance of deductive-nomological explanation for social science and accordingly assess participant observation from within a different epistemological framework than that of many 'quantitative' sociologists. The argument for fieldwork presented here does not derive from their position.

2 See Whyte (1955), Dalton (1964), Myrdal (1969), Polsky (1971).

3 Junker (1960), for example, has stressed that participant observation is a loose term covering a continuum of degrees of participation and observation.

4 Particularly Johnson (1976) and Bruyn (1966). A reading of Cicourel (1964) might also lead to such a position.

5 See Cicourel (1964), especially chapter 2. This methodological appendix leans heavily, though not entirely, on this chapter.

6 Where I would disagree with Schutz (1962) is that this theoretical construction must be both derived from and intelligible within the actors' world. This necessarily leads itself towards a theoretical humanism and a methodological individualism which inadequately conceives of social structure as ultimately explicable in terms of mediated social reality. See Hindess (1972).

7 See Goffman (1959, 1963, 1969). Since Cicourel's *Method and Measurement* (1964) what is loosely called 'ethnomethodology' has occasionally addressed itself to the general properties of reality construction. For a useful general review, see Atewell (1974).

8 This, of course, does not deny the importance of the two concerns to each other. In a purist light it might be argued that the general properties of communication need to be explicated before the specific content of any communicative message becomes knowable. That is, however, not the case in language. The same may or may not be true of non-verbal communications. The relevant section in Johnson (1976) is Part 4, 'Developing Trust'.

Bibliography

Books and periodicals

ALLPORT, G. (1954), *The Nature of Prejudice*, Addison Wesley, Cambridge, Mass.

ALTHUSSER, L. (1971), *Lenin and Philosophy and other Essays*, New Left Books, London.

ATEWELL, P. (1974), 'Ethnomethodology since Garfinkel', *Theory and Society*, vol. 1, no. 2.

BARRITT, D. and BOOTH, A. (1972), *Orange and Green*, Northern Friends Peace Board, Sedbergh.

BARRITT, D. and CARTER, C. (1972), *The Northern Ireland Problem*, Oxford University Press, London.

BARTON, A. (1969) *Communities in Disaster*, Ward Lock Educational, Columbia.

BAYLEY, F. and LOIZOS, P. (1969), 'The Bogside Off Its Knees', *New Society*, 21 August 1969.

BECKER, H. (1958), 'Problems of Proof and Inference in Participant Observation', *American Sociological Review*, no. 23.

BECKETT, F. and GLASSOCK, R. (1967), *Belfast: Origin and Growth*, BBC Publications, London.

BECKETT, J. C. (1969), *The Making of Modern Ireland*, Faber and Faber, London.

BOAL, F. (1969), 'Territoriality on the Shankill Falls Divide in Belfast', *Irish Geography*, vol. 6, no. 1.

BOAL, F. (1971), 'Territory and Class: A Study of Two Residential Areas in Belfast', *Irish Geography*, vol. 6, no. 3.

BOAL, F. (1972), 'The Urban Residential Subcommunity', *Area*, vol. 4, no. 3.

BOSERUP, A. (1972), *Who is the Principal Enemy? Contradictions and Struggle in Northern Ireland*, ILP, London. (Also in J. Saville and R. Miliband (eds) (1972), *Socialist Register*, Merlin Press, London.)

BOULTON, D. (1973), *The UVF, 1966–73*, Gill & Macmillan, Dublin.

BOWYER-BELL, F. (1970), *The Secret Army*, Blond, London.

BOWYER-BELL, F. (1971), 'The Escalation of Insurgency: The Provisional IRA Experience, 1969–71', *Review of Politics*, no. 35.

BIBLIOGRAPHY

BOX, S. (1971), *Deviance, Reality and Society*, Holt, Rinehart & Winston, London.

BOYD, A. (1970), *Holy War in Belfast*, Anvil Books, Tralee.

BOYD, A. (1972), *Brian Faulkner and the Crisis of Ulster Unionism*, Anvil Books, Tralee.

BOYLE, K., HADDEN, T. and HILLYARD, P. (1975), *Law and State: The Case of Northern Ireland*, Martin Robertson, London.

BRAIDWOOD, F. (1964), 'Ulster and Elizabethan English' in G. Adams (ed.), *Ulster Dialects*, Ulster Folk Museum, Belfast.

BRENNAN, I. (1975), *Northern Ireland: A Programme for Action*, CPGB, London.

BRITISH AND IRISH COMMUNIST ORGANIZATION (BICO) (1969), *Catholic Political Culture and the Constitution of Ireland*, BICO, Belfast.

BICO (1973), *The Birth of Ulster Unionism*, BICO, Belfast.

BICO (1972), *The Economics of Partition*, BICO, Belfast.

BRITISH SOCIETY FOR THE SOCIAL RESPONSIBILITY OF SCIENCE (1974), *The New Technology of Repression, Paper Two*, Russell Press, Nottingham.

BRUYN, S. (1966), *The Humanist Perspective in Sociology*, Prentice-Hall, Englewood Cliffs, N.J.

BUDGE, I. and O'LEARY, C. (1973), *Belfast: Approach to Crisis, 1613–1970*, Macmillan, London.

BURTON, F. and CARLEN, P. (1977), 'Official Discourse', *Economy and Society*, vol. 6, no. 4.

CALLAGHAN, F. (1973), *A House Divided*, Collins, Glasgow.

CAMERON (1969), *Disturbances in Northern Ireland: Report of the Cameron Commission*, Cmd 532, HMSO, London.

CAMPBELL, F. (1967), 'Between the Wars', in F. Beckett and R. Glassock (1967), *Belfast: Origin and Growth*, BBC Publications, London.

CHIBNALL, S. (1975), 'The Crime Reporter: A Study of the Production of Commercial Knowledge', *Sociology*, no. 1.

CICOUREL, A. (1964), *Method and Measurement in Sociology*, Free Press, New York.

CLUTTERBUCK, R. (1973), *Protest and the Urban Guerrilla*, Cassell, London.

CLUTTERBUCK, R. (1975), *Living with Terrorism*, Faber and Faber, London.

COATES, K. and SILBURN, R. (1972), *Poverty: The Forgotten Englishman*, Penguin, Harmondsworth.

COBDEN TRUST (1973), *Justice in Northern Ireland* (T. Hadden and P. Hillyard), Cobden Trust, London.

COHEN, S. and YOUNG, J. (1973), *Manufacture of News*, Constable, London.

COMMUNITY RELATIONS COMMISSION, see Northern Ireland Community Relations Commission.

COMPTON (1971), *Report of the Enquiry into the Allegations against the Security Forces of physical brutality in Northern Ireland arising out of events on the 9th August 1971*, Cmd 4823, HMSO, London.

COOGAN, T. P. (1970) (paperback, 1971), *The IRA*, Fontana, London.

COOPER, J. (1958), 'Prejudicial Attitudes and the Identification of Their Stimulus: A Phenomenological Approach', *Journal of Social Psychology*, no. 48.

198

DALTON, M. (1964). 'Preconceptions in "Men Who Manage"', in P. Hammond (1964), *Sociologists at Work*, Doubleday, Garden City, N.J.

DE PAOR, L. (1970), *Divided Ulster*, Penguin, Harmondsworth.

DEUTSCH, A. and MAGOWAN, V. (1973), *Northern Ireland, 1968–73: A Chronology of Events, vol. 1: 1968–71*, Blackstaff Press, Belfast.

DEUTSCH, A. and MAGOWAN, V. (1974), *Northern Ireland 1968–73: A Chronology of Events, vol. 2: 1972–3*, Blackstaff Press, Belfast.

DEVLIN, B. (1969), *The Price of My Soul*, André Deutsch, London.

DICKSON, R. (1966), *Ulster Emigration to Colonial America, 1718–1775*, Routledge & Kegan Paul, London.

DILLON, M. and LEHANE, D. (1973), *Political Murder in Northern Ireland*, Penguin, Harmondsworth.

DIPLOCK (1972), *Report of the Commission to Consider Legal Procedures to Deal with Terrorist Activities in Northern Ireland*, Cmd 5185, HMSO, London.

DORN, R. (1973), *Irish Nationalism and British Imperialism*, Plough Book Service, Dublin.

DOUGLAS, J. (ed.) (1972), *Research on Deviance*, Random House, New York.

DOUGLAS, M. (1966), *Purity and Danger*, Penguin, Harmondsworth.

DOUGLAS, M. (1970), *Natural Symbols*, Penguin, Harmondsworth.

DOUGLAS, M. (ed.) (1973), *Rules and Meanings*, Penguin, Harmondsworth.

DURKHEIM, E. (1915), *Elementary Forms of the Religious Life*, George Allen and Unwin, London.

DURKHEIM, E. (1933), *The Division of Labour in Society*, Macmillan, New York.

EDWARDS, O. (1970), *The Sins of Our Fathers*, Gill & Macmillan, Dublin.

EGAN, B. and MCCORMACK, V. (1969), *Burntollet*, L.R.S., London.

ELLIS, P. BERESFORD (1972), *A History of the Irish Working Class*, Gollancz, London.

EVANS-PRITCHARD, E. (1947), *The Nuer*, Clarendon Press, Oxford.

FAUL, D. and MURRAY, R. (1972), *British Army and RUC Special Branch Brutalities*, Abbey Printers, Cavan.

FIELDS, R. (1973), *A Society on the Run*, Penguin, Harmondsworth.

Flight (1971), see Northern Ireland Community Relations Commission.

FOLEY, G. (1972), *Problems of the Irish Revolution*, Pathfinder Press, New York.

FOX, R. (1957), *Jim Larkin*, Lawrence & Wishart, London.

FRASER, M. (1971), 'How Children see Conflict', *New Society*, 15 April.

FRASER, M. (1973), *Children in Conflict*, Penguin, Harmondsworth.

FREEDOM STRUGGLE (1973), see PROVISIONAL IRA (1973).

GANS, H. (1962), *The Urban Villagers*, Free Press, New York.

GARFINKEL, H. (1967), *Studies in Ethnomethodology*, Prentice Hall, Englewood Cliffs, N.J.

GEORGE, D. (1971), 'These are the Provisionals', *New Statesman*, 19 November, 1971.

GIBBON, P. (1972), 'The Origins of the Orange Order and the United Irishmen', *Economy and Society*, vol. 1.

GIBBON, P. (1975), *The Origins of Ulster Unionism*, Manchester University Press.

GOFFMAN, E. (1959), *The Presentation of Self in Everyday Life*, Doubleday, Garden City, N.J.

GOFFMAN, E. (1961), *Encounters*, Bobbs-Merrill, Indianapolis, Ind.

GOFFMAN, E. (1963), *Behaviour in Public Places*, Free Press, New York.

GOFFMAN, E. (1967), *Interaction Ritual*, Doubleday, New York.

GOFFMAN, E. (1969), *Strategic Interaction*, University of Pennsylvania Press, Philadelphia.

GOLDMAN, L. (1975), *Towards a Sociology of the Novel*, Tavistock, London.

HABERMAS, J. (1970), 'Towards a Theory of Communicative Competence', in H. Drietzel, *Recent Sociology*, no. 2, Macmillan, London.

HABERMAS, J. (1973), *Legitimation Crisis*, Beacon Press, Boston.

HALL, S. (1973), 'The Determination of New Photographs', in S. Cohen and J. Young (eds), *The Manufacture of News*, Constable, London.

HANNERZ, V. (1970), *Soulside*, Columbia University Press, New York.

HARRIS, R. (1972), *Prejudice and Tolerance in Ulster*, Manchester University Press.

HASTINGS, M. (1969), *Ulster*, Gollancz, London.

HERBSTEIN, D. (1973), article in *Sunday Times*, 2 December 1973.

HEZLET, A. (1972), *The 'B' Specials*, Pan, London.

HICKIE, J. and ELLIOTT, R. (1971), *Ulster: A Case Study in Conflict Theory*, Longmans, London.

HIMMELFARB, S. (1966), 'Studies in the Perception of Ethnic Group Members: Accuracy, Response Bias, and Anti-Semitism', *Journal of Personality and Social Psychology*, vol. 18.

HINDESS, B. (1972), 'The Phenomenology of Alfred Schutz', *Economy and Society*, vol. 1, no. 1.

HIRST, P. (1976), 'Althusser and the Theory of Ideology', *Economy and Society*, vol. 5, no. 4.

HUNT (1969), *Report of the Advisory Committee on Police in Northern Ireland* (The Hunt Report), Cmnd 535, HMSO, London.

Intimidation in Housing (1974), see Northern Ireland Community Relations Commission.

JACKSON, H. (1971), *The Two Irelands* (*MRG Two*), Minority Group Report, London.

JOHNSON, J. (1976), *Doing Fieldwork*, Wiley, New York.

JONES, E. (1960), *A Social Geography of Belfast*, Oxford University Press, London.

JUNKER, B. (1960), *Fieldwork: An Introduction to the Social Sciences*, University of Chicago Press.

KATZENBACH, E. (1964), 'Time, Space and Will: The Politico-Military Views of Mao-Tse-Tung', in T. Greene (1969), *The Guerrilla – and How to Fight Him*, Praeger, London.

KELLY, J. (1972), *How Stormont Fell*, Gill & Macmillan, Dublin.

KENNALLY, D. and PRESTON, E. (1971), *Belfast, August 1971: A Case to be Answered*, ILP, London.

KITSON, F. (1971), *Low Intensity Operations*, Faber and Faber, London.

LABOV, W. (1973), *Sociolinguistic Patterns*, Princeton University Press, New Jersey.

LÉVI-STRAUSS, C. (1962 edn), *Totemism*, Penguin, Harmondsworth.

LOFLAND, J. (1969), *Deviance and Identity*, Prentice Hall, Englewood Cliffs, N.J.

LUKÁCS, G. (1971), *History and Class Consciousness*, Merlin Press, London.

LUKES, S. (1975), *Emile Durkheim*, Penguin, Harmondsworth.

LYSAGHT, D. R. O'CONNOR (1973), 'Basis for a Statement on the Situation in Northern Ireland', in R. Dorn (1973), *Irish Nationalism and British Imperialism*, Plough Book Service, Dublin.

MCCANN, E. (1971), *The British Press and Northern Ireland*, Pluto Press, London.

MCCANN, E. (1972a), *What Happened in Derry*, Pluto Press, London.

MCCANN, E. (1972b), 'After 5th October 1968', *International Socialist*, no. 51.

MCCANN, E. (1974), *War and an Irish Town*, Penguin, Harmondsworth.

MCGUFFIN, F. (1973), *Internment*, Anvil Books, Tralee.

MCGUFFIN, F. (1974), *The Guinea Pigs*, Penguin, Harmondsworth.

MCLYSAGHT, E. (ed.) (1975), *Some Ulster Surnames*, (*publisher unknown*), Belfast.

MAGEE, J. (1971), *The Teaching of Irish History in Irish Schools*, NICRC Research Paper, Belfast.

MALINOWSKI, B. (1922), *Argonauts of the Western Pacific*, Routledge & Kegan Paul, London.

MANNHEIM, K. (1968a), *Essays in the Sociology of Knowledge*, Routledge & Kegan Paul, London.

MANNHEIM, K. (1968b), *Ideology and Utopia*, Routledge & Kegan Paul, London.

MARX, K. (1926 edn), *The 18th Brumaire of Louis Bonaparte*, Allen and Unwin, London.

MARX, K. and ENGELS, F. (1968 edn), *Selected Works*, Lawrence & Wishart, London.

MARX, K. and ENGELS, F. (1972 edn), *Ireland and the Irish Question*, International Publishers Co., New York.

MOODY, T. and MARTIN, F. (1967), *The Course of Irish History*, Mercier, Cork.

MOORE, R. (1971), 'Race Relations in the Six Counties', paper given at Lancaster Conference on Northern Ireland, 1971. See also R. Moore, 'Race Relations in the Six Counties: Colonialism, Industrialization, and Stratification in Ireland', *Race*, vol. XIV, 1972.

MOSS, R. (1972), *Urban Guerrillas*, Temple Smith, London.

MYRDAL, G., (1969), *Objectivity in Social Research*, Duckworth, London.

NISBET, R. (1970), *The Sociological Tradition*, Heinemann, London.

NORTHERN IRELAND COMMUNITY RELATIONS COMMISSION (NICRC) (1971), *Flight*, NICRC, Belfast.

NICRC (1974), *Intimidation in Housing*, NICRC, Belfast.

O'BRIEN, C. C. (1974), *States of Ireland*, Panther, St Albans.

O'FARRELL, M. (1976), *The Orange State*, Pluto Press, London.

OPPENHEIMER, M. (1970), *The Urban Guerrilla*, Penguin, Harmondsworth.

O'SNODAIGH, P. (1972), *Hidden Ulster*, Codhanna Teo, Belfast.

OWEN, D. (1921), *A Short History of the Port of Belfast*, Moyne, Boyd and Son, Belfast.

PAKENHAM, T. (1969), *The Year of Liberty*, Panther, London.

PALMER, J. (1972), 'The Gombeen Republic', *International Socialism*, no. 51.

PARKER (1972), *Report of the Committee of Privy Councillors appointed to consider Authorised Procedure for the Interrogation of Persons Suspected of Terrorism*, Cmnd 4901, HMSO, Belfast.

PARLIAMENTARY PAPERS (1865), *Report of Commission of Enquiry into 1864 Disturbances. Minutes of Evidence to Select Commission on the Belfast Riots 1864*, vol. XXVIII (1865) and Appendix B, xxviii (1865).

PARLIAMENTARY PAPERS (1896), *Minutes of Evidence Taken Before the Select Committee on the Belfast Corporation Bill*, vol. VIII (1896).

POLSKY, N. (1971), *Hustlers, Beats and Others*, Penguin, Harmondsworth.

PROVISIONAL IRA (1973), *Freedom Struggle*, (*no publisher shown*), Dublin.

PURDIE, B. (1972), *Ireland Unfree, Red Pamphlet no. 2*, International Marxist Group, London.

REDMOND, T. (1973), editorial in the *Irish Socialist Review*, no. 1.

REMMLING, G. (1976), *The Sociology of Karl Mannheim*, Routledge & Kegan Paul, London.

REVOLUTIONARY COMMUNIST GROUP (1976), *Ireland: British Labour and British Imperialism*, RCG Publications, London.

ROBERTS, R. (1973), *The Classic Slum*, Penguin, Harmondsworth.

ROCK, P. (1973), *Deviant Behaviour*, Hutchinson, London.

ROSE, R. (1971), *Governing Without Consensus*, Faber and Faber, London.

ROSS, N. (1971), 'The Identification from Faces of Religious Affiliation in a Sectarian Social Milieu: An Introductory Survey', unpublished BA (Hons) thesis, Queens University, Belfast.

RUSSELL, J. (1972), 'Childrens' Attitudes towards Political Change and Conflict', *Community Forum*, no. 2, NICRC Research Unit, Belfast.

RUSSELL, J. (1973), *Civic Education in Northern Ireland*, NICRC, Belfast.

SAHLINS, M. (1965), 'On the Sociology of Primitive Exchange', in M. Banton (ed.), *The Relevance of Models for Social Anthropology*, A.S.A. Monograph no. 1, Tavistock, London.

SCARMAN (1972), *Violence and Civil Disturbance in Northern Ireland in 1969*, (The Scarman Report), 2 volumes, Cmnd 566, HMSO, London.

SCHERVISH, P. (1975), 'The Labelling Perspective, Its Bias and Potential in the Study of Political Deviance', *American Sociology*, vol. 81, no. 1.

SCHUTZ, A. (1962), (1964), (1966), *Collected Papers*, vols 1–3, Nijhoff, The Hague.

SCHUTZ, A. (1967), 'Phenomenology and the Social Sciences', in J. Kockelmans, *Phenomenology*, Doubleday Anchor, New York.

SENIOR, H. (1966), *Orangeism in Ireland and Britain, 1795–1836*, Routledge & Kegan Paul, London.

SINN FÉIN (*c*. 1970), *Where Sinn Féin Stands Now*, (no publisher shown), Dublin.

SINN FÉIN (1971), *Eire Nua. The Social and Economic Programme of Sinn Féin*, ELO Press, Dublin.

SMYTH, C. (1974), *Rome, Our Enemy*, Puritan Publishing Ltd, Belfast.

SMYTH, M. (*c*. 1972), *Battle for Northern Ireland*, Orange Order Publications, Belfast.

STALIN, J. (1913, edn), 'Marxism and the National Question', in J. Stalin (1953), *Works*, vol. 2, Lawrence & Wishart, London.

STRAUSS, A. (1959), *Mirrors and Masks*, Glencoe, Illinois.

SUNDAY TIMES 'INSIGHT' TEAM (1972), *Ulster*, Penguin, Harmondsworth.

SUTTLES, G. (1968), *The Social Order of the Slum*, University of Chicago Press.

SUTTLES, G. (1972), *The Social Construction of Communities*, University of Chicago Press.

TABER, R. (1970), *The War of the Flea*, Paladin, St Albans.

TAFJEL, H. (1969), 'Social and Cultural Factors in Perception', in A. Lindzey and E. Aronson, *Handbook of Social Psychology*, vol. 3, Addison Wesley, London.

TAYLOR, I., WALTON, P. and YOUNG, J. (1974), *The New Criminology*, Routledge & Kegan Paul, London.

TÖNNIES, F. (1957), *Community and Association*, Harper & Row, New York.

TRENCH, B. (1972), 'The Two Nations Fallacy', *International Socialism*, no. 51.

VIDICH, A. (1955), 'Participant Observation and the Collection and Interpretation of Data', *American Journal of Sociology*, no. 60.

WALTON, P. (1973), 'The Case of the Weathermen', in I. Taylor and L. Taylor (eds), *Politics and Deviance*, Penguin, Harmondsworth.

WHYTE, W. (1955), *Street Corner Society*, University of Chicago Press.

WIDGERY (1972), *Report of the Tribunal to Inquire into the Events on Sunday, 30th January 1972. Which Led to Loss of Life in Connection with the Procession in Londonderry on that Day* (The Widgery Report), HL 100/HC 220, HMSO, London.

WOLFF, J. (1975), *Hermeneutic Philosophy and the Sociology of Art*, Routledge & Kegan Paul, London.

WRIGHT, F. (1973), 'Protestant Ideology and Politics in Ulster', *Archives européennes de sociologie*, vol. 14, 1973.

ZEITLIN, I. (1967), *Revolutionary Politics in the Cuban Working Class*, Princeton University Press, New Jersey.

Newspapers 1970–6

Guardian
Irish News
Newsletter
Republican News
Sunday Times

Index

Routledge Social Science Series

Routledge & Kegan Paul   London, Henley and Boston

39 Store Street, London WC1E 7DD
Broadway House, Newtown Road, Henley-on-Thames,
Oxon RG9 1EN
9 Park Street, Boston, Mass. 02108

Contents

*Authors wishing to submit manuscripts for any series in
this catalogue should send them to the Social Science Editor,
Routledge & Kegan Paul Ltd, 39 Store Street,
London WC1E 7DD*

● *Books so marked are available in paperback
All books are in Metric Demy 8vo format (216 × 138mm approx.)*

nternational Library of Sociology

;eneral Editor John Rex

;ENERAL SOCIOLOGY

3arnsley, J. H. The Social Reality of Ethics. *464 pp.*
3elshaw, Cyril. The Conditions of Social Performance. *An Exploratory Theory. 144 pp.*
Brown, Robert. Explanation in Social Science. *208 pp.*
  Rules and Laws in Sociology. *192 pp.*
Bruford, W. H. Chekhov and His Russia. *A Sociological Study. 244 pp.*
Cain, Maureen E. Society and the Policeman's Role. *326 pp.*
Fletcher, Colin. Beneath the Surface. *An Account of Three Styles of Sociological Research. 221 pp.*
Gibson, Quentin. The Logic of Social Enquiry. *240 pp.*
Glucksmann, M. Structuralist Analysis in Contemporary Social Thought. *212 pp.*
Gurvitch, Georges. Sociology of Law. *Preface by Roscoe Pound. 264 pp.*
Hodge, H. A. Wilhelm Dilthey. *An Introduction. 184 pp.*
Homans, George C. Sentiments and Activities. *336 pp.*
Johnson, Harry M. Sociology: *a Systematic Introduction. Foreword by · Robert K. Merton. 710 pp.*
Keat, Russell, and **Urry, John.** Social Theory as Science. *278 pp.*
Mannheim, Karl. Essays on Sociology and Social Psychology. *Edited by Paul Keckskemeti. With Editorial Note by Adolph Lowe. 344 pp.*
  Systematic Sociology: *An Introduction to the Study of Society. Edited by J. S. Erös and Professor W. A. C. Stewart. 220 pp.*
Martindale, Don. The Nature and Types of Sociological Theory. *292 pp.*
Maus, Heinz. A Short History of Sociology. *234 pp.*
Mey, Harald. Field-Theory. *A Study of its Application in the Social Sciences. 352 pp.*
Myrdal, Gunnar. Value in Social Theory: *A Collection of Essays on Methodology. Edited by Paul Streeten. 332 pp.*
Ogburn, William F., and **Nimkoff, Meyer F.** A Handbook of Sociology. *Preface by Karl Mannheim. 656 pp. 46 figures. 35 tables.*
Parsons, Talcott, and **Smelser, Neil J.** Economy and Society: *A Study in the Integration of Economic and Social Theory. 362 pp.*
Podgórecki, Adam. Practical Social Sciences. *About 200 pp.*
Rex, John. Key Problems of Sociological Theory. *220 pp.*
  Sociology and the Demystification of the Modern World. *282 pp.*
Rex, John (Ed.) Approaches to Sociology. *Contributions by Peter Abell, Frank Bechhofer, Basil Bernstein, Ronald Fletcher, David Frisby, Miriam Glucksmann, Peter Lassman, Herminio Martins, John Rex, Roland Robertson, John Westergaard and Jock Young. 302 pp.*
Rigby, A. Alternative Realities. *352 pp.*
Roche, M. Phenomenology, Language and the Social Sciences. *374 pp.*

Sahay, A. Sociological Analysis. *220 pp.*

Simirenko, Alex (Ed.) Soviet Sociology. *Historical Antecedents and Current Appraisals. Introduction by Alex Simirenko. 376 pp.*

Strasser, Hermann. The Normative Structure of Sociology. *Conservative and Emancipatory Themes in Social Thought. About 340 pp.*

Urry, John. Reference Groups and the Theory of Revolution. *244 pp.*

Weinberg, E. Development of Sociology in the Soviet Union. *173 pp.*

FOREIGN CLASSICS OF SOCIOLOGY

●**Durkheim, Emile.** Suicide. *A Study in Sociology. Edited and with an Introduction by George Simpson. 404 pp.*

●**Gerth, H. H.,** and **Mills, C. Wright.** From Max Weber: *Essays in Sociology. 502 pp.*

●**Tönnies, Ferdinand.** Community and Association. (*Gemeinschaft und Gesellschaft.) Translated and Supplemented by Charles P. Loomis. Foreword by Pitirim A. Sorokin. 334 pp.*

SOCIAL STRUCTURE

Andreski, Stanislav. Military Organization and Society. *Foreword by Professor A. R. Radcliffe-Brown. 226 pp. 1 folder.*

Carlton, Eric. Ideology and Social Order. *Preface by Professor Philip Abrahams. About 320 pp.*

Coontz, Sydney H. Population Theories and the Economic Interpretation. *202 pp.*

Coser, Lewis. The Functions of Social Conflict. *204 pp.*

Dickie-Clark, H. F. Marginal Situation: *A Sociological Study of a Coloured Group. 240 pp. 11 tables.*

Glaser, Barney, and **Strauss, Anselm L.** Status Passage. *A Formal Theory. 208 pp.*

Glass, D. V. (Ed.) Social Mobility in Britain. *Contributions by J. Berent, T. Bottomore, R. C. Chambers, J. Floud, D. V. Glass, J. R. Hall, H. T. Himmelweit, R. K. Kelsall, F. M. Martin, C. A. Moser, R. Mukherjee, and W. Ziegel. 420 pp.*

Johnstone, Frederick A. Class, Race and Gold. *A Study of Class Relations and Racial Discrimination in South Africa. 312 pp.*

Jones, Garth N. Planned Organizational Change: *An Exploratory Study Using an Empirical Approach. 268 pp.*

Kelsall, R. K. Higher Civil Servants in Britain: *From 1870 to the Present Day. 268 pp. 31 tables.*

König, René. The Community. *232 pp. Illustrated.*

●**Lawton, Denis.** Social Class, Language and Education. *192 pp.*

McLeish, John. The Theory of Social Change: *Four Views Considered. 128 pp.*

Marsh, David C. The Changing Social Structure of England and Wales, 1871-1961. *288 pp.*

Menzies, Ken. Talcott Parsons and the Social Image of Man. *About 208 pp.*

Mouzelis, Nicos. Organization and Bureaucracy. *An Analysis of Modern Theories. 240 pp.*

Mulkay, M. J. Functionalism, Exchange and Theoretical Strategy. *272 pp.*

Ossowski, Stanislaw. Class Structure in the Social Consciousness. *210 pp.*

Podgórecki, Adam. Law and Society. *302 pp.*

Renner, Karl. Institutions of Private Law and Their Social Functions. *Edited, with an Introduction and Notes, by O. Kahn-Freud. Translated by Agnes Schwarzschild. 316 pp.*

SOCIOLOGY AND POLITICS

Acton, T. A. Gypsy Politics and Social Change. *316 pp.*

Clegg, Stuart. Power, Rule and Domination. *A Critical and Empirical Understanding of Power in Sociological Theory and Organisational Life. About 300 pp.*

Hechter, Michael. Internal Colonialism. *The Celtic Fringe in British National Development, 1536–1966. 361 pp.*

Hertz, Frederick. Nationality in History and Politics: *A Psychology and Sociology of National Sentiment and Nationalism. 432 pp.*

Kornhauser, William. The Politics of Mass Society. *272 pp. 20 tables.*

Kroes, R. Soldiers and Students. *A Study of Right- and Left-wing Students. 174 pp.*

Laidler, Harry W. History of Socialism. *Social-Economic Movements: An Historical and Comparative Survey of Socialism, Communism, Co-operation, Utopianism; and other Systems of Reform and Reconstruction. 992 pp.*

Lasswell, H. D. Analysis of Political Behaviour. *324 pp.*

Martin, David A. Pacifism: *an Historical and Sociological Study. 262 pp.*

Martin, Roderick. Sociology of Power. *About 272 pp.*

Myrdal, Gunnar. The Political Element in the Development of Economic Theory. *Translated from the German by Paul Streeten. 282 pp.*

Wilson, H. T. The American Ideology. *Science, Technology and Organization of Modes of Rationality. About 280 pp.*

Wootton, Graham. Workers, Unions and the State. *188 pp.*

CRIMINOLOGY

Ancel, Marc. Social Defence: *A Modern Approach to Criminal Problems. Foreword by Leon Radzinowicz. 240 pp.*

Cain, Maureen E. Society and the Policeman's Role. *326 pp.*

Cloward, Richard A., and **Ohlin, Lloyd E.** Delinquency and Opportunity: *A Theory of Delinquent Gangs. 248 pp.*

Downes, David M. The Delinquent Solution. *A Study in Subcultural Theory. 296 pp.*

Dunlop, A. B., and **McCabe, S.** Young Men in Detention Centres. *192 pp.*

Friedlander, Kate. The Psycho-Analytical Approach to Juvenile Delinquency: *Theory, Case Studies, Treatment. 320 pp.*

Glueck, Sheldon, and **Eleanor.** Family Environment and Delinquency. *With the statistical assistance of Rose W. Kneznek. 340 pp.*

Lopez-Rey, Manuel. Crime. *An Analytical Appraisal. 288 pp.*

Mannheim, Hermann. Comparative Criminology: *a Text Book. Tw‹ volumes. 442 pp. and 380 pp.*

Morris, Terence. The Criminal Area: *A Study in Social Ecology. Forewor‹ by Hermann Mannheim. 232 pp. 25 tables. 4 maps.*

Rock, Paul. Making People Pay. *338 pp.*

●**Taylor, Ian, Walton, Paul,** and **Young, Jock.** The New Criminology. *For ‹ Social Theory of Deviance. 325 pp.*

●**Taylor, Ian, Walton, Paul,** and **Young, Jock** (Eds). Critical Criminology *268 pp.*

SOCIAL PSYCHOLOGY

Bagley, Christopher. The Social Psychology of the Epileptic Child. *320 pp*

Barbu, Zevedei. Problems of Historical Psychology. *248 pp.*

Blackburn, Julian. Psychology and the Social Pattern. *184 pp.*

●**Brittan, Arthur.** Meanings and Situations. *224 pp.*

Carroll, J. Break-Out from the Crystal Palace. *200 pp.*

●**Fleming, C. M.** Adolescence: Its Social Psychology. *With an Introduction to recent findings from the fields of Anthropology, Physiology, Medicine, Psychometrics and Sociometry. 288 pp.*

● The Social Psychology of Education: *An Introduction and Guide to Its Study. 136 pp.*

●**Homans, George C.** The Human Group. *Foreword by Bernard DeVoto. Introduction by Robert K. Merton. 526 pp.*

● Social Behaviour: *its Elementary Forms. 416 pp.*

●**Klein, Josephine.** The Study of Groups. *226 pp. 31 figures. 5 tables.*

Linton, Ralph. The Cultural Background of Personality. *132 pp.*

●**Mayo, Elton.** The Social Problems of an Industrial Civilization. *With an appendix on the Political Problem. 180 pp.*

Ottaway, A. K. C. Learning Through Group Experience. *176 pp.*

Plummer, Ken. Sexual Stigma. *An Interactionist Account. 254 pp.*

●**Rose, Arnold M.** (Ed.) Human Behaviour and Social Processes: *an Interactionist Approach. Contributions by Arnold M. Rose, Ralph H. Turner, Anselm Strauss, Everett C. Hughes, E. Franklin Frazier, Howard S. Becker, et al. 696 pp.*

Smelser, Neil J. Theory of Collective Behaviour. *448 pp.*

Stephenson, Geoffrey M. The Development of Conscience. *128 pp.*

Young, Kimball. Handbook of Social Psychology. *658 pp. 16 figures. 10 tables.*

SOCIOLOGY OF THE FAMILY

Banks, J. A. Prosperity and Parenthood: *A Study of Family Planning among The Victorian Middle Classes. 262 pp.*

Bell, Colin R. Middle ʼClass Families: *Social and Geographical Mobility. 224 pp.*

Burton, Lindy. Vulnerable Children. *272 pp.*
Gavron, Hannah. The Captive Wife: *Conflicts of Household Mothers.*
190 pp.
George, Victor, and **Wilding, Paul.** Motherless Families. *248 pp.*
Klein, Josephine. Samples from English Cultures.
  1. Three Preliminary Studies and Aspects of Adult Life in England.
  447 pp.
  2. Child-Rearing Practices and Index. *247 pp.*
Klein, Viola. The Feminine Character. *History of an Ideology. 244 pp.*
McWhinnie, Alexina M. Adopted Children. *How They Grow Up. 304 pp.*
● **Morgan, D. H. J.** Social Theory and the Family. *About 320 pp.*
● **Myrdal, Alva,** and **Klein, Viola.** Women's Two Roles: *Home and Work.*
238 pp. 27 tables.
Parsons, Talcott, and **Bales, Robert F.** Family: Socialization and Inter-
action Process. *In collaboration with James Olds, Morris Zelditch and
Philip E. Slater. 456 pp. 50 figures and tables.*

SOCIAL SERVICES

Bastide, Roger. The Sociology of Mental Disorder. *Translated from the
French by Jean McNeil. 260 pp.*
Carlebach, Julius. Caring For Children in Trouble. *266 pp.*
George, Victor. Foster Care. *Theory and Practice. 234 pp.*
  Social Security: *Beveridge and After. 258 pp.*
George, V., and **Wilding, P.** Motherless Families. *248 pp.*
●**Goetschius, George W.** Working with Community Groups. *256 pp.*
Goetschius, George W., and **Tash, Joan.** Working with Unattached Youth.
416 pp.
Hall, M. P., and **Howes, I. V.** The Church in Social Work. *A Study of
Moral Welfare Work undertaken by the Church of England. 320 pp.*
Heywood, Jean S. Children in Care: *the Development of the Service for the
Deprived Child. 264 pp.*
Hoenig, J., and **Hamilton, Marian W.** The De-Segregation of the Mentally
Ill. *284 pp.*
Jones, Kathleen. Mental Health and Social Policy, 1845-1959. *264 pp.*
King, Roy D., Raynes, Norma V., and **Tizard, Jack.** Patterns of Residential
Care. *356 pp.*
Leigh, John. Young People and Leisure. *256 pp.*
●**Mays, John.** (Ed.) Penelope Hall's Social Services of England and Wales.
About 324 pp.
Morris, Mary. Voluntary Work and the Welfare State. *300 pp.*
Nokes, P. L. The Professional Task in Welfare Practice. *152 pp.*
Timms, Noel. Psychiatric Social Work in Great Britain (1939-1962).
280 pp.
● Social Casework: *Principles and Practice. 256 pp.*
Young, A. F. Social Services in British Industry. *272 pp.*

SOCIOLOGY OF EDUCATION

Banks, Olive. Parity and Prestige in English Secondary Education: a Study in Educational Sociology. *272 pp.*

Bentwich, Joseph. Education in Israel. *224 pp. 8 pp. plates.*

●**Blyth, W. A. L.** English Primary Education. *A Sociological Description.*
1. Schools. *232 pp.*
2. Background. *168 pp.*

Collier, K. G. The Social Purposes of Education: *Personal and Social Values in Education. 268 pp.*

Dale, R. R., and **Griffith, S.** Down Stream: *Failure in the Grammar School. 108 pp.*

Evans, K. M. Sociometry and Education. *158 pp.*

●**Ford, Julienne.** Social Class and the Comprehensive School. *192 pp.*

Foster, P. J. Education and Social Change in Ghana. *336 pp. 3 maps.*

Fraser, W. R. Education and Society in Modern France. *150 pp.*

Grace, Gerald R. Role Conflict and the Teacher. *150 pp.*

Hans, Nicholas. New Trends in Education in the Eighteenth Century. *278 pp. 19 tables.*

● Comparative Education: *A Study of Educational Factors and Traditions. 360 pp.*

●**Hargreaves, David.** Interpersonal Relations and Education. *432 pp.*

● Social Relations in a Secondary School. *240 pp.*

Holmes, Brian. Problems in Education. *A Comparative Approach. 336 pp.*

King, Ronald. Values and Involvement in a Grammar School. *164 pp.*

School Organization and Pupil Involvement. *A Study of Secondary Schools.*

●**Mannheim, Karl,** and **Stewart, W. A. C.** An Introduction to the Sociology of Education. *206 pp.*

Morris, Raymond N. The Sixth Form and College Entrance. *231 pp.*

●**Musgrove, F.** Youth and the Social Order. *176 pp.*

●**Ottaway, A. K. C.** Education and Society: An Introduction to the Sociology of Education. *With an Introduction by W. O. Lester Smith. 212 pp.*

Peers, Robert. Adult Education: *A Comparative Study. 398 pp.*

Pritchard, D. G. Education and the Handicapped: *1760 to 1960. 258 pp.*

Stratta, Erica. The Education of Borstal Boys. *A Study of their Educational Experiences prior to, and during, Borstal Training. 256 pp.*

Taylor, P. H., Reid, W. A., and **Holley, B. J.** The English Sixth Form. *A Case Study in Curriculum Research. 200 pp.*

SOCIOLOGY OF CULTURE

Eppel, E. M., and **M.** Adolescents and Morality: *A Study of some Moral Values and Dilemmas of Working Adolescents in the Context of a changing Climate of Opinion. Foreword by W. J. H. Sprott. 268 pp. 39 tables.*

●**Fromm, Erich.** The Fear of Freedom. *286 pp.*

● The Sane Society. *400 pp.*

Mannheim, Karl. Essays on the Sociology of Culture. *Edited by Ernst Mannheim in co-operation with Paul Kecskemeti. Editorial Note by Adolph Lowe. 280 pp.*

Weber, Alfred. Farewell to European History: *or The Conquest of Nihilism. Translated from the German by R. F. C. Hull. 224 pp.*

SOCIOLOGY OF RELIGION

Argyle, Michael and **Beit-Hallahmi, Benjamin.** The Social Psychology of Religion. *About 256 pp.*

Glasner, Peter E. The Sociology of Secularisation. *A Critique of a Concept. About 180 pp.*

Nelson, G. K. Spiritualism and Society. *313 pp.*

Stark, Werner. The Sociology of Religion. *A Study of Christendom.*
   Volume I. *Established Religion. 248 pp.*
   Volume II. *Sectarian Religion. 368 pp.*
   Volume III. *The Universal Church. 464 pp.*
   Volume IV. *Types of Religious Man. 352 pp.*
   Volume V. *Types of Religious Culture. 464 pp.*

Turner, B. S. Weber and Islam. *216 pp.*

Watt, W. Montgomery. Islam and the Integration of Society. *320 pp.*

SOCIOLOGY OF ART AND LITERATURE

Jarvie, Ian C. Towards a Sociology of the Cinema. *A Comparative Essay on the Structure and Functioning of a Major Entertainment Industry. 405 pp.*

Rust, Frances S. Dance in Society. *An Analysis of the Relationships between the Social Dance and Society in England from the Middle Ages to the Present Day. 256 pp. 8 pp. of plates.*

Schücking, L. L. The Sociology of Literary Taste. *112 pp.*

Wolff, Janet. Hermeneutic Philosophy and the Sociology of Art. *150 pp.*

SOCIOLOGY OF KNOWLEDGE

Diesing, P. Patterns of Discovery in the Social Sciences. *262 pp.*

●**Douglas, J. D.** (Ed.) Understanding Everyday Life. *370 pp.*

●**Hamilton, P.** Knowledge and Social Structure. *174 pp.*

Jarvie, I. C. Concepts and Society. *232 pp.*

Mannheim, Karl. Essays on the Sociology of Knowledge. *Edited by Paul Kecskemeti. Editorial Note by Adolph Lowe. 353 pp.*

Remmling, Gunter W. The Sociology cf Karl Mannheim. *With a Bibliographical Guide to the Sociology of Knowledge, Ideological Analysis, and Social Planning. 255 pp.*

Remmling, Gunter W. (Ed.) Towards the Sociology of Knowledge. *Origin and Development of a Sociological Thought Style. 463 pp.*

Stark, Werner. The Sociology of Knowledge: *An Essay in Aid of a Deeper Understanding of the History of Ideas. 384 pp.*

URBAN SOCIOLOGY

Ashworth, William. The Genesis of Modern British Town Planning: *A Study in Economic and Social History of the Nineteenth and Twentieth Centuries. 288 pp.*

Cullingworth, J. B. Housing Needs and Planning Policy: *A Restatement of the Problems of Housing Need and 'Overspill' in England and Wales. 232 pp. 44 tables. 8 maps.*

Dickinson, Robert E. City and Region: *A Geographical Interpretation 608 pp. 125 figures.*

The West European City: *A Geographical Interpretation. 600 pp. 129 maps. 29 plates.*

● The City Region in Western Europe. *320 pp. Maps.*

Humphreys, Alexander J. New Dubliners: *Urbanization and the Irish Family. Foreword by George C. Homans. 304 pp.*

Jackson, Brian. Working Class Community: *Some General Notions raised by a Series of Studies in Northern England. 192 pp.*

Jennings, Hilda. Societies in the Making: *a Study of Development and Re-development within a County Borough. Foreword by D. A. Clark. 286 pp.*

●**Mann, P. H.** An Approach to Urban Sociology. *240 pp.*

Morris, R. N., and **Mogey, J.** The Sociology of Housing. *Studies at Berinsfield. 232 pp. 4 pp. plates.*

Rosser, C., and **Harris, C.** The Family and Social Change. *A Study of Family and Kinship in a South Wales Town. 352 pp. 8 maps.*

●**Stacey, Margaret, Batsone, Eric, Bell, Colin,** and **Thurcott, Anne.** Power, Persistence and Change. *A Second Study of Banbury. 196 pp.*

RURAL SOCIOLOGY

Haswell, M. R. The Economics of Development in Village India. *120 pp.*

Littlejohn, James. Westrigg: *the Sociology of a Cheviot Parish. 172 pp. 5 figures.*

Mayer, Adrian C. Peasants in the Pacific. *A Study of Fiji Indian Rural Society. 248 pp. 20 plates.*

Williams, W. M. The Sociology of an English Village: *Gosforth. 272 pp. 12 figures. 13 tables.*

SOCIOLOGY OF INDUSTRY AND DISTRIBUTION

Anderson, Nels. Work and Leisure. *280 pp.*

●Blau, Peter M., and Scott, W. Richard. Formal Organizations: *a Comparative approach. Introduction and Additional Bibliography by J. H. Smith.* *326 pp.*

Dunkerley, David. The Foreman. *Aspects of Task and Structure. 192 pp.*

Eldridge, J. E. T. Industrial Disputes. *Essays in the Sociology of Industrial Relations. 288 pp.*

Hetzler, Stanley. Applied Measures for Promoting Technological Growth. *352 pp.*

Technological Growth and Social Change. *Achieving Modernization. 269 pp.*

Hollowell, Peter G. The Lorry Driver. *272 pp.*

●Oxaal, I., Barnett, T., and Booth, D. (Eds). Beyond the Sociology of Development. *Economy and Society in Latin America and Africa. 295 pp.*

Smelser, Neil J. Social Change in the Industrial Revolution: *An Application of Theory to the Lancashire Cotton Industry, 1770–1840. 468 pp. 12 figures. 14 tables.*

ANTHROPOLOGY

Ammar, Hamed. Growing up in an Egyptian Village: *Silwa, Province of Aswan. 336 pp.*

Brandel-Syrier, Mia. Reeftown Elite. *A Study of Social Mobility in a Modern African Community on the Reef. 376 pp.*

Dickie-Clark, H. F. The Marginal Situation. *A Sociological Study of a Coloured Group. 236 pp.*

Dube, S. C. Indian Village. *Foreword by Morris Edward Opler. 276 pp. 4 plates.*

India's Changing Villages: *Human Factors in Community Development. 260 pp. 8 plates. 1 map.*

Firth, Raymond. Malay Fishermen. *Their Peasant Economy. 420 pp. 17 pp. plates.*

Gulliver, P. H. Social Control in an African Society: a Study of the Arusha, Agricultural Masai of Northern Tanganyika. *320 pp. 8 plates. 10 figures.*

Family Herds. *288 pp.*

Ishwaran, K. Tradition and Economy in Village India: *An Interactionist Approach.*
Foreword by Conrad Arensburg. 176 pp.

Jarvie, Ian C. The Revolution in Anthropology. *268 pp.*

Little, Kenneth L. Mende of Sierra Leone. *308 pp. and folder.*

Negroes in Britain. *With a New Introduction and Contemporary Study by Leonard Bloom. 320 pp.*

Lowie, Robert H. Social Organization. *494 pp.*

Mayer, A. C. Peasants in the Pacific. *A Study of Fiji Indian Rural Society. 248 pp.*

Meer, Fatima. Race and Suicide in South Africa. *325 pp.*

Smith, Raymond T. The Negro Family in British Guiana: *Family Structure and Social Status in the Villages. With a Foreword by Meyer Fortes. 314 pp. 8 plates. 1 figure. 4 maps.*

Smooha, Sammy. Israel: Pluralism and Conflict. *About 320 pp.*

SOCIOLOGY AND PHILOSOPHY

Barnsley, John H. The Social Reality of Ethics. *A Comparative Analysis of Moral Codes. 448 pp.*

Diesing, Paul. Patterns of Discovery in the Social Sciences. *362 pp.*

●**Douglas, Jack D.** (Ed.) Understanding Everyday Life. *Toward the Reconstruction of Sociological Knowledge. Contributions by Alan F. Blum. Aaron W. Cicourel, Norman K. Denzin, Jack D. Douglas, John Heeren, Peter McHugh, Peter K. Manning, Melvin Power, Matthew Speier, Roy Turner, D. Lawrence Wieder, Thomas P. Wilson and Don H. Zimmerman. 370 pp.*

Gorman, Robert A. The Dual Vision. *Alfred Schutz and the Myth of Phenomenological Social Science. About 300 pp.*

Jarvie, Ian C. Concepts and Society. *216 pp.*

●**Pelz, Werner.** The Scope of Understanding in Sociology. *Towards a more radical reorientation in the social humanistic sciences. 283 pp.*

Roche, Maurice. Phenomenology, Language and the Social Sciences.*371 pp.*

Sahay, Arun. Sociological Analysis. *212 pp.*

Sklair, Leslie. The Sociology of Progress. *320 pp.*

Slater, P. Origin and Significance of the Frankfurt School. *A Marxist Perspective. About 192 pp.*

Smart, Barry. Sociology, Phenomenology and Marxian Analysis. *A Critical Discussion of the Theory and Practice of a Science of Society. 220 pp.*

International Library of Anthropology

General Editor Adam Kuper

Ahmed, A. S. Millenium and Charisma Among Pathans. *A Critical Essay in Social Anthropology. 192 pp.*

Brown, Paula. The Chimbu. *A Study of Change in the New Guinea Highlands. 151 pp.*

Gudeman, Stephen. Relationships, Residence and the Individual. *A Rural Panamanian Community. 288 pp. 11 Plates, 5 Figures, 2 Maps, 10 Tables.*

Hamnett, Ian. Chieftainship and Legitimacy. *An Anthropological Study of Executive Law in Lesotho. 163 pp.*

Hanson, F. Allan. Meaning in Culture. *127 pp.*

Lloyd, P. C. Power and Independence. *Urban Africans' Perception of Social Inequality. 264 pp.*

Pettigrew, Joyce. Robber Noblemen. *A Study of the Political System of the Sikh Jats. 284 pp.*

Street, Brian V. The Savage in Literature. *Representations of 'Primitive' Society in English Fiction, 1858–1920. 207 pp.*

Van Den Berghe, Pierre L. Power and Privilege at an African University. *278 pp.*

International Library of Social Policy

General Editor Kathleen Jones

Bayley, M. Mental Handicap and Community Care. *426 pp.*

Bottoms, A. E., and McClean, J. D. Defendants in the Criminal Process. *284 pp.*

Butler, J. R. Family Doctors and Public Policy. *208 pp.*

Davies, Martin. Prisoners of Society. *Attitudes and Aftercare. 204 pp.*

Gittus, Elizabeth. Flats, Families and the Under-Fives. *285 pp.*

Holman, Robert. Trading in Children. *A Study of Private Fostering. 355 pp.*

Jones, Howard, and Cornes, Paul. Open Prisons. *About 248 pp.*

Jones, Kathleen. History of the Mental Health Service. *428 pp.*

Jones, Kathleen, with Brown, John, Cunningham, W. J., Roberts, Julian, and Williams, Peter. Opening the Door. *A Study of New Policies for the Mentally Handicapped. 278 pp.*

Karn, Valerie. Retiring to the Seaside. *About 280 pp. 2 maps. Numerous tables.*

Thomas, J. E. The English Prison Officer since 1850: *A Study in Conflict. 258 pp.*

Walton, R. G. Women in Social Work. *303 pp.*

Woodward, J. To Do the Sick No Harm. *A Study of the British Voluntary Hospital System to 1875. 221 pp.*

International Library of Welfare and Philosophy

General Editors Noel Timms and David Watson

● **Plant, Raymond.** Community and Ideology. *104 pp.*

● **McDermott, F. E.** (Ed.) Self-Determination in Social Work. *A Collection of Essays on Self-determination and Related Concepts by Philosophers and Social Work Theorists. Contributors: F. P. Biestek, S. Bernstein, A. Keith-Lucas, D. Sayer, H. H. Perelman, C. Whittington, R. F. Stalley, F. E. McDermott, I. Berlin, H. J. McCloskey, H. L. A. Hart, J. Wilson, A. I. Melden, S. I. Benn. 254 pp.*

Ragg, Nicholas M. People Not Cases. *A Philosophical Approach to Social Work. About 250 pp.*

● **Timms, Noel,** and **Watson, David** (Eds). Talking About Welfare. *Readings in Philosophy and Social Policy. Contributors: T. H. Marshall, R. B. Brandt, G. H. von Wright, K. Nielsen, M. Cranston, R. M. Titmuss, R. S. Downie, E. Telfer, D. Donnison, J. Benson, P. Leonard, A. Keith-Lucas, D. Walsh, I. T. Ramsey. 320 pp.*

Primary Socialization, Language and Education

General Editor Basil Bernstein

Adlam, Diana S., *with the assistance of Geoffrey Turner and Lesley Lineker.* Code in Context. *About 272 pp.*

Bernstein, Basil. Class, Codes and Control. *3 volumes.*
　　1. *Theoretical Studies Towards a Sociology of Language. 254 pp.*
　　2. *Applied Studies Towards a Sociology of Language. 377 pp.*
● 　3. *Towards a Theory of Educatiomal Transmission. 167 pp.*

Brandis, W., and **Bernstein, B.** Selection and Control. *176 pp.*

Brandis, Walter, and **Henderson, Dorothy.** Social Class, Language and Communication. *288 pp.*

Cook-Gumperz, Jenny. Social Control and Socialization. *A Study of Class Differences in the Language of Maternal Control. 290 pp.*

● **Gahagan, D. M.,** and **G. A.** Talk Reform. *Exploration in Language for Infant School Children. 160 pp.*

Hawkins, P. R. Social Class, the Nominal Group and Verbal Strategies. *About 220 pp.*

Robinson, W. P., and **Rackstraw, Susan D. A.** A Question of Answers. *2 volumes. 192 pp. and 180 pp.*

Turner, Geoffrey J., and **Mohan, Bernard A.** A Linguistic Description and Computer Programme for Children's Speech. *208 pp.*

Reports of the Institute of Community Studies

● **Cartwright, Ann.** Parents and Family Planning Services. *306 pp.*
　　Patients and their Doctors. *A Study of General Practice. 304 pp.*

Dench, Geoff. Maltese in London. *A Case-study in the Erosion of Ethnic Consciousness. 302 pp.*

● **Jackson, Brian.** Streaming: *an Education System in Miniature. 168 pp.*

Jackson, Brian, and **Marsden, Dennis.** Education and the Working Class: *Some General Themes raised by a Study of 88 Working-class Children in a Northern Industrial City. 268 pp. 2 folders.*

Marris, Peter. The Experience of Higher Education. *232 pp. 27 tables.*
　　Loss and Change. *192 pp.*

Marris, Peter, and **Rein, Martin.** Dilemmas of Social Reform. *Poverty and Community Action in the United States. 256 pp.*

Marris, Peter, and **Somerset, Anthony.** African Businessmen. *A Study of Entrepreneurship and Development in Kenya. 256 pp.*

Mills, Richard. Young Outsiders: *a Study in Alternative Communities. 216 pp.*

Runciman, W. G. Relative Deprivation and Social Justice. *A Study of Attitudes to Social Inequality in Twentieth-Century England. 352 pp.*

Willmott, Peter. Adolescent Boys in East London. *230 pp.*

Willmott, Peter, and **Young, Michael.** Family and Class in a London Suburb. *202 pp. 47 tables.*

Young, Michael. Innovation and Research in Education. *192 pp.*

● **Young, Michael,** and **McGeeney, Patrick.** Learning Begins at Home. *A Study of a Junior School and its Parents. 128 pp.*

Young, Michael, and **Willmott, Peter.** Family and Kinship in East London. *Foreword by Richard M. Titmuss. 252 pp. 39 tables.*

   The Symmetrical Family. *410 pp.*

Reports of the Institute for Social Studies in Medical Care

Cartwright, Ann, Hockey, Lisbeth, and **Anderson, John L.** Life Before Death. *310 pp.*

Dunnell, Karen, and **Cartwright, Ann.** Medicine Takers, Prescribers and Hoarders. *190 pp.*

Medicine, Illness and Society

General Editor   W. M. Williams

Robinson, David. The Process of Becoming Ill. *142 pp.*

Stacey, Margaret, *et al.* Hospitals, Children and Their Families. *The Report of a Pilot Study. 202 pp.*

Stimson, G. V., and **Webb, B.** Going to See the Doctor. *The Consultation Process in General Practice. 155 pp.*

Monographs in Social Theory

General Editor   Arthur Brittan

● **Barnes, B.** Scientific Knowledge and Sociological Theory. *192 pp.*

Bauman, Zygmunt. Culture as Praxis. *204 pp.*

● **Dixon, Keith.** Sociological Theory. *Pretence and Possibility. 142 pp.*

Meltzer, B. N., Petras, J. W., and **Reynolds, L. T.** Symbolic Interactionism. *Genesis, Varieties and Criticisms. 144 pp.*

● **Smith, Anthony D.** The Concept of Social Change. *A Critique of the Functionalist Theory of Social Change. 208 pp.*

Routledge Social Science Journals

The British Journal of Sociology. *Editor – Angus Stewart; Associate Editor – Leslie Sklair. Vol. 1, No. 1 – March 1950 and Quarterly. Roy. 8vo. All back issues available. An international journal publishing original papers in the field of sociology and related areas.*

Community Work. *Edited by David Jones and Marjorie Mayo. 1973. Published annually.*

Economy and Society. *Vol. 1, No. 1. February 1972 and Quarterly. Metric Roy. 8vo. A journal for all social scientists covering sociology, philosophy, anthropology, economics and history. All back numbers available.*

Religion. Journal of Religion and Religions. *Chairman of Editorial Board, Ninian Smart. Vol. 1, No. 1, Spring 1971. A journal with an inter-disciplinary approach to the study of the phenomena of religion. All back numbers available.*

Year Book of Social Policy in Britain, The. *Edited by Kathleen Jones. 1971. Published annually.*

Social and Psychological Aspects of Medical Practice

Editor Trevor Silverstone

Lader, Malcolm. Psychophysiology of Mental Illness. *280 pp.*

● **Silverstone, Trevor,** and **Turner, Paul.** Drug Treatment in Psychiatry. *232 pp.*

Printed in Great Britain by
Lowe & Brydone Printers Limited, Thetford, Norfolk